THE PATRIARCHS

The Origins of Inequality

Angela Saini

BEACON PRESS
BOSTON

BEACON PRESS
Boston, Massachusetts
www.beacon.org

Beacon Press books
are published under the auspices of
the Unitarian Universalist Association of Congregations.

26 25 24 23   8 7 6 5 4 3 2

This book is printed on acid-free paper that meets the uncoated paper
ANSI/NISO specifications for permanence as revised in 1992.

Text design and composition by Kim Arney

Cover image: Gift of Landon T. and Lavinia Clay in honor of Malcolm Rogers,
collection of the Museum of Fine Arts Boston.

Library of Congress Cataloguing-in-Publication Data is available for this title.
Hardcover ISBN: 978-0807-0-1454-7
E-book ISBN: 978-0807-0-1456-1

CONTENTS

TIME LINE

13 MILLION TO 4 MILLION BCE—The human lineage diverges from other apes, including chimpanzees and bonobos, according to various scientific estimates.

ROUGHLY 300,000 BCE—Our species *Homo sapiens* appears in the archaeological record in Africa.

10,000 BCE—An agricultural revolution begins in the Middle East's Fertile Crescent, following many thousands of years of plant cultivation across the world, marking the start of this region's Neolithic period.

7400 BCE—Large Neolithic communities in Çatalhöyük in Southern Anatolia are relatively gender-blind, according to the archaeologist Ian Hodder.

AROUND 7000 BCE—The body of a female hunter of big game is buried in the Peruvian Andes.

5000 TO 3000 BCE—A genetic "bottleneck" emerges in Europe and parts of Asia and Africa, suggesting that a small number of men are having disproportionately more children than other men.

3300 BCE—The start of the Bronze Age in North Africa, the Middle East, the Indian subcontinent, and parts of Europe.

2500 BCE—Kubaba founds the third dynasty of Kish in Mesopotamia, ruling as a king in her own right.

2500 BCE TO 1200 BCE—A movement of people from the Eurasian Steppe into Europe and then into Asia, bringing apparently more violent and male-dominated cultures, according to the archaeologist Marija Gimbutas.

750 BCE—Wealthier ancient Greek homes are divided into separate spaces for women and men.

700 BCE—The ancient Greek poet Hesiod describes women as a "deadly race and tribe" with "a nature to do evil," in his history of the world, the *Theogony*.

AROUND 622 BCE—An early form of the Old Testament book of Deuteronomy is written, which has instructions for men on how to treat women taken captive in battle.

AROUND 950 CE—A high-status female Viking leader and warrior is buried in Birka, Sweden.

1227—Death of the Mongol leader Chinggis (Genghis) Khan, whose descendants are thought to include one in two hundred of all the men alive today.

1590—Meeting of Native American Haudenosaunee women in Seneca Falls to demand peace between their peoples.

1680—The English political theorist Sir Robert Filmer's *Patriarcha* defends the divine right of kings by arguing that a monarch has natural authority over his people the way a father does over his household.

1765—The English jurist Sir William Blackstone's *Commentaries on the Laws of England* reinforce the principle that a woman's legal existence is incorporated into her husband's during marriage.

1848—The world's first women's rights convention is held at the Wesleyan Chapel in Seneca Falls, New York.

1870—The Married Women's Property Act is passed in the United Kingdom, allowing married women to legally keep their own earnings

1884—The German socialist philosopher Friedrich Engels writes that matriarchal human societies were overthrown by a "world historical defeat of the female sex."

1900—The Asante Queen Mother Nana Yaa Asantewaa in Ghana leads a war of independence against the British Empire.

1917—The Russian Revolution leads to the creation of the first socialist state.

1920—Soviet Russia becomes the first country in the world to legalize abortion.

1960—Sirimavo Bandaranaike is elected the world's first woman prime minister, in Sri Lanka.

1976—The Kerala legislature in India abolishes matriliny.

1979—The Iranian Revolution overthrows the ruling monarchy, leading to the creation of a conservative Islamic republic.

1989—The Berlin Wall falls, marking the start of the collapse of the Soviet Union.

1994—Bride kidnapping is made illegal in Kyrgyzstan.

2001—The Netherlands becomes the world's first country to legalize same-sex marriage.

2017—The International Labour Organization includes forced marriage in its statistical estimates of modern slavery for the first time.

2021—The Taliban returns to power in Afghanistan after twenty years of war, immediately restricting access to education and work for women and girls.

2022—The Supreme Court in the United States overturns the 1973 *Roe v. Wade* ruling establishing the federal right to abortion.

MAP OF MATRILINY

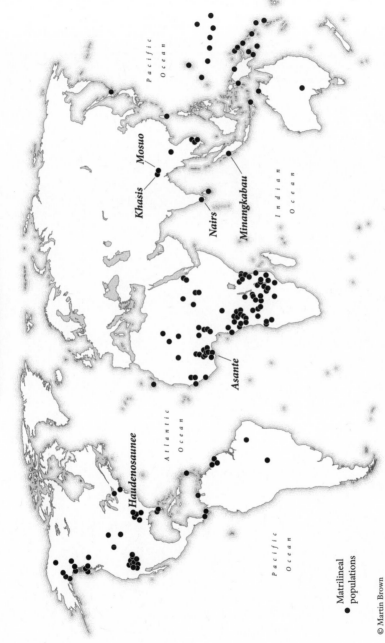

Matrilineal
populations

© Martin Brown

Illustration by Martin Brown based on fig. 1 in Alexandra Surowiec, Kate T. Snyder, and Nicole Creanza, "A Worldwide View of Matriliny: Using Cross-Cultural Analyses to Shed Light on Human Kinship Systems," Philosophical Transactions of the Royal Society B, vol. 374, no. 1780, 2 September 2019.

INTRODUCTION

've been preoccupied by images of goddesses while writing this book. But there's one to which I keep coming back.

It's a popular lithograph produced in India just over a century ago. Kali, slayer of demons, symbol of death and time, dares us to survey the carnage she's wrought. Eyes wide and tongue protruding, her bright blue skin pops from the page. Wavy black hair falls below her waist, circled by a skirt of disembodied arms. Severed heads are strung like flowers around her neck. In one hand she holds a sword; in another, the head of a demon; in her third is a plate to catch his dripping blood; the fourth gestures, outstretched, to the bloody scene around her.

Ancient Indian goddesses and gods are routinely transgressive, as though they've been summoned from other universes. But in the era of empire, British authorities and Christian missionaries in India were so terrified of Kali in particular that nationalist revolutionaries adopted her as a symbol against colonial rule. There are depictions in which she wears corpses as earrings, whole bodies threaded through her lobes. "What an awful picture!" one Englishwoman wrote in a tract published by the Bible Churchmen's Missionary Society in 1928. "Yet this savage female deity is called the gentle mother!"

The paradox of Kali is that she is a divine mother, one who challenges every modern-day assumption about womanhood and power. Whether she's a reflection of humanity or a subversion of it, the fact that she was imagined at all continues to amaze. In the twenty-first century, she has been embraced by women's rights activists from New Delhi to New York, described as the "feminist icon we need today." In her, we can still recognize our potential to destroy the social order. We can visualize the unstoppable rage in the heart of the oppressed. We might even wonder if those are the heads of history's patriarchs suspended from her neck.

This is the power the past has over us. Why do we in the twenty-first century turn to a figure from ancient history for reassurance of our capacity to change the world? What does Kali give us that we can't find within ourselves? The philosopher Kwame Anthony Appiah once asked, in a similar vein, why some of us feel the need to believe in a more equal past to picture a more equal future. Historians, scientists, anthropologists, archaeologists, and feminists have all been fascinated by this question. As a science journalist who writes about racism and sexism, I often find myself thinking about it as well. We want to know how our societies came to be structured the way they are—and what they were like before. When we look to Kali, I wonder if we're reaching for the possibility that there was a time in which men didn't rule, a lost world where femininity and masculinity didn't mean what they do now.

That desire for a historical precedent tells us something else, too. It hints at how hopeless our lives can feel at times. The word we use now to describe women's oppression—"patriarchy"—has become devastatingly monolithic, drawing in all the ways in which women and girls around the world are abused and treated unfairly, from domestic violence and rape to the gender pay gap and moral double standards. Taken together, the sheer scale and breadth of it appear out of our control. Patriarchy begins to look like one vast conspiracy stretching all the way back into deep time. Something terrible must have happened in our forgotten past to bring us to where we are now.

If only it were that straightforward.

■   ■   ■

People have long struggled to understand the origins of patriarchy.

It was in 1680 that the English political theorist Sir Robert Filmer defended the divine right of kings by arguing in his *Patriarcha* that the state was like a family, meaning kings were effectively the fathers and their subjects, the children. The royal head of state was the ultimate earthly patriarch, ordained by God, whose authority went back to the patriarchs of biblical times. In Filmer's vision of the universe—an obviously self-serving one for an aristocrat—patriarchy was natural. It began small, in people's families, with the father having dominion over his household, and ended large, marbled through institutions of politics, law, and religion.

For a while in the middle of the nineteenth century, and then in the latter half of the twentieth, intellectuals were again exercised by what patriarchy was and how it came about. Was it the overarching domination of all men over all women, or was it something more specific? Was it about sex, or was it about work? Was it underpinned by capitalism, or did it stand independently of it? Did it have a history at all, or was it a universal pattern determined by our natures?

Hundreds of years later, there was still something compelling about Robert Filmer's fractal-like explanation. In *Sexual Politics*, a classic feminist text of 1970, the American activist Kate Millett defined patriarchy as the control of younger men by older men, as well as the control of women by men more generally. Starting with the father, gendered power was still thought to radiate outwards from the home to the community and the state.

But there remained the question of how men came to have that power in the first place. In 1979, surveying what had by then become a rich seam of feminist writing about patriarchy, the British sociologist Veronica Beechey noticed that male domination was often assumed to have its basis in sex and reproduction. Women's oppression was seen to lie in men's pathological urge to control women's bodies. "Yet," she wrote, "it is never made clear what it is about men which makes them into sexual oppressors nor, more importantly, what characteristics of particular forms of society place men in positions of power over women."

As Beechey found, what complicates any universal theory of patriarchy is that gender inequality and oppression have never been the same for everyone everywhere. In the goddess Kali, after all, we have a symbol of female power. She may belong to legend, but she wouldn't have the following she does if we didn't also recognize a part of ourselves in her.

In India, where I used to live, upper- and middle-class Indian women often employ male as well as female staff to cook and clean for them at subsistence wages. I was twenty-two and living alone when I had two men working for me. Those at the bottom of the caste hierarchy do most of the country's dirtiest and lowest-paid jobs, including cleaning human and animal waste. During the first pandemic lockdown of 2020, when domestic servants returned to their homes and couldn't work, the country's wealthiest women suddenly found themselves having to do household labor for possibly the first time in their lives. Early the following year (coincidentally or not), a political party in the Indian state of Tamil Nadu began campaigning for housewives to be paid a monthly wage.

As the professor of women's studies Chandra Talpade Mohanty has asked, "How is it possible to refer to 'the' sexual division of labor when the *content* of this division changes radically from one environment to the next, and from one historical juncture to another?" If there were some fundamental aspects of male and female natures that put men in control of women, that divided us up neatly into separate roles, we would expect everyone all over the world and throughout history to share similar living and working patterns.

Of course, we don't. The low status of some women has never stopped others in the same society from having enormous wealth or power in their own right. There have been queens, empresses, female pharaohs, and powerful women warriors for as long as humans have kept records. In the last two centuries, women have reigned as monarchs over Britain for longer than men have. Women all over the world have kept slaves and servants, and still do. There are cultures that prioritize mothers, in which children aren't even seen to belong to the same households as their fathers.

"Women of different classes have different historical experiences," wrote Gerda Lerner, one of the founders of the academic field of women's history in the United States, grappling with these contradictions. "Yes, women are part of the anonymous in history, but unlike them, they are also and always have been part of the ruling elite. They are oppressed, but not quite like either racial or ethnic groups, though some of them are. They are subordinate and exploited, but not quite like lower classes, though some of them are."

In 1989, the legal scholar Catharine MacKinnon wrote about realizing that, save for a few exceptions, "feminism had no account of male power as an ordered yet deranged whole. Feminism began to seem an epic indictment in search of a theory, an epic theory in need of writing." The end products of male power are well documented—in the greater proportion of men in positions of authority, in the preference for sons in many parts of the world, in rates of sexual harassment, in statistic after statistic—but that in itself isn't an explanation for how men came to rule to begin with. "The subject to be explained—the development of male supremacy—is effectively presumed," observed MacKinnon.

"Social power is not explained, it is only restated."

What actually brought us here takes on a mythic quality. If women were exploited more than men, wrote MacKinnon, it was their *character* that was seen to be the cause rather than their material condition. The fault lay inside us, not outside us. Even Karl Marx, who dreamed of abolishing class inequality through communism, couldn't escape the suspicion that sexual inequality was an exception to other forms of oppression, resting in biological difference rather than in history.

For a while, efforts to find a universal basis for women's oppression turned into exercises in simplification, occasionally to the point of absurdity. There were accounts of the origins of patriarchy that ended with women being just plain unable to resist male domination. They were too weak and men were too strong, this story goes. In the most vivid of these narratives, the big turning point in prehistory came when peaceful, women-centered societies were suddenly overthrown by violent marauding men who shared an unstoppable lust for power and sexual control. Patriarchal gods replaced soft, nurturing mother goddesses.

"In other words," wrote the French sociologist Christine Delphy, cautioning against these speculative histories, "the culture of our own society is attributed to the 'nature' of a hypothetical society."

The American anthropologist Michelle Rosaldo was also skeptical. "We find ourselves the victims of a conceptual tradition that discovers 'essence' in the natural characteristics which distinguish us from men and then declares that women's present lot derives from what, 'in essence,' women are," she wrote in 1980. Based on her anthropological observations of societies all over the world, Rosaldo thought that male domination was indeed widespread. But she also came to see that it manifested in such different ways that it made no sense to imagine there was some globally common experience or cause to it.

"We would do well to think of biological sex, like biological race," she suggested, "as an excuse rather than a cause for any sexism we observe."

■   ■   ■

The exceptions are what truly test our assumptions. It's not in the big, simplistic accounts of history that we discover who we are but in the margins, where people live differently from how we might expect. Evidence across cultures proves that what we imagine to be fixed biological rules or neat, linear histories are usually anything but. We are a species that shows enormous variation in how we choose to live, with remarkable leeway for change. By thinking about gendered inequality as rooted in something unalterable within us, we fail to see it for what it is: something more fragile that has had to be constantly remade and reasserted.

We're in the process of remaking it even now.

There is little convincing proof for the existence of matriarchal utopias that were overthrown in one fatal swoop. Nor is there much evidence that women's oppression started in the home. Instead, we can see it in the historical record around the same time that the earliest states and empires began to grow, as they tried to expand their populations and maintain armies to defend themselves. The elites that ran these societies needed young women to have as many children as possible, and for the young men they raised to be willing warriors. It's at this point that it's possible to spot gendered rules appearing, curbing the behavior and freedom of everyday individuals. Virtues such as loyalty and honor became recruited into service of these basic goals. Traditions and religions, in turn, developed around the same social codes.

Society's pressures filtered down into households, affecting power dynamics inside relationships. In the parts of the world where brides left their childhood families to live with their husbands' families, institutions of marriage appear to have been informed by the widespread, dehumanizing practices of captive-taking and slavery. Wives might be treated as outsiders in their own communities, their status rising only as they grew older and had children of their own. Women's oppression may not have begun in the home, but it did end there.

The debris of the past suggests that the reality of male-dominated ideologies and institutions as they emerged couldn't have been one flat system in which all men exercised power over all women at once; rather there were variations depending on local circumstances. Patriarchal power could be wielded in myriad ways by everyone in a society. But all the time this was happening, people also pushed back. There was always resistance and compromise. The changes we see through time are gradual and fitful, often stealing into people's lives over generations until they couldn't imagine themselves any other way. After all, this is how social transformation usually works: by normalizing what would have been unthinkable before.

Ultimately, this is the story of individuals and groups fighting for control over the world's most valuable resource: other people. If patriarchal ways of organizing society happen to look eerily similar at opposite ends of the globe now, this isn't because societies magically (or biologically) landed on them at the same time, or because women everywhere rolled over and accepted subordination. It's because power is inventive. Gendered oppression was cooked up and refined not only within societies; it was also deliberately exported to others for centuries, through proselytism and colonialism.

The most insidious part of this racket is how it has shaped so many of our beliefs about human nature. If the Indian goddess Kali tells us something about our past, it's that how people have pictured the world has never been static. Those in power have worked desperately hard over time to give the illusion of solidity to the gendered codes and hierarchies they invented. Today, these myths have become our convictions. We live by them. We don't dare to ask whether the reason we find Kali so radical, as breaking the rules of womanhood, might be because she comes from a time when the rules were different.

After centuries of living in the societies we have made, we call what we see "patriarchy." From here it appears almost conspiratorial, as though it was cleverly planned out from the start—when, in truth, it has always been a slow grift. We can see this for ourselves in the patriarchs still trying to stretch their tentacles into our lives today. We can look to the Taliban's resurgence in Afghanistan, the clampdowns on gender freedoms in Russia and Eastern Europe, the overturning of abortion rights in the United States. This isn't a done-and-dusted origin story. It's one that we're actively in the process of writing.

This book has taken years of research and travel. The biggest challenge was untangling the mass of assumptions that bog down this subject, disguised as objective knowledge but often turning out to be husks of conjecture. The further back you go into prehistory, the more ambiguous the evidence becomes. Myth and legend interact with fact until it's almost impossible to tell them apart. I've come as close as I could to identifying the earliest signs of male domination, of the social and ideological shoots of gendered oppression, and to trace their slow growth into our own time. The account I offer is of course imperfect and incomplete. Even if we're able to see beyond the sleights of hand, we're constrained by our own experiences and beliefs. For all of us who have gone in search of the origins of patriarchy, our efforts may say less about the past than they do about the present.

But maybe it's the present we really want to understand, anyway.

CHAPTER 1

Domination

Imagine remaking the world from scratch.

That's where the plot of the multibillion-dollar Hollywood movie franchise *Planet of the Apes* takes us. The dystopian fantasy, adapted from the 1963 work of the French novelist and former secret agent Pierre Boulle, sees unsuspecting humans ousted as the world's most powerful creatures by a collective of chimpanzees, gorillas, and orangutans, who go on to build their own civilization, to create their own political and social institutions. At a stroke, *we* become the inferior species. It's about as fundamental a revolution as there could be.

The movies, starting with the original starring Charlton Heston in the 1960s and followed by sequels and remakes for another fifty years, are deliberately provocative. It's hard to miss the commentary on war, animal rights, the fragility of humanity's belief in its own exceptionalism. There's an obvious racial subtext, with echoes of civil rights struggles that have struck critics as offensive. But there's a part of *Planet of the Apes* that often passes audiences by unnoticed: whether human or ape, males are almost always at the center of the action.

The original film had one strong female character. But in the 2014 installment, Cornelia, the most visible female chimpanzee and the wife of ape protagonist Caesar, is on screen for no longer than a few minutes. What's more, she's a bundle of gendered stereotypes. After the revolution, she rapidly transforms into a caregiver and companion, beaded adornments in her hair, clutching an infant, looking vulnerable.

The thrill of science fiction should be its license to break with convention. The radical promise of this genre is that it can help us push back against the world we're in. The late Ursula K. Le Guin once wrote that her novels, like so much of the speculative fiction she admired, hoped to offer "an imagined but persuasive alternative reality, to dislodge my mind, and so the reader's mind, from the lazy, timorous habit of thinking that the way we live now is the only way people can live."

But even our fantasies seem to have their limits. We can't help but look for threads of familiarity on which to suspend our disbelief. Maybe that's why the filmmakers behind *Planet of the Apes* deliberately lend the other primates a touch more humanness than they have in real life. Chimpanzees aren't so distant from us on the evolutionary tree already, but nudged a little closer still, we can start to believe they might actually be able to overpower us. We can see ourselves in them—a species blinking into global dominance.

So, how does society look at the dawn of this brave new world in which everything starts over? Oddly, not so different from the ones we have now. Even as we swallow the possibility of a chimpanzee-led uprising, we fall short of questioning why it is that the males in these films still end up in charge. We don't ask why another species would automatically adopt heterosexual marriage customs, with females quickly disappearing into the domestic shadows.

Somehow, the apes have wound up with what looks like another patriarchy.

For it to be any other way, we're left to think to ourselves (if we think about it at all), would need a separate science fiction plot of its own. That would demand another revolution.

■   ■   ■

I had reached California's San Diego Zoo just in time to see the aftermath of the attack.

Peering into the enclosure, I couldn't help but pity the ape nursing a wound on his hand, crouched to one side with his back to the group, looking to my eyes as though he was scared or embarrassed. Amy Parish, a primatologist from the University of Southern California who had studied bonobo apes here for so long that the animals recognized her, explained to me that male bonobos usually rely on their mothers for protection and status. Without his mother around, this one had fallen immediate victim to a violent attack from an older female.

In the five years since I met Parish that day at the zoo, her work with bonobos has only further reinforced the scientific consensus that female domination is the norm for this species. Bonobo females are known to chase and attack males. And this matters to the human story because bonobos are at least as close to us in evolutionary terms as chimpanzees are, making them one of our two nearest genetic relatives in the animal kingdom. The primate expert Frans de Waal, a professor of psychology at Emory University, confirms that no bonobo colony has ever been found to be led by a male, not in captivity, nor in the wild. "There used to be a little bit of doubt about that, like twenty years ago," he tells me, but "people don't say that anymore.

"We now say that females are dominant."

Male domination is certainly common in the animal kingdom. It's seen among chimpanzees, for instance. "Most people do think patriarchy is a given," says Parish. But it's not a hard-and-fast rule. The more researchers look in detail, the more variation they find. Female leadership is seen not just among bonobos but also among killer whales, lions, spotted hyenas, lemurs, and elephants.

When it comes to understanding how dominance works, "there is so much we can learn from bonobos," adds Parish. For this species at least, it has nothing to do with size. Bonobo females are on average slightly smaller than the males, the same way that chimpanzee females are slightly smaller than their males. What sets them apart is that bonobo females form tight social bonds with each other even when they're not related, cementing those relationships and easing tensions by rubbing their genitals together. These intimate social networks create power, locking out the possibility for individual males to dominate the group.

"We have this storyline that males are naturally dominant over females, and that males make better leaders than females. And I think that storyline just doesn't work," de Waal continues. The evidence doesn't stack up. Yet, as he and Parish have seen for themselves, convincing others of this has taken longer than it perhaps should have. "It's very hard for men to accept that women would be in charge," says de Waal. If facts were overlooked in the *Planet of the Apes* movies, blame might be placed at the feet of sexist myths that have bogged down studies of animal behavior for generations.

"It's sort of interesting for me as a man to write about gender and bonobos, because I think if a woman would write about the things that I write about bonobos, she would probably be dismissed," he adds. Even fellow primatologists have been reluctant to accept the existence of a clearly female-dominated species. Once, while giving a lecture in Germany about the power of the alpha female bonobo, de Waal recalls, "at the end of the discussion there was a German professor, an older man, who stood up and said, 'What is *wrong* with those males?'"

But there's more to it than sexism. When we observe other species, we search for what we observe in ourselves. If humans have patriarchal societies, how can our nearest primate cousins, the ones who we imagine represent our primordial past, not be the same? What does that say about the evolutionary roots of male domination?

Five years after the first *Planet of the Apes* film opened in theatres in 1968, a professor of sociology at the City University of New York, Steven Goldberg, published a book arguing that the fundamental biological differences between men and women ran so deep that in every iteration of human society a patriarchal system would win out eventually. His claim in *The Inevitability of Patriarchy* was that whichever way people happened to cut the pie, men—in his view being naturally more powerful and aggressive—would always end up with the bigger slice.

Goldberg wrote that he valued scientific truths and hard biological data above all. But his argument actually rested on what he gauged to be other people's sense of their own status. "Male dominance refers to the *feeling* [his emphasis] acknowledged by the emotions of both men and women that the woman's will is somehow subordinate to the male's," he explained. "Every society accepts the existence of these feelings, and conforms to their existence by socializing children accordingly, because every society must." Goldberg might have interpreted this behavior as a self-fulfilling prophecy, of culture affecting how we behave over generations. Instead, he saw it as a biological instinct, as nature playing out its script.

Hand-wavy though his explanation might sound to us today, there are actually few differences between Goldberg's conclusion and the writings of scientists and philosophers through the centuries. Naturalist Charles Darwin thought that "man has ultimately become superior to woman" as a result of evolution. Biologist Edward O. Wilson wrote in 1975 that one of the basic human patterns was that adult males "are dominant over females." It's a belief that plays out, again and again, in popular culture. In a 1988 episode of the science fiction series *Star Trek: The Next Generation*, the crew beams down to a planet that happens to be governed by women who treat men as their inferiors. The mystery of this matriarchal planet is resolved for the audience by a simple visual cue: the men of this world are noticeably shorter and physically slighter than the women. Of course, the women are in charge because they're bigger!

But as we know from bonobos, we can't assume that average physical differences in size or strength between the sexes necessarily lead to a steep imbalance of power at the level of society as a whole. There's no biological rule here.

Why, then, do we routinely assume there must be? Even feminists, argues the sociologist Christine Delphy, have leaned on biological arguments to explain women's status, seeing patriarchy as having its roots in a natural division of labor between the sexes, or in an overwhelming male instinct to control female sexuality. "Naturalism is, of course, even more obvious in anti-feminist thinking," she writes, "but it is still present in large measure in feminism."

■　■　■

Steven Goldberg was eventually made chair of the Department of Sociology at the City University of New York. When I speak to him nearly five decades after *The Inevitability of Patriarchy* was published, I find his faith in his theory only slightly weather-beaten. Goldberg insists that he was politically uninterested in the topic when he first started researching it all those years ago, that he was just trying to make sense of a neutral observation.

"Curiosity . . . That's my real motivation," he tells me over the phone. "When I was in sociology, it was disturbing to me, basically, how mushy a lot of it was. And when I happened upon the fact that societies were *all* patriarchal, that fascinated me."

At the core of his argument was a single fact: in 1973, when his book was published, many of the world's most powerful countries, including the United States, China, and the Soviet Union, were led by men. One might have countered that Indira Gandhi was prime minister of India, and there was Golda Meir running Israel. Unknown to Goldberg at the time, obviously, was that Margaret Thatcher would be leading Britain by 1979. But Goldberg did hit upon an uncomfortable truth: there seemed to be a stubborn endurance to male authority. Even in the states that had women as leaders, most of the politicians underneath them tended to be men. Thatcher was a prime example, choosing only one woman to be in her cabinet in the eleven years she was in power.

"Patriarchy is universal," Goldberg tells me. "The fact that every society is that way, to me suggests strongly that there is some biological element, and to some extent it's inevitable."

In a book review at the time for the journal *American Anthropologist*, Eleanor Leacock, the chair of anthropology at the City College of New York, was exasperated with the lack of science linking Goldberg's theory to something measurable in our bodies. His answer to male domination was a frustratingly tautological one. It was natural for it to exist, and it existed because it was natural. "If I had the wit I would write a parody rather than a straight review," she wrote. "Perhaps, however, Goldberg's argument is itself a parody."

When his book came out, the data around women in leadership leaned in Goldberg's favor. But in the decades since, it has moved in the other direction. The first woman in the world to be elected prime minister was in Sri Lanka in 1960. Sirimavo Bandaranaike ended up serving three separate terms. After 1960, the number of countries in which the highest position of executive power was held by a woman rose steadily with only the occasional dip, reaching eighteen in 2019. By the start of 2020, United Nations data showed that fourteen countries had governments in which at least half the ministers were women: Spain, Finland, Nicaragua, Colombia, Austria, Peru, Sweden, Rwanda, Albania, France, Andorra, Canada, Costa Rica, and Guinea-Bissau.

"Science speaks only of what is and what, within the limits of mathematical probability, must be," Goldberg had written in 1973, fully convinced that the future would turn out to reinforce his claims. In light of fifty years of social change, mostly the other way, "the tendency has been to move away from what my book argues," he admits. "When you have a theory, you always have to be prepared to be incorrect." But he still believes that he'll be proven right in the long run. "I think it's a somewhat muddier situation now," he tells me. "If things remained the way they were a hundred years ago, my theory would be stronger, but I think it's still strong."

He leaves me with a prediction: "We're never going to come to the point where any society completely lacks patriarchy." For him, male domination is a biological tide that cultural pressure can stem only so far. Sexual equality is something that must be fought for against our natural instincts.

Goldberg's argument, then, falls back again on his personal feelings. His implication is that female power is something new, a modern interference with a universal, timeless order. Patriarchy is the way life has always been. But the problem remains one of hard evidence. What proof do we have that life has always been this way? If it were universal and timeless, we should at least be able to find some of the same patriarchal patterns we see in humans among other species, particularly the ones closest to us on the evolutionary tree.

But as primatologist Frans de Waal explains, when animal researchers talk about male dominance, they're almost always referring to males trying to assert dominance over each other—not over females. "Even in a chimp society where males dominate, you have female leaders," he says.

Sexual coercion of females does happen, but how violently and to what degree varies enormously between species. And between males, size and aggression don't necessarily give them the deciding edge. The alpha wins not always by beating others into submission but by building networks of strategic allies. Primates don't like to be ruled by bullies or treated unfairly. Some of the key traits linked to dominance are kindness, sociability, and cooperation. Even the physically smallest chimpanzee can end up being the alpha if he shows an ability to win trust and loyalty, adds de Waal. Conflict management strategies to keep the peace also exist among ravens and domestic dogs, according to the Bristol University biologist Amy Morris-Drake, who in 2021 was part of a team that showed that dwarf mongooses, too, remember which of their group picked fights with others and later give them the cold shoulder.

Identifying what is and what isn't "natural" behavior in animals isn't as simple as it sounds either. In 2010, researchers from the Max Planck Institute spotted a chimpanzee at a wildlife trust in Zambia tucking a blade of grass in her ear for no apparent reason. Soon, other chimps started doing the same, continuing with the trend after she had died. Scientists described it as a "tradition." And this raised a dilemma: if other primates can forge what look like traditions or social customs, how are we supposed to identify an immutable, never-changing nature in a species as culturally complex as our own? As de Waal tells me, there are some chimpanzee communities in West Africa that, in contrast to those in East Africa, are more cohesive. In these societies, females have a stronger hand. He believes that the difference, here too, may be partly a cultural one.

"I think when people say that patriarchy is sort of natural for the human species, . . . that male dominance and male violence are natural, I think they are totally exaggerating," he says. "I don't think that's necessarily the natural condition of our species."

When compared with other primates, the "patriarchal" human family with the father at its head in fact looks quite odd. In a special issue of a Royal Society journal in 2019, anthropologist Melissa Emery Thompson at the University of New Mexico found that "no primate species provides a direct analogue to humans." On the contrary, she found that kin relationships in other primates are consistently organized through mothers rather than fathers. This may mean nothing at all. It could well be that humans are just different from non-human primates. But ties to mothers were so persistent a feature that it led Thompson to wonder whether scientists who had studied humans might actually have underestimated the importance of maternal links through generations. Experts were so sure that human patriarchy could be explained using biology that they had become blind to the possibility that mothers could hold power as well as fathers.

■   ■   ■

One monsoon morning in July 1968, Robin Jeffrey was traveling through the Indian state of Kerala by bus. Now an academic who studies the modern history and politics of India, he had been working as a schoolteacher in Punjab in the north of the country at the time. Kerala's climate tends to be humid, and after a while, the bus steamed up. So, he opened the tarpaulin on his window at the first stop to let in some air. A few meters away, he noticed an old woman dressed in white, sitting comfortably dry on her veranda.

She peered intently through thick spectacles. Propped up against her leg, he saw her morning newspaper.

That moment felt so remarkable to him that he's never forgotten it. "It's so fixed in my mind," he tells me. It was unusual for Jeffrey to see anyone reading a local language newspaper in public, at least in Punjab. Literacy across India was low, as it was in much of the world then, but female literacy was even lower. People rarely owned reading glasses. Yet, here was this woman, leisurely reading her paper. "It's just one of those vivid, vivid pictures that strikes you when it's so out of keeping with what you expect."

Adult literacy in India is far higher today, around three-quarters of the population, but there remains a pronounced gender gap in most states. In Kerala, though, women's literacy rates have been around the same as men's for as long as records have been kept. They currently sit at more than 95 percent. Running along India's verdant southwest coast, the state is famous for being one where women can travel alone and walk the streets relatively safe and unbothered. And this is no small thing. In my first job at an Indian current affairs magazine in the busy, dusty capital New Delhi, I quickly learned not to go out after dark without a friend or relative. A misogynistic disregard for women and girls, leaning toward contempt, was matched only by a no-nonsense resilience that women had learned to adopt. Kerala, on the other hand, was spoken about in almost fabled terms as a place where gender roles were reversed, where women had always ruled and daughters were prized over sons.

To this day, Kerala is often referred to by outsiders as matriarchal. In reality, misogyny and abuse exist there just like they do elsewhere, and women are far from holding all the power, especially lower-caste women. But there is some truth to the legends. At least some of the state's record on gender equality can be laid at the door of the ancient Nairs, a powerful caste-based community that once dominated parts of this region, organizing itself along matrilineal lines, tracing ancestry through mothers rather than fathers.

They're often treated as exceptions, but societies with a matrilineal bias are in fact dotted across Asia, parts of North and South America, and a wide "matrilineal belt" stretching through the middle of Africa. Matriliny doesn't guarantee that women are better treated, or that men won't be in positions of power and authority, but it is one part of the picture of how a society thinks about gender. At its simplest, it tells children that their female ancestors matter, that girls have an important place in their families. It can also determine a woman's status and how much wealth and property she can expect to inherit. In 2020, the economist Sara Lowes at the University of California, San Diego, published a survey of more than six hundred people living in an urban area along Africa's matrilineal belt in Kananga, Democratic Republic of Congo, comparing their responses to independent demographic and health surveys across the country as a whole. She found that "matrilineal women report greater autonomy in decision-making, are less supportive of domestic violence, and, crucially, experience less domestic violence."

Lowes also found that children of matrilineal women were less likely than others to have been sick in the month before the survey was taken and had on average almost half a year more of education.

Researchers estimate that around 70 percent of societies around the world are patrilocal, meaning people tend to live with their fathers' families. Matrilocality, where people stay with or near their mothers' families throughout their lives, often goes hand in hand with matriliny. And at least some of these matrilocal societies are believed to be thousands of years old. In 2009, biologists and anthropologists writing in the scientific journal *Proceedings of the Royal Society B* used genetic evidence, together with cultural data and family trees, to prove that matrilocal communities in the Pacific, for example, may go as far back as five millennia. Living habits have changed since then, but there was still a "theme" of matrilineality and matrilocality running through them.

In his 1991 memoir in the local language Malayalam, later translated into English with the title *The Village Before Time*, the journalist Madhavan Kutty offers an intimate portrait of everyday life in his matrilineal childhood home in Kerala. Rather than small nuclear families splitting off after marriage, Nairs would live together in large *taravads*, joint households with possibly dozens of family members, each sharing an older female ancestor. Sisters and brothers stayed under one roof all of their lives. Women were allowed more than one sexual partner, none of whom would necessarily live with her. This meant that fathers weren't expected to play a big part in raising their own children but would instead help to raise their sisters' children. Born into a huge *taravad*, Kutty recounts that his was a family tree in which only the children of daughters were listed.

Kutty's grandmother, Karthiyayani Amma, eventually became the head of their household. As local custom had it, she never covered her breasts. "A deep, subconscious wealth of history was contained within her," he writes. "This matriarch of our extended family, a personality of great fortitude and understanding, was deeply concerned about women's liberty."

Theirs wasn't a small or unimportant community. Nairs had high standing in a country that pays acute attention to social status. The Kerala-born author Manu Pillai has traced the history of the Kingdom of Travancore, which stretched over parts of southern Kerala for at least two hundred years until the middle of the twentieth century. "Nair women always had the security of the homes they were born in throughout their lives and were not dependent on their husbands," he writes in his book *The Ivory Throne*. "Widowhood was no catastrophic disaster and they were effectively at par with men when it came to sexual rights, with complete control over their bodies."

For those on the inside, of course, this was nothing remarkable. It was family life as it had been for generations. But from the moment they encountered Kerala's Nairs, European visitors were transfixed. It wasn't just the reality that fascinated them but also the creative potential of what looked to them like "normal" society upended. Some were shocked, according to G. Arunima, a scholar of women's studies at Jawaharlal Nehru University and the director of the Kerala Council for Historical Research. In the seventeenth century, one Dutch traveler found theirs to be the "most lecherous and unchast nation in all the Orient," she writes. Others were inspired. Around the end of the eighteenth century, James Henry Lawrence, a young British novelist and son of a slave owner, wrote a romance later titled *The Empire of the Nairs*. Lawrence used Kerala's example to advocate for women in Europe to be better educated and allowed to have multiple lovers. He also called for an end to marriage.

But whichever way they reacted, writes Arunima, outsiders usually looked upon Nairs as an oddity, betraying their belief that patriliny was the normal way of life. Matrilineal societies were described as "uncivilized" and "unnatural." Their existence needed to be explained.

Even today, Western academics treat them with a mix of confusion and surprise. Matriliny has been described in recent anthropological literature as a paradox, a state that's inherently unstable. The phrase "matrilineal puzzle" has been used for seventy years by researchers studying societies such as Kerala's Nairs: Why would a father invest his time and energy looking after his nieces and nephews, rather than his own children? Why would a man tolerate his brother-in-law having authority over his own children and their mother? How could men put up with this for centuries without forcing a change?

When change did come to Kerala in the nineteenth century, the irony is that it was in large part because of the attitudes of curious and scandalized outsiders. British colonialists who took over the region, together with missionaries looking to convert people to Christianity, pressured matrilineal Keralans to bring gender norms into line with their Victorian sensibilities. "In seeking a psychological advantage over their subjects colonial ideology felt compelled to assert the moral superiority of the rulers in many subtle and not so subtle ways," writes the historian Uma Chakravarti.

Over the course of the nineteenth century, power that had been held by older brothers in the *taravads* swung from being shared with the women of their households, always contingent on circumstance or seniority, to being sole and incontestable. Colonial-era legal rulings with one eye on "civilizing" matrilineal communities helped to raise the status of the eldest men in the *taravads*. Family disputes followed. In one court case in 1855, a judge in Calicut, one of Kerala's largest cities and then under direct British rule, stated that "it would indeed be a violent inference that . . . the authority resides in women only."

The question of how much power a woman could naturally possess had already come up when Travancore's queen, Rani Gowri Lakshmi, began her reign in 1810. When she gave birth to a son, she was asked to pass the throne to him, explains Manu Pillai. The queen would instead have the watered-down caretaker title of "regent" until he was old enough to rule. As much as the British authorities tried to dilute her status, though, local people couldn't help but see her as the rightful monarch anyway. Pillai notes that she carried on with unrestrained authority. And this continued when her sister took over after her death. The queen was even addressed in official documents as "Maharajah," the title usually given to an Indian king.

Under the matrilineal system, where the sexes were relatively more equal than in a patrilineal system, "the monarch's gender was of little consequence," writes Pillai. "It was the position and its dignity that mattered and whoever exercised supreme authority in the state and in the royal house was held to be the Maharajah."

But as the decades passed, the pressure on Nair families to change began to have its intended effect. Young, educated reformers became eager to make a break with the past, having learned to see their traditions through the eyes of others as embarrassing and backward. Monogamous marriage and smaller families were slowly accepted as more modern. Literature and art started to reflect shifting opinions about women and their place in society. The cultural dial moved and, with it, people's ideas about themselves.

■   ■   ■

There's a local saying in the million-strong Khasi community in the grassy hills of Meghalaya, northeast India: *Long Jaid na ka Kynthei*. It means "all people sprang from the woman." Khasis are matrilineal, but unlike Kerala's Nairs, their tribal society remains matrilineal to this day. A child is seen to belong to her mother. She, in turn, belongs to her own mother, and so on, all the way back to the root ancestress. The birth of a daughter is cause for celebration because there's nobody to carry on the family line without her.

"Men do not have rights over property, and men also do not have rights over children, because the children belong to the mother's clan, the mother's family," I'm told by Tiplut Nongbri, a retired professor of sociology at Jawaharlal Nehru University, who grew up in the Khasi Hills. After marriage, a Khasi husband will move to his wife's family home. But his ancestral place is still back with his own mother's clan—sometimes his remains will be sent to rest with them after death. "Traditionally, inheritance among the Khasis flows from mother to daughter, with the youngest daughter getting the bulk of the property," adds Nongbri. It becomes her responsibility to take care of her parents and any unmarried siblings. She's the family's custodian.

Theirs isn't strictly a matriarchal society. Family authority rests formally with the mother's brother, although his power isn't absolute. Women also play a marginal role in local politics. But even then, Nongbri tells me that they're better off on average than they would be in patrilineal communities elsewhere in India. Khasi women divorce and remarry more often than other Indian women. They have relatively more freedom and agency. Having experienced life both ways, as a woman inside a matrilineal society and outside it, Nongbri says there's no comparison.

"I'm happy that I was born into that society," she tells me.

But just like in Kerala, there has been pressure to change. This is where the story of modern-day Khasis overlaps with the history of Nairs. When Welsh Christian missionaries came to the Khasi Hills in the nineteenth century, they chipped away at some of the roots of local kinship customs, pushing out religious rituals that brought clans together. This weakened the ties between brothers and sisters, which sat at the heart of the matrilineal family. More recently, as the world has become more interconnected, Khasi men have been able to see patriarchal alternatives to their own society in the rest of India. A few have started pushing for adjustments to inheritance laws to benefit sons as well as daughters.

"They want the same kinds of power and privilege and authority that men in non-matriarchal societies enjoy," explains Nongbri. "Men with exposure to the outside world, when they see themselves, compare themselves with the men in patriarchal societies who have rights over children, rights over property, and exercise control over everything in the nuclear household; they see themselves as being disadvantageous in many respects," she adds. "It brings on an inferiority complex."

International news outlets have been captivated by what they've framed as a topsy-turvy struggle for gender equality. "Meet the Men's Libbers of Meghalaya," went one headline in the *Times of India*. Khasi men feel undervalued and marginalized, treated like breeders who are only good for making babies, other journalists have reported. This is "where women rule, and men are suffragettes," according to the BBC News.

The amused reactions of the press feed into how some Khasi men see themselves. "Women are everywhere, in the bazaars, at the government offices," *Deutsche Welle* quoted Keith Pariat, former president of the men's rights group Synkhong Rympei Thymmai (roughly translated to Association for Reformation of the Family Structure). Pariat went against tradition by passing his own surname onto his daughter. According to him, the discomfort felt by Khasi men living in a matrilineal society had driven some of them to drink, to drugs, and into the arms of other women.

But Pariat is an outlier. Others have defended their community's traditions. Support for matriliny remains strong. As far back as 1936, the Khasi writer David Roy Phanwar, born in the hill station of Shillong and educated in Calcutta, pushed back against the hypocrisy of foreigners who framed his community as simple and superstitious, yet saw the relatively recent fight for women's suffrage as modern and progressive. "Women amongst the Khasis enjoy a position of unusual dignity and importance," he wrote. "The enslavement of the wife where she is a mere chattel of the family of men has been the cause of the feminist movement in the world, but in Khasi the woman is the glorified person, free to act."

The tension between newer patriarchal forces and time-honored ones, between what's seen to be modern and what's valued because it's ancient, is shared by matrilineal societies elsewhere. In West Sumatra in Indonesia, Minangkabau communities have households traditionally made up of women and their children, with husbands joining wives upon marriage. While men are able to inherit land from their mothers, ownership lasts only for their lifetime—they're not allowed to pass their inheritance onto their own children. Evelyn Blackwood, an anthropologist at Purdue University, writes that when this region was under Dutch rule in the nineteenth century, colonialists routinely assumed that senior Minangkabau men must have been the chiefs and leaders. They selected men to work with them in enforcing their rules. Over time, the Dutch authorities passed decrees that only men could register land or represent their ancestral families in disputes.

This may not have had much of an impact on how Minangkabau families thought about themselves in the short term, but Blackwood argues that the presence of this different worldview did leave "a strong impression on those elite Minangkabau men educated in Dutch schools." When Islam arrived, it again gave men fresh routes into positions of authority that they didn't have before, this time as religious leaders. Eventually, the country would have a Muslim majority. To this day, there's a struggle between those who want to live by the new ways and those who want to stick to the old customs, known in the local language as *adat*.

The late Indonesian anthropologist Mochtar Naim, who chronicled the changes in Minangkabau society, explained that part of the problem was that a father was seen as a guest in his children's family. In a society in which young, unmarried men also already felt marginalized, without firm footholds in their mother's homes after reaching adulthood yet with no wives whose homes they could go to, it's small surprise that some were willing to entertain alternatives. People began migrating in search of property and wealth. Couples wanting more independence split off into nuclear families or found compromises to old marriage traditions.

It wasn't that they were necessarily rejecting matriliny. It was more that they wondered whether life might be better another way.

■   ■   ■

In the Nair *taravads* of nineteenth-century Kerala, just like in the matrilineal societies negotiating their survival in the present, change didn't come like a violent storm. It crept in slowly.

A celebrated Malayalam novel in 1889 featured a new brand of woman, writes Manu Pillai. "She has all the qualities of a self-assured woman but (and this is crucial) she is tremendously dedicated to her one man, has the graces of an English lady, and is horrified when her virtue is questioned." Four years later, a painting by the renowned Indian artist Raja Ravi Varma showed a young, upper-class Nair woman in traditional dress, with a baby perched on her hip and a dog at her feet, all three awaiting the arrival of a mysterious person in the distance. The picture's title, *There Comes Papa*, explained the identity of that fourth figure. The father, who had never before been a central figure in the matrilineal *taravad*, was moving into its heart.

What was happening was a gradual realignment of where family authority was seen to naturally lie. This didn't come about just through the efforts of colonial authorities and zealous missionaries; it was also supported by those who thought they might be advantaged by the new ways, who welcomed the end of their communal households as a chance to seize a slice of family power, property, and wealth.

Gender norms changed, pushed along by legislation. By 1912, writes Arunima, matriliny was undermined by new laws in Travancore that tried to shift partnerships between women and men, which until then could be easily ended, into the territory of legal, monogamous marriages. Newly minted husbands were able to pass on property, which had previously been shared by their mother's families, to their own wives and children. Wives could receive maintenance but only if they weren't "adulterous," adds Arunima, meaning the sexual freedom they had before was effectively gone. The changes were slow and piecemeal, but they added up.

The final blow to the *taravad* would come in 1976, decades after India's independence from British rule. That year, the Kerala legislature abolished matriliny altogether.

By the end of the twentieth century, the sprawling homes of former matrilineal clans lay in disrepair. The ones that were in better shape were sold. Others were demolished. The sociologist Janaki Abraham at the University of Delhi, who has carried out fieldwork in Kerala, notes how dramatic the collapse of the *taravads* looked by then. Those who were alive in the old days could recall how many people, particularly children, used to live in the houses once. "Sometimes there were even enough for one side of a cricket team!" Now the buildings that survived had "only one or two old people living in them, and many were locked up, with greenery growing tall and wild around them."

The transition away from matriliny in Kerala had stretched achingly across more than a century. There was no single cause, and neither had it been inevitable. Toward the end, people were carried along, noticing what they had lost only after it was gone.

■   ■   ■

For decades, biologists and anthropologists have come up with hypothesis after hypothesis to try to explain the conditions under which matriliny thrives or declines.

Some have claimed, for instance, that it can exist only among hunter-gatherers or simple agriculturalists, not in larger-scale societies. Others say that matriliny works best when men are away at war for most of the time, leaving women in charge. Many argue that as soon as people start keeping cattle or other big animals, matriliny ends, because men want to control these resources. Even more have claimed that land or property ownership automatically brings patriarchy, for similar reasons. The very existence of these explanations assumes that societies that land on matriliny are unusual cases, "beset by special strains, as fragile and rare, possibly even doomed to extinction," the Washington State University anthropologist Linda Stone has written. In academic circles, the problem has its own name: the "matrilineal puzzle."

Patriliny, on the other hand, is seen to need no explanation at all. It just is.

In 2019, researchers at Vanderbilt University attempted to solve the matrilineal puzzle. They analyzed known matrilineal communities across the world to see if they did actually have anything in common. They were looking for shared evolutionary threads, some pattern that might connect them. Of the 1,291 societies they looked at, 590 were traditionally patrilineal and 160 were traditionally matrilineal. Another 362 societies were bilateral, meaning they acknowledged descent through both parents. Nicole Creanza, one of the biologists who worked on the study, tells me that not one of the popular anthropological ideas about matriliny they tested held true in every case.

"I thought that if we scaled up the patterns to worldwide, we would likely only see some of them being significant, and that's basically what we saw," she says. "A lot of the hypotheses that we catalogued from the literature didn't really hold up to a worldwide evolutionary analysis."

The single factor that did seem to affect a society's move away from matriliny, says Creanza, was "when populations had property, not in terms of land, but movable, transmissible wealth, where if your offspring inherited this thing that you have, they would be potentially better off." But even this correlation didn't hold true all of the time. In the end, each society was just too socially complicated to reduce to simple factors, be they biological, environmental, or anything else. "As far in as you can zoom," she says, "you can find more and more complexity."

Western anthropologists have long insisted that there are no real matriarchies in the world, if by "matriarchy" we mean the opposite of "patriarchy." But if patriarchy begins with the dominion of the father over his family and ends with the ruler over his subjects, as the English political theorist Robert Filmer wrote centuries ago in his *Patriarcha*, it's hard to argue that matrilineal and matrilocal societies are really patriarchal at all. Even if a great deal of authority lies with the brother or uncle, this power is more often diffuse, rather than the absolute kind of power that Filmer referred to. What characterizes matrilineal societies, as Linda Stone has written, is "considerable variation" in "authority, power and influence among both males and females."

As much variation as there is now, there would have been even more in the past. In prehistory, social norms were changing all the time. The late anthropologist David Graeber and his colleague the archaeologist David Wengrow have written that human life before the widespread adoption of agriculture was "one of bold social experiments, resembling a carnival parade of political forms." For them, the evidence for institutional inequality in prehistory has proven sporadic. "Even if we put this down to the patchiness of the evidence, we still have to ask why the evidence is so patchy."

If the only way of thinking about gender and power is a binary opposition between women and men, it becomes impossible to imagine men sharing status and importance with women, or of the balance of power changing with circumstances. But this is often what we have in matrilineal societies. For Asante people in Ghana, for instance, leadership is divided between the queen mother (a position she holds in her own right, not because she is anyone's mother or wife) and the (male) chief, whom she has a role in selecting. It was the powerful Asante ruler Nana Yaa Asantewaa who famously commanded her army in rebellion against British colonial rule in 1900.

"To some extent, the matrilineal puzzle is primarily a puzzle if you think about the default being male transmission of things," Creanza reflects. "Nobody ever calls the patriarchy 'the patriarchal puzzle.'"

Yet we know that human history is full of transitions, with societies dramatically changing how they're organized or how they operate. What can appear from one point of view to be an instability resolving itself—a shift from matriliny to patriliny, for instance—may from another point of view be a move from one relatively stable state to another, explains Creanza. Scholars almost never look at feminist movements in more patriarchal societies and ask whether this might mean *they* are socially unstable. Maybe the real puzzle isn't the existence of a relatively small number of matrilineal societies, but that patriarchal ones have become so common.

■　■　■

For Choo Waihong, matriliny was a life-changing experience.

In her memoir *The Kingdom of Women*, the corporate lawyer describes visiting the Mosuo, a goddess-worshipping society in Southwest China. Living between the Sichuan and Yunnan border since what's thought to be at least the thirteenth century, they've so far resisted being absorbed into the wider patriarchal Han Chinese culture like their neighbors have been. Mosuo children live in their mother's homes. A man's place is in his own mother's house, helping to raise his sisters' children. Instead of marriage, when a young woman comes of age, she's given her own room in which to invite her lovers in the night, with the expectation that they will leave in the morning.

Having lived and worked in the capitalist metropolis of Singapore, Waihong found the Mosuo way of life so liberating—calling it not just a matriarchy but a "feminist utopia"—that she chose to live with them.

"I really believe I am accepted because I am a woman welcomed into a woman's world," she writes with undisguised thrill. "The Mosuo woman positively rocks with confidence. It is not an aggressive confidence but a self-assurance that comes from deep within. I see it in her tall and straight-backed gait." Bathing in hot springs, she marvels at a sixty-six-year-old grandmother who has a six-pack from physical labor. At a bar, she sees a young woman confidently stride up to a group of men to buy them a round of beer. She's made to wait before talking business with a Mosuo grandfather because he's busy changing his granddaughters' nappies.

In the galaxy of alternative worlds, there are the imaginary ones, the ones we see in science fiction. But none are as radical as the ones that are real. This kingdom of women, Waihong writes, "has shown that it is possible to have an alternative model." It's a living memory that things can be different.

But no society is forged without effort. James Suzman and Christopher Boehm, anthropologists who have both studied egalitarian societies, particularly smaller hunter-gathering communities, learned that social equality doesn't come easily. It takes complex, ongoing negotiation, keeping power, jealousy, and greed in check, sometimes using criticism or ridicule of those in power. Yet all over the world, we keep trying to achieve it. As Suzman writes, "As much as modern human history has been shaped by the pursuit of wealth, status and power, it has also been defined by popular movements determined to flatten established hierarchies."

Everywhere, people are pushing for societies to be structured differently, for the marginalized to have more freedoms or privileges. "Anyone, given half a chance, will prefer equality and justice to inequality and injustice," writes the political theorist Anne Phillips. "Subservience does not, on the whole, come naturally to people." We generally don't submit to power or aggression without resistance.

The heart of sociologist Steven Goldberg's argument in *The Inevitability of Patriarchy* back in 1973 was that if a pattern of behavior is seen universally, it probably has a biological basis. It's a line of reasoning that has run through the work of biologists, too, for centuries. The best way to understand a species is to observe how it behaves. But if we're to follow this approach and take as a scientific fact that all the members of one sex are naturally subordinate to another, that there are innate differences between us that make it impossible for women to have equality or as much power as men, we also have to be able to explain why women fight for more rights and privileges at all. If subordination is knitted into our bodies and minds, it's hard to understand why we struggle against it. To use Goldberg's own argument against him, why do so many people *feel* aggrieved about gendered expectations and oppression? If there is only one natural way for us to live, just one that is biologically inevitable, why do we have different ways at all?

"I consider the oppression of women *to be a system*," argues the sociologist Christine Delphy. "An institution which exists today cannot be explained by the simple fact that it existed in the past, even if this past is recent." If we resign ourselves to accepting our lot as part of who we are, we give up on understanding how it might have come about. When we settle for resting the case for "patriarchy" on something as simple as biological difference, when the evidence points to a reality that's far more complex and contingent, we lose the capacity to see just how precarious it might be. We stop asking how it works or the ways in which it's being reinvented. We don't dissect the circumstances that might help us undermine its ideological power right now.

The most dangerous part of any form of oppression is that it can make people believe that there are no alternatives. We see this in the old fallacies of race, caste, and class. The question for any theory of male domination is why this one form of inequality should be treated as an exception.

CHAPTER 2

Exception

The small town of Seneca Falls, surrounded by picturesque lakes and vineyards in Upstate New York, is unnervingly quiet when I visit on a freezing day in March.

The original Wesleyan Chapel on the corner of Fall Street is long gone. What little was left of the building has been turned sympathetically into a museum, now a pilgrimage site for women's rights activists. But even women's rights activists know not to come in winter. I'm the only one here. I take a pew and stare at the bare brick walls, imagining for a moment the summer of 1848 when this spot would have been crowded with people, some of them supporters, some opponents, and some here to just witness the first-ever women's rights convention.

Historians remember that time as the dawn of the American suffrage movement. One of the most prominent speakers at the convention was Frederick Douglass, the Black social reformer and abolitionist who had escaped slavery in 1838. The organizers themselves were exclusively white, middle-class, and fairly well-connected Christian women. Among them was thirty-two-year-old Elizabeth Cady Stanton, who on the first day of the convention made the radical announcement that women had gathered here "to declare our right to be free as man is free." Stanton would later be heralded as a pioneer, writing influential articles and books. She contributed to *The Woman's Bible*, which controversially challenged religious assumptions about women's inferiority and subservience to men.

Today, there are pictures of Stanton all over Seneca Falls. An elementary school is named after her. The story of this town has been written around people like her. Its status owes everything to their efforts and the legend they built around their struggle. These women didn't just fight for themselves, we are told; they fought for all women everywhere.

But in the shadows of that history is a neglected one. The significance of Seneca Falls to women's rights actually goes back much further than the middle of the nineteenth century. It goes back to long before the United States was even founded.

■   ■   ■

"History is a story Western culture buffs tell each other," writes the feminist scholar Donna Haraway.

I think about this as I wander the dimly lit halls of the American Museum of Natural History in New York City, around five hours southeast of Seneca Falls. In 1939, a diorama was constructed here depicting a scene titled "Old New York." It told the story of the birth of the city in 1660, when European colonists first started to settle in the state. And it survives to this day. Behind glass, a life-sized model of Dutch colonial leader Peter Stuyvesant welcomes a delegation of Lenape, Native Americans on whose land the city now sits. There's a Dutch-style wooden windmill in the background and a fleet of European sailing ships shimmering behind it. All the Dutch people in this scene are fully clothed. Stuyvesant is in a hat and cape. All the Lenape figures, on the other hand, including one representing a leader and respected delegate, the sachem Oratamin, are dressed in simple red loincloths. In the middle distance I can see images of Native American women carrying heavy loads on their naked backs, with their faces lowered. Their posture implies subservience.

In 2018, the curators of the museum did something unusual. Acknowledging that the diorama was historically inaccurate, they decided that instead of removing it, they would add large explanatory labels to the window in front. The story wasn't deleted or replaced but corrected in full view of visitors, like a teacher with a red pen. Where the original creators of the image had got their facts wrong, where the complex reality of colonization had been replaced by misleading stereotypes, would now be clear to the public. It would serve a double lesson: both correcting the facts and explaining how history had been filtered by those in power.

The whole scene looks strange in retrospect. It's odd enough that a diorama depicting a *political* event would feature in a museum of *natural* history, one that's equally famous for its animal taxidermy and dinosaur fossils. But then, maybe in 1939 this encounter was considered natural history of a kind, as one "race" of people locked in an existential struggle with another. Indeed, throughout the museum, people are treated not unlike animal species, our cultural features equivalent to plumage or fur. This was the politics of the United States at the time.

Stuyvesant is clearly labeled in the original diorama. Oratamin on the other hand, isn't mentioned by name at all. One of the new labels on the glass apologizes for how the faces of the two Lenape men in the foreground, one of whom is supposed to be Oratamin, look strangely identical. They're almost caricatures. The European figures, meanwhile, look like real people with physically distinct features. When this historical encounter actually happened, if it did indeed happen this way, Lenape delegates would in all likelihood have been dressed in finery, not as simply as they are here. Putting them in loincloths served to emphasize a perceived civilizational difference between the conquering Europeans and the Indigenous inhabitants of the land. The intention is clear—one is superior to the other.

As the labels reveal, there was error after error in this diorama. But of them all, it's the Indigenous women who were perhaps the most misrepresented.

We know that Lenape women held leadership roles and acted as keepers of knowledge in the seventeenth century. Modern-day Lenape women still do. All we see in the diorama, though, are three anonymous women too far away to identify, bent over like beasts of burden. The image had been designed to suggest that they were treated like slaves in their own communities, when nothing could have been further from the truth. The female sachem Mamanuchqua had been actively involved in treaty negotiations around this time. But she's not depicted here.

The historical journey to this narrative was a complex one. There wasn't always the gulf between European settlers and Native Americans that the diorama suggests. In the early decades of colonization, when the military strength of Indigenous communities for a time matched that of the colonists, European settlers and Native Americans interacted constantly. "For over 150 years most Europeans had lived in frequent, even daily, contact with Indian people," writes Randall McGuire, an archaeologist at the State University of New York at Binghamton, whose work examines power relations between peoples in the past. It was only after the formal end of the American Revolutionary War, in 1783, and the ensuing battles, that this changed. On the East Coast of North America at least, close links between white and Indigenous communities would fade.

Racist ethnic stereotypes slid in to fill the gap, of "Red Indians" and "squaws" recognizable from old Hollywood Westerns. There were some Europeans who saw Native Americans as savage. There were others who recognized the strengths and beauties of their cultures. But whichever way they were seen, as noble savages or savage savages, depending on the observer's persuasion, McGuire explains, the headline was that they were primitive first. By the nineteenth century, archaeologists were so steeped in this belief that they consistently framed Native Americans as objects of nature or its fading remnants, he writes.

"By 1870 this view was firmly institutionalized and taken for granted." The past had been rewritten to serve the myth of Manifest Destiny, a nation-building origin story that claimed that Americans of European descent were destined to move westward and obtain more land for themselves. Even liberals, adds McGuire, "upheld the humanity of Indian people but allowed them a place in the nation only if they gave up their Indianness."

The anthropologist Adam Kuper, whose work has shown how the idea of "primitive" societies was invented, tells me that this was nineteenth-century doctrine. Europeans believed that Native Americans, like Indigenous people everywhere, belonged to the past and that they were lower down the chain of development, closer to a primordial state. If humanity was advancing from savagery to civilization, then Western Europe was at the peak of this ladder of progress. Everyone else was on the lower rungs.

In this worldview, it wasn't just certain "races" that were overtaking others; it was also men who were taking their place as the dominant sex. Many European naturalists and philosophers came to the conviction that the female was closer to nature, while the male was more rational. He was capable of taming nature. European intellectuals imagined a transition from savagery to civilization, from irrationality to rationality, from immorality to morality, as humans were shifting from being governed by nature to themselves governing it. Male authority, then, was believed to be another marker of humanity's progress.

"It was Enlightenment doctrine," Kuper repeats. "There's a direction in history."

This was the philosophical bedrock upon which the United States was founded, later inspiring the exhibits at the American Museum of Natural History. European assumptions about race and gender had been imported into the New World by the Founding Fathers, men such as Thomas Jefferson, John Adams, and George Washington, who drew up the Declaration of Independence and the country's Constitution toward the end of the eighteenth century. They were "urbane gentlemen of the Enlightenment," writes McGuire. "They accepted the primacy of nature and the theory that scholars could arrive at a rational understanding of the world by uncovering the laws of nature."

One scholar has gone so far as to suggest that Jefferson, the third president, was driven by a "patriarchal rage" to keep women in their place. In the society in which he had been raised, built on tobacco plantations and slavery, governed by an elite of white men supported by their wives, the model he hoped to instill in his own family was also the one that he wanted for the new nation he was helping to create. He believed that for women, "it was through domesticity that they could achieve their highest potential and realize their longed-for happiness, a happiness men pursued in the public sphere," I'm told by Brian Steele, a historian at the University of Alabama at Birmingham.

"For most of the Founding Fathers, and I think this is true of almost all Western political thought, there were gendered assumptions that underlay all of their positive pronouncements about what societies ought to be like," Steele continues. Jefferson's view was that women were formed to be "objects of our pleasures." They were there to be enjoyed, to be dependent on men. This paternalism was woven into the nation's laws and values, not through error or oversight but by design.

For those making these rules, though, what they were doing felt radical for the age—even anti-patriarchal. If one aspect of patriarchy is the control of society by an undemocratic elite of powerful men, the Founding Fathers did reject it, according to Linda Kerber, an expert in gender and American legal history at the University of Iowa. In the New World, they saw themselves forging a society based not on artificial hierarchies like the decadent old aristocracies of Europe but on rules underpinned by what they considered to be biological. They turned their backs on monarchy, in which power was exercised at the state-level by an unelected king or queen. The United States would be a republic in which all free men would be equal. They would be governed instead by man-made laws guided by human nature. In that sense, men such as Thomas Jefferson and John Adams were making a break with some of the inequalities of the past.

In 1840, in his second volume of *Democracy in America*, the French political scientist Alexis de Tocqueville was delighted by what he saw in the United States. Here, French revolutionary ideals of freedom had been put into practice, creating a society that looked to him to be even more enlightened than any in Europe when it came to offering women of a certain class a valued place. In the American republic, "while they have allowed the social inferiority of woman to continue, they have done all they could to raise her morally and intellectually to the level of man," he wrote. "I do not hesitate to avow that although the women of the United States are confined within the narrow circle of domestic life, and their situation is in some respects one of extreme dependence, I have nowhere seen women occupying a loftier position."

As paradoxical as it might sound now to hear women being described as fortunate to be unable to vote, work, or have public lives, this would have made perfect sense to the Founding Fathers. Thomas Jefferson thought that women were lucky if they were under the full care of their husbands, because this freed them to look after their children and homes as nature intended. This was emancipation of a kind. It liberated women into an equality befitting their nature, says Steele. People would go so far as to describe it as "an exaltation of women."

"The tender breasts of ladies were not formed for political convulsion," Jefferson once advised. This brand of patriarchy had been instilled in him from a young age. It was part of the air that he breathed as a Virginia planter of the elite class, adds Steele. For "white men, Jefferson emphasized unalienable rights, but when he came to white women, Jefferson shifted focus to natural roles and the happiness of society." Those roles were firmly in the home as wives and mothers.

The problem for us now looking back at the freedom they offered is that it also had its limits. As revolutionary as it was, American democracy chose to draw the line at women and the enslaved, for the simple reason that neither group was seen as being naturally worthy of having the vote. Indigenous peoples weren't recognized as citizens in the first place. This worldview explains both the sexism and the racism of the exhibits at the American Museum of Natural History. Indigenous women must always have been subordinates in their own communities, the designers of the diorama would have thought, because nature had placed women beneath men—and Indigenous people were even closer to nature. Those documenting history were unable to imagine a universe ordered any other way.

■ ■ ■

From the start, there were wives of free white men in the United States who were bothered by the double standards at the heart of their democracy. In

1776, Abigail Adams, the thoughtful and intelligent wife of John Adams, who would later become the second president of the United States, wrote to urge him to "Remember the Ladies, and be more generous and favourable to them than your ancestors." What did freedom and equality really mean if they were for some people and not for everyone?

His wife's question gave him pause. But in the end, Adams decided that women already exercised power vicariously through their husbands at home. They didn't need to have a political presence outside it as well. "We know better than to repeal our Masculine systems" to the "Despotism of the Petticoat," he replied.

By the middle of the nineteenth century, though, the legal and moral arguments for equality were mounting all over the world. "The contradiction between principle and practice cannot be explained away," the British feminist and philosopher Harriet Taylor Mill observed in her 1851 essay "Enfranchisement of Women." Ironically, it would be the United States' own lofty rhetoric about freedom, liberty, and equality that would eventually foment its powerful movements against slavery and for women's suffrage. It was impossible to read the Declaration of Independence of 1776 with its "self-evident" truths about all men being "created equal" and for people not to ask why the same shouldn't apply to them.

At the Woman's Rights Convention in Seneca Falls in 1848, the Declaration of Independence became the very basis for their demands. "They issue a Declaration of Sentiments that essentially takes Jefferson's language in the Declaration and applies it explicitly and directly to women," explains Brian Steele. Activists rewrote the Founding Fathers' own words. In the new version, all men *and women* were created equal.

But the road ahead was a long one. Women weren't just barred from voting. Until the passage of the Nineteenth Amendment, in 1920, they were the property of their fathers, brothers, and husbands, without the right to their own children. Under common law, a husband could beat and rape his wife. And this mirrored laws throughout Europe. "She could not sue, be sued, enter into contracts, make wills, keep her own earnings, or control her own property," writes the lawyer Renée Jacobs. "Married women were civilly dead."

Laws were put in place based on a principle that a married woman could be "covered" by her husband's legal identity, writes the historian and legal expert Linda Kerber. She existed as a citizen only through her husband. This meant that as recently as 1922 an American woman could lose her citizenship if she married a foreign man who wasn't a citizen, even if they both lived in the country. American-born women were denied passports in the 1950s, adds Kerber, "because they had married aliens before 1922." The United States wasn't alone in having these rules. Indeed, to this day there are nationality laws in dozens of countries, including Nepal, Saudi Arabia, and Malaysia, which prevent women from automatically passing on citizenship to their children, or to a spouse who isn't a citizen.

In the nineteenth century, as people began interrogating what reasons there were in nature to deny women the same rights as men, patriarchal beliefs began to be challenged on multiple fronts. European scientists, anthropologists, and philosophers questioned basic assumptions about human hierarchies. If humanity really was proceeding toward modernity and civilization, how had it started? Was there a simpler state of nature that might explain who humans were biologically, deep down? Some asked whether, by studying "savages" living in "primitive" states, they might be able to understand humanity's shared past and explain the origins of human society.

A few wondered if they could even isolate the source of early gender relations. Studying the past, they believed they might once and for all identify the reasons for male domination.

But there were problems. The answers they uncovered weren't what they were expecting. For one, civilizational progress didn't follow a single universal pattern. Exploring the world, studying history and cultures that weren't their own, they found that human societies didn't slot into neat models of progress from primitive to advanced. Instead, civilizations could be seen rising and falling over millennia, becoming technological powerhouses and then slipping into dark ages, or surviving with simpler, more sustainable ways for tens of thousands of years. Some communities were remarkably egalitarian. Others had women in powerful leadership positions. There was no single model that could explain human cultural change through time.

Assumptions about the biological facts of women's subordination were confounded by the fact that human communities weren't structured the same way everywhere. The world was full of exceptions. So many that the rules no longer made sense.

In the United States, watching Native American cultures at close quarters, scholars here found their own ways of understanding natural gender relations quickly undermined. In some Indigenous societies, so-called savages lived traditionally in matrilineal clans, family groups united by a common female ancestor, names passed down over generations by mothers. "Nothing is more real . . . than the women's superiority," observed Joseph-François Lafitau, a French Jesuit missionary who lived with a Native American community not far from Montreal in the eighteenth century. "It is they who really maintain the tribe, the nobility of blood, the genealogical tree, the order of generations and conservation of families. In them resides all the real authority."

There were Indigenous women in the Americas who owned and managed property. They played physically demanding outdoor sports, including ball games and wrestling matches, both for fun and competitively. Young Navajo girls would run races to prove their strength of character. Seri women from the Mexican state of Sonora could run more than seventy kilometers in a night, noted one European ethnologist.

This was an age in which the United States saw itself as a beacon for the rest of the world, building a society at the peak of Western civilization. Yet much to their surprise, nineteenth-century women's rights activists—including some who attended the Seneca Falls Convention in 1848—learned that more egalitarian and democratic models for arranging gender relations already existed right under their noses. They were struck with the earth-shattering realization that perhaps male domination wasn't natural at all. In societies right alongside theirs was the prospect that the rulebook could be rewritten.

In Seneca Falls, these women's stories intersect.

■   ■   ■

"I live here on the Onondaga Nation," I'm told by the community organizer Awhenjiosta Myers. "I think it's such a grand place to live. I wouldn't want to live anywhere else." Her homeland sits in the center of territory belonging to the Haudenosaunee Confederacy, a group of six tribal nations that were once referred to by outsiders as the Iroquois. They've been called the "People of the Longhouse," for the huge long wooden homes that families shared, with space for cooking inside.

The land they have now does little justice to how her ancestors used to live. "It's so sad, because we're only five miles by five miles, when our entire lands were beyond the horizon," she says. When European colonists arrived, their world shrank. "They came in with all these restrictions to make us a better American, to wipe out the Native American in us. But all the time we were able to hang on to as much as we could. For some of us, it wasn't everything. But it was as much as we could hang onto, our language, our ceremonies, our culture, and our way of life."

As Myers explains, part of that way of life was that women were seen as the equals of men. "Growing up here, I've never felt that my role as the woman was any less than the men." Her mother had one sister and eight brothers. "She could split wood just like her brothers could. She could cook a meal just like her brothers could. That's how they were raised.

"I never felt I had to sit in my place as a woman."

The story of Haudenosaunee women in Seneca Falls is far older than any building in this town. In 1590, more than 250 years before the famous convention for women's rights took place at the Wesleyan Chapel on Fall Street, women from across the Seneca, Mohawk, Oneida, Onondaga, and Cayuga Nations met to call for peace as war raged between their peoples. These Haudenosaunee women weren't powerless activists railing against male authority. Far from it. They belonged to communities in which they already wielded significant control, as they had done for generations. They were in the process of consolidating it further. By the 1600s, the women would secure veto power over any future wars.

So, the white, middle-class women who met to fight for equality in Seneca Falls in 1848 were asking for a small slice of what Native American women in the same area had enjoyed as a matter of course for centuries before them. The battle for suffrage in the United States would prove to be long and bitter. Yet full democracy was already an everyday part of Haudenosaunee life. Indigenous people remain steeped in those customs to this day. This isn't to say that life is a matriarchal utopia. Jobs have long been divided between men and women in gendered ways. Women were traditionally in charge of agricultural production, while men hunted, for example—and farming is hard work. But control over food production did give women economic agency, and with it, social freedom. This included the freedom to divorce.

In Haudenosaunee origin stories, divided into epochs that carry into the present, life begins with a woman. According to Barbara Alice Mann, a scholar of Native American history and culture based at the University of Toledo, Ohio, it's here that we can see their society's ideological basis for female authority. There are some versions of this story in which, before the world came into being, there was an island in the sky on which the Sky People lived. Sky Woman fell through a hole but was guided by birds until she landed safely on the Great Turtle. Other animals fetched mud from the ocean until an island began to form on the turtle's back, marking the beginning of the first epoch. Versions vary, but some say that Sky Woman arrived with seeds in her hands brought from her world, which became the basis of agriculture.

Since Sky Woman is considered a literal forebear, not a metaphor, it's taken as fact that everyone's genealogical line begins with her and travels through their mothers.

In the second epoch of this origin story, set sometime around the first half of the previous millennium, we meet Jikonhsaseh, the Mother of Nations. Along with two men, the Great Peacemaker and Hiawatha, the legendary Chief of the Onondaga tribe, these three formed the Haudenosaunee Confederacy. Clan mothers still help run the local level of government, from which political power radiates out to the federal level. They are the ones who select honorary male chiefs to lead their clans, influencing their decisions and wielding the power to oust them if they don't do a good job. Myers tells me that a chief is nothing like a king or absolute ruler. "He's working for the people. He's not working above them or below them, but he's working with them."

While traditions have changed over the decades, women remain at the core of contemporary Haudenosaunee public life as community leaders. As the first clan mother, Jikonhsaseh remains an archetype for those who have followed. There were clan mothers, then, long before there were Founding Fathers.

In a 1900 edition of the *Journal of American Folklore*, the ethnologist William Martin Beauchamp, who had spent time with the Haudenosaunee, described a condolence song that revealed just how much harder it was for the community when a woman passed away than when a man did. It was seen as being worse even than the death of a chief, he wrote, "because with her the line is lost." When Indigenous people began learning English after colonization, he added, they would routinely "speak of a man as *she*, and a woman as *he*." They swapped the pronouns, consciously or subconsciously, because they could see that *he* represented the more important gender in the English language. One teacher noticed that when learning the Bible, Indigenous children would also persistently switch the fifth commandment from "thy father and thy mother" to "thy mother and thy father."

Every Native American society is organized differently. Midwestern Omaha tribes, for instance, are patrilineal. But as I'm told by Jennifer Nez Denetdale, a professor of American studies at the University of New Mexico, in the Navajo Nation she also traced her family history through her mother and grandmothers, and the stories they passed down. She learned about her great-great-great-grandfather only through United States military reports dating from 1866, when he had been known for his role in resisting American occupation. "I was in my late twenties when I finally recognized that my mother was saying we are descended from a *couple*."

"We continue to be a matrilineal people," Denetdale adds. "My mom, she was our matriarch, so I very much acknowledge that women's leadership and women's power and authority from living in a matrilineal system."

Like many matrilineal societies, theirs isn't a simple reverse of patriliny. Only relatively recently have Western scholars begun to appreciate the complexity of gender in some Indigenous traditions. "We have the discussion of a third gender in the creation stories, which is the person that is called a *nádleehí*, or a third gendered person," explains Denetdale. "This was the person who displayed skills and talents of being a negotiator and a mediator between men and women, usually dressed as a feminine person." There are others who believe their forebears recognized four, five, or perhaps more manifestations of gender, which they suggest might correspond to something like gay, lesbian, "feminine" man, and "masculine" woman. The Indigenous term "Two Spirit" has also resurfaced into common usage to recapture this concept of fluidity beyond the gender binary.

A "female cross-gender role in certain Native American tribes constituted an opportunity for women to assume the male role permanently and to marry women," the anthropologist Evelyn Blackwood has written. These cultural practices confounded Western ideas about gender and were poorly documented by outsiders. According to Blackwood, it may have been easier for people to cross genders in egalitarian Native American communities, because neither men nor women carried out jobs that were more highly valued than the other. Without a difference in status, there were fewer barriers to negotiate.

While many of the nuances of gender relations may have been lost on them, the flattened, egalitarian form of government seen among the Haudenosaunee didn't go unnoticed by early European colonists. "The settlers came in and learned from us," says Awhenjiosta Myers. "Democracy itself was learned from the Haudenosaunee. A lot of their symbolism within their government was stolen from our peoples." Official recognition of this came in October 1988, when the United States Senate passed a resolution confirming that when its first colonies were brought together into one republic in the eighteenth century, leading to the formation of its representative democracy, the political system of the Haudenosaunee people influenced its founders.

Oren Lyons, the faithkeeper of the Turtle Clan of the Onondaga and Seneca Nations, told an interviewer in 2007 that when Christopher Columbus set sail for the New World from Spain, the Haudenosaunee "already had several hundred years of democracy, organized democracy. We had a constitution here based on peace, based on equity and justice, based on unity and health."

So, the paradox of American democracy becomes further complicated. In the middle of the nineteenth century, women in Seneca Falls were fighting for the right to vote in a country that, by its own admission, had drawn at least some of its democratic principles from matrilineal Indigenous societies in which women already held significant power. Yet the ideology underpinning the expansion of the United States saw those same Indigenous people as backward, as remnants of the past, perhaps even doomed to go extinct. How could they argue that women's equality represented modernity and progress when Haudenosaunee women had so many more rights and much more autonomy in their societies than European and American women did in theirs?

Circles needed to be squared.

And this was how the question of the origins of patriarchy became one of the most important of that age. It attracted the attention of influential thinkers across the Western world, from English naturalist Charles Darwin and German political theorist Friedrich Engels to America's foremost women's rights activists.

■　■　■

Matilda Joslyn Gage was a firebrand even by the standards of suffragists.

Born in 1826 into a family of liberal thinkers in New York state, active in the movement to end slavery, she would go on to become almost as important a figure in the women's rights movement as its leader, Elizabeth Cady Stanton. Gage wasn't there for the Seneca Falls Convention in 1848, but she did become the youngest speaker at the third National Women's Rights Convention four years later.

There's an anecdote that sums up the kind of activist she was: In October 1886, at a ceremony on what would be known as Liberty Island, to dedicate the Statue of Liberty, a gift from France, Gage turned up to protest. Learning that women weren't allowed on the island that day, she and her group barged a rented steamship into the harbor so they could make their point. "It is the sarcasm of the nineteenth century to represent liberty as a woman," they declared, "while not one single woman throughout the length and breadth of the land is as yet in possession of political liberty!"

Gage looked to Haudenosaunee women, living in New York state just like she did, and saw another world. She was struck by how differently they were treated in their own communities. When a young Haudenosaunee woman got married, her husband came to live with his mother-in-law. He was obliged to hand over to her whatever spoils he won from hunting. If the couple separated, the children went to their mother. For Gage, this was nothing short of a revelation. The double standards of her own life fell into sharp relief.

The white men of New York "are this very moment lower in the scale of humanitarian civilization than were the Iroquois," she wrote, because at least Indigenous peoples recognized that if a couple separated, the children belonged to the mother and not the husband.

In an article in New York's *Evening Post* newspaper in 1875, Gage could barely contain her excitement at discovering a society in which women had this much authority. "Division of power between the sexes in this Indian republic was nearly equal," she wrote. She formed such close associations with the Haudenosaunee that in 1893 she was adopted into one of their clans and given the name Karonienhawi, meaning "She Who Holds the Sky."

But there was a dilemma that needed to be resolved. Many white women's rights activists at the time, including Gage, made their case for sexual equality by arguing that it represented the future. It was a sign of a mature, advanced civilization. By extending the right to vote to women, they argued, Americans would be leading the way for the rest of the world. So, how would they explain the egalitarian, matrilineal setup of far older Native American communities? How did these Indigenous societies manage to leapfrog a nation as supposedly modern as the United States?

Among those also looking to answer the same question around this time was Lewis Henry Morgan, an ethnologist and lawyer from New York who belonged to a secret fraternity that studied the traditions of the Haudenosaunee. As well as lobbying for land claims on behalf of Native Americans, Morgan also (unsuccessfully) petitioned President Abraham Lincoln to make him commissioner of Indian Affairs. In 1847, Morgan was adopted into the Hawk clan, one of the four bird clans of the Seneca Nation, and given the name Tayadawahkugh, meaning "One Lying Across," perhaps to symbolize that he had a foot in both worlds or that he was a bridge between them.

Morgan's fascination with Native American customs had a different flavor from Gage's. Unlike her, he didn't look to them for political inspiration. On the contrary, he thought Native Americans were barbarians, far down the scale on which he thought, as self-servingly as other European colonialists

did then, that the white "Aryan family represents the central stream of human progress," as he put it. His was instead an anthropological interest, to
better understand what he believed to be the shared roots of human society.
Indigenous people, he assumed, were a window into the past.

As far as he could tell, Morgan explained in his 1877 book *Ancient Society*,
the Haudenosaunee organized themselves on the building blocks of family
relationships. If a society wanted to be built around kinship this way, women
had to take center stage because children could always be reliably traced back
to their mothers. It was harder to be certain of paternity. Morgan assumed
that if "primitive" people adopted matrilineal patterns of inheritance, it was
because they hadn't yet come up with better ways of assuring themselves
who a child's father was. If they had, they would surely have been patrilineal.

For Morgan, then, Haudenosaunee traditions represented humankind's
shared distant past, an earlier stage of development when people were more
promiscuous, lived communally, and didn't know which baby belonged to
which man. By his reasoning, these old societies had no choice but to prioritize women. Female-centered Native American society wasn't superior in
his view. It was just simpler.

A Swiss anthropologist and writer on the law named Johann Jakob Bachofen had already suggested in 1861 that the earliest structure of human
families might have been matriarchal. He used the phrase *Mutterrecht*, meaning "Mother-right," to refer to inheritance through the female line. Morgan
linked male power to reproduction, just like Bachofen had and other thinkers
of his age would—including the father of evolutionary theory, Charles Darwin, with whom Morgan corresponded. As Morgan saw it, more "advanced"
societies like the ones in Europe tended to be male-dominated because men,
in their wisdom and rationality, had finally taken control of women's sexuality to make sure their children were their own and not someone else's. The
invention of strictly enforced monogamous marriage allowed families to be
organized along patrilineal lines. And this meant that whatever property
men owned could transfer to their true heirs. With men in charge of women,
inheritance could run from father to son, just as Morgan believed it should.

"Morgan regarded this as natural and proper," writes the anthropologist
Adam Kuper. With this feat of intellectual acrobatics, Morgan could equate
male domination, monogamy, and heterosexual marriage with progress and
modernity—and comfortably square the circle of Western patriarchy.

How Morgan's theories were read depended on the reader. In particular,
on the reader's politics. While for Morgan there was no endorsement of

gender equality in what he had written (quite the opposite, actually), his work nevertheless offered a thrilling new narrative to women's rights activists like Matilda Joslyn Gage. Men like Morgan saw a matriarchal past as sexually corrupt and backward. For suffragists, on the other hand, it proved that it was possible for women to have power. If the Haudenosaunee were not cultural oddities but remnants of a universally shared matriarchal past, living in a primitive state closer to nature, those who argued that male domination was the way it had been from the start could be fundamentally challenged. The United States' failure to grant women the same rights as men on the basis of their different natures could be framed as a forcible denial of the rights women had in the first place.

Smashing the patriarchy was not an affront to nature but a return to it.

This proved to be the perfect origin story for the burgeoning American women's rights movement. And it received a further shot in the arm when it was taken up by the German socialist philosopher Friedrich Engels, co-author with Karl Marx of *The Communist Manifesto*.

■   ■   ■

Friedrich Engels was so inspired by Lewis Henry Morgan's *Ancient Society* that in 1884 he published an ambitious theory around it to explain the origins of the state itself. His was a grand suite of explanations for how family and property had come to be organized the way they were in modern societies. Engels argued, like Bachofen and Morgan before him, that "Mother-right" was a primitive system that ended with the arrival of the civilized, monogamous patriarchal family. Where he parted ways from Morgan was that he saw this transition from matriarchy to patriarchy as a tragic destruction of women's freedoms, a moment that brought about "the world historical defeat of the female sex."

Those words—"the world historical defeat of the female sex"—would ring through feminist literature for the next century or more. They would shape how generations of people would think about patriarchy.

Engels's narrative was as stirring as it was dramatic. Men's drive to control paternity and inheritance not only forced women into becoming little more than vessels for their babies, Engels wrote; it also transformed them into men's property. "The man took command in the home also; the woman was degraded and reduced to servitude, she became the slave of his lust and a mere instrument for the production of children," he wrote. Modern-day legal inequality between the sexes was the product of this "economic oppression," as he put it, relegating women to subordinates within the institution of marriage in their own homes. The husband and father became the head of household, and "the wife became the head servant."

Engels saw salvation for women through the creation of an egalitarian, classless society. Quoting Morgan directly, Engels hoped that by redistributing wealth to everyone equally and by eliminating hierarchies, people could bring about "a revival, in a higher form, of the liberty, equality and fraternity" of the ancient matriarchies. Engels didn't advocate living like modern-day Indigenous peoples any more than Morgan did, because he also saw them as primitive, as belonging to the past. But he did believe they contained the germ of sexual equality that would eventually be reclaimed once people revolted against capitalism.

Engels's theory seemed to tie everything together. It was easy to get swept away by its argument, and indeed it would have a profound impact on how generations of people would think about patriarchy and women's oppression. But the theory also had a fundamental problem.

■   ■   ■

Are humans really on some ladder of progress, reaching ever upward to some mythical point of perfection? Is it fair to think about all societies as progressing through the same stages of civilization, some faster and some slower?

The trouble with the entire line of reasoning employed by Johann Jakob Bachofen in 1861, then Lewis Morgan and Friedrich Engels soon after him, is that, as the anthropologist Adam Kuper notes in his book *The Invention of Primitive Society*, human societies don't all necessarily trace back to one single point, to a time when everyone lived the same way. We may be able to draw some common threads, writes Kuper, but there are no "fossils of social organization." Within the Americas, Indigenous practices, customs, and languages vary from nation to nation, place to place, time to time, just as they do anywhere else in the world. No cultures are homogenous, nor static. There's no basis for assuming that Haudenosaunee families in the nineteenth century were living the way that people in Europe used to live thousands of years earlier.

The issue of perspective struck even Benjamin Franklin, one of the Founding Fathers of the United States, when he was thinking about Native American societies. "Savages we call them, because their manners differ from ours, which we think the Perfection of Civility," he wrote sometime between 1783 and 1784. "They think the same of theirs."

Efforts by nineteenth-century thinkers such as Engels and Morgan to come up with a single, coherent story that might explain human development as a progression from matriarchal to patriarchal betrayed these biases. Rather than seeing the Haudenosaunee as a modern, breathing community of people who happened to have developed rules that worked better for women in some ways than other societies, Engels and Morgan treated them as living skeletons. To their eyes, they were just residues of their past. Native American lives were picked over only to understand where all modern humans came from, forgetting what should have been obvious: Native Americans aren't who everyone else used to be but present-day people with their own rich, changing histories, interwoven with the world around them.

The anthropologist Gail Landsman at the University at Albany, New York, who has studied the writings of nineteenth-century suffragists, warns that we need to be mindful of the intentions of those who invoked Native Americans as models for an alternative politics. Landsman points out that, while on the one hand looking to Indigenous societies for inspiration, even Matilda Joslyn Gage believed that she was observing a primitive culture. Gage sat firmly within the European Enlightenment tradition of imagining that all people sat on a ladder of progress—and that people like her were at the top. She wasn't hoping to live like the Haudenosaunee did but looking instead to reform the laws of her own nation. It was the United States that represented her future.

"Indians were of value and interest primarily for how they moved forward white American history," writes Landsman.

Gage could have embraced Haudenosaunee society as an opportunity to fold Indigenous ideas and practices back into a model for a different United States, one that fully appreciated the rights and cultures of Native Americans, that didn't see them as dispensable. But her gaze fell back instead on herself. Rather than including Indigenous women in their fight for equality, activists like her used them as intellectual pawns. Haudenosaunee people became a tool to serve political ideals. For men like Lewis Henry Morgan, they functioned as a dark reminder of a corrupt matriarchal past, confirming why male domination was more "civilized." For others, like Friedrich Engels, they dangled the promise of a return to egalitarianism through revolution. And for Gage, they offered dazzling reassurance that female power was natural because it existed even in a "primitive" society like theirs.

None was seeing Indigenous communities for who they really were, only for what they wanted them to be. Along the way, living people were reduced to relics. And this would mean that some women's rights and freedoms would end up being sacrificed for the rights of others.

■ / ■   ■

It's difficult to overestimate just how central the domesticated housewife was in the founding of the United States.

Centuries before the Declaration of Independence was written, Europeans had come to believe that patriarchy was the divine order of the universe, from the father with authority over his family, to the monarch with dominion over the nation, and higher still to God himself. The historian David Veevers at Queen Mary University of London, who has researched Empire-era attitudes to gender, writes that from the sixteenth century onward, English "institutions of state and society were obsessed with reinforcing this patriarchal principal at the familial, local and national levels." By the 1700s, there was an explosion in manuals on household management, each throbbing with an anxiety to maintain proper gender relations, seeing them as "the cornerstone of political stability as well."

If the family was under control, if everyone was following gender norms to the letter, the state would be safe. The Founding Fathers of the United States inherited the same philosophy. The "American republic would remain safe as long as its women remained domestic," explains the historian Brian Steele.

By the middle of the nineteenth century, around the same time that the women's rights convention was being held in Seneca Falls, this idea had become firmly embedded in class relations in New York City, according to Christine Stansell, a historian at the University of Chicago. The wealthier middle classes saw it as their job to uphold traditional family values—and not just in their own households. Women in particular "strengthened their role as dictators of domestic and familial standards," she adds, passing judgement on those who didn't fulfil the American ideal of domestic motherhood.

Women policed other women. New York's middle-class social reformers, Stansell explains, were among those who believed that "female self-support was synonymous with indigence." Even prominent suffragists, while pushing for their right to vote, shared a commitment to the ideal of the domesticated wife and mother. Among the moral reformers of the age, for instance, was Lydia Maria Child, a contemporary of Elizabeth Cady Stanton and Matilda

Joslyn Gage, and a prominent activist for women's and Native American rights. Seeing impoverished children on the streets of New York City, Child wondered whether the "squalid little wretches" might not be better off as orphans. Reformers like her set up asylums, schools, and institutions designed to help these children.

The problem was that girls in some of these places ended up being trained not for the kind of paid work they would actually need but in how to become future wives and mothers. As Stansell has documented, they would be molded into perfect housewives. Despite their good intentions, these reformers failed to recognize that working-class women worked not out of rejection to the ideal but because they often had no other choice. Almost two-thirds of the women sampled in two neighborhoods of New York for the 1855 census had no men in their households, Stansell writes. Not taking up paid work would have condemned them to poverty and homelessness.

The domesticated housewife had from the beginning only ever been an aspiration for the wealthiest. Until slavery ended, it was the labor of enslaved men, women, and children that afforded rich white women the luxury to avoid work at all. Small surprise that by the middle of the twentieth century it had become a middle-class status symbol. "It was the only ambition I ever had," the actress Doris Day is reported to have said. "Not to be a dancer or Hollywood movie star, but to be a housewife in a good marriage." If a man earned enough for his wife to stay at home, he was judged to be doing well for himself. Employers assumed that when a woman got married, she would give up work. This was how educated women in the 1950s found themselves channeling their energies into housekeeping, shaping what we now recognize as the stereotype of the chirpy, manicured suburban wife and mother.

This ideal also gave birth to what the historian Linda Kerber has called the "Republican Mother." This was a woman whose job was to raise healthy, sturdy sons in service of the state. Rosemarie Zagarri, a historian of early America at George Mason University in Virginia, has described this paradoxical arrangement, which accepted the family unit as politically vital but women not as political actors in their own right, as a form of "Anglo-American Womanhood." It gave women a respected and visible place in society but only as defined by their capacity to have children and raise them. If they wanted to exercise political or economic power outside the home, they would have to do it vicariously through their husbands and sons.

In some ways, this was Thomas Jefferson's brand of womanhood. It didn't view women as men's inferiors. But neither did it offer them a place beyond being a wife and mother. It "straddled a boundary between tradition and innovation," writes Zagarri.

Nobody would embrace being a Republican Mother quite as fully as the anti-feminist author and lawyer Phyllis Schlafly, who devoted herself to promoting the American housewife until she died in 2016. She was an early supporter of Donald Trump's campaign for president (at her funeral service, he described her as a "truly great American patriot"). In the 1970s, Schlafly mobilized likeminded housewives to mount a successful campaign to stop the United States ratifying the Equal Rights Amendment to its Constitution, which until then had bipartisan political support. She railed against abortion rights and working women.

Yet throughout her life, Schlafly was also living proof of the constraints of the domestic dream. While lobbying against equality, she studied, worked, and eventually sought national political prominence. She would never admit it, but her career contradicted the very rules she fought to defend.

But then, the ideal of the domesticated housewife always had its limitations. It made little sense for most everyday women, even when Thomas Jefferson was alive. The families of poorer and immigrant women couldn't survive without working outside their homes, whether they lived in rural areas or cities. And it certainly wouldn't extend to Black women whose work was being exploited. The fixed roles of domestic wife and public-facing working husband had the capacity to provide happiness only to those with the wealth and slave labor to remove their drudgery, says Brian Steele.

For Haudenosaunee women, it made no sense at all. They had long traditions of working and managing the land. Ethnologists have noted that in Jefferson's time Haudenosaunee women were noticeably physically stronger than white American women from outdoor work. They also tended to have fewer children than white American women and likely practiced some form of abortion to achieve that limit. And of course, Haudenosaunee women held positions of power outside the home as well as inside it. Their very existence challenged the ideals of the Founding Fathers to the point of subversion.

Yet their lives, too, would be sacrificed to the goal of female domesticity. The patriarchal belief that women should stay at home would ride roughshod over the traditions of Indigenous communities. Believing outdoor work to be unsuited to women, American political leaders, well-intentioned social reformers, and Christian missionaries saw ushering women into domestic roles and men into agricultural labor and leadership as vital to assimilating Native Americans into their "modern" society. "Missionary discourse promoted a particular understanding of gender roles that elevated the standing of white, middle-class American women," writes Rosemarie Zagarri. In the process, she adds, its goal was to reaffirm the superiority of Western civilization.

In effect, white Americans would seek to civilize Native Americans into patriarchy.

■　■　■

"As an Indian woman I was free."

These words were collected by the controversial anthropologist Alice Cunningham Fletcher in interviews with Native American women in the nineteenth century. She read them out loud in 1888 for an audience at the First Convention of the International Council of Women.

"I owned my home; my person, the work of my own hands, and my children could never forget me. I was better as an Indian woman than under white law," Fletcher continued narrating. The men she had spoken to told her much the same thing. "Your laws show how little your men care for their women," they had told her. "The wife is nothing of herself. She is worth little but to help a man to have one hundred and sixty acres."

Already, Indigenous families bore the scars of colonization.

In the nineteenth century, writes the anthropologist Gail Landsman, middle-class white suffragists were united against oppression on the basis of gender. At the same time, though, some held power that many other women didn't have. They "were generally well placed within the dominant society in terms of race and class," writes Landsman. This situation divided their loyalties when it came to deciding who should be granted rights first.

"Even those who saw themselves as friends of the Indian, those who sought to reform government policy, saw Native people as essentially children—undeveloped primitives newly born into American culture," observes Melissa Ryan at Alfred University in New York, who researches race, class, and gender in American literature. Matilda Joslyn Gage, for instance, for all of her support of Native American rights, veered between celebrating Haudenosaunee societies for their matrilineal traditions on the one hand and admitting how backward she found them on the other. This was an attitude among some white suffragists that extended to views of Black Americans and immigrants, too. When it came to suffrage, writes Ryan, Gage's language "implies that the juxtaposition of voting barbarians with disenfranchised white women is an outrage not just to women, but to the principles of civilization itself."

Elizabeth Cady Stanton, who famously spoke on the first morning of the Woman's Rights Convention in Seneca Falls, also believed that it "was better and safer to enfranchise educated white women than former slaves or ignorant immigrants," writes the historian Elisabeth Griffith in her biography of Stanton. When the social reformer and abolitionist Frederick Douglass, who had been an outspoken supporter of women's suffrage from the start, told a meeting in 1869 that there was an urgency to Black suffrage because of the brutal murders and persecution that Black men were suffering in some states, Stanton betrayed her prejudices by telling him, "If you will not give the whole loaf of suffrage to the entire people, give it to the most intelligent first."

In her book *White Tears/Brown Scars*, the journalist Ruby Hamad documents a discomfiting history of women betraying other women on race, class, and other grounds. It's a common strategy, writes Hamad, "to align with women of color when it suits, trumpeting a nonexistent sisterhood as a mask for appropriating our work to advance the myth of a better world run by women." While many white suffragists were vehemently opposed to slavery and were themselves active in the abolitionist movement (Stanton organized the Seneca Falls convention after seeing women like her being marginalized at an anti-slavery conference in London), this didn't mean they necessarily saw Black, brown, or immigrant women as their equals. Some canvassed for white women's suffrage, notes Landsman, with the argument that this would help "dilute" the Black and immigrant vote if suffrage became universal. Black women found themselves thrown under the bus because of disagreements over slavery and race between white suffragists in the north and south of the country. At the Woman Suffrage Procession of 1913, which saw thousands of women march through Washington, DC, this confusion led to Black activists being told to stay at the back. Journalist Ida B. Wells-Barnett, a founding member of the National Association for the Advancement of Colored People, refused.

American women would eventually secure the right to vote in 1920 with the ratification of the Nineteenth Amendment to the United States Constitution. In reality, the franchise wasn't universal. Some states prevented Black women and men from voting using poll taxes, tests, and segregation. The Indian Citizenship Act of 1924 opened the possibility for Native Americans to vote but left it to individual states to extend them that right in practice—which in some cases took many decades. Even then, Native Americans continued to face the same barriers as Black voters.

The underlying belief that some people were more deserving of rights than others would continue to affect Indigenous women in other ways. In the mid-nineteenth century, for instance, there was no such thing as an illegitimate child in the Seneca Nation, notes Nancy Shoemaker, an expert in Native American history based at the University of Connecticut. All children born to Seneca mothers were automatically legitimate citizens. "And there is no suggestion in the records that within Seneca society there was any social stigma attached to unmarried women having children," she writes. But in the 1865 US census, Seneca women found themselves being forced by the American authorities to name their children after the fathers. Hemmed in, they tried instead to name them after their own grandfathers or other male relatives in their mothers' families.

The Seneca ended up adopting a patrilineal naming system. They did manage to retain matrilineal tribal membership, though. Both men and women in the Seneca Nation sought to safeguard women's social rights, inheritance, property rights, and freedom to marry and divorce. Yet the pressure from outside remained on men to take up leadership roles.

"Missionaries and government agents always treated men as heads of families and disregarded other patterns of family authority," Shoemaker writes. As this happened, "Seneca political life did come to resemble that of whites' in that the constitution identified men as the community's leader." The anthropologist Eleanor Leacock has also noted that when European Americans transacted political or military business with Indigenous communities, they preferred to deal with the men. Patriarchy, then, wasn't introduced overnight. It was the product of one battle after another, stretching out over centuries. It slowly chipped away at existing laws and customs, just as it did in India in the nineteenth century among Kerala's matrilineal Nairs.

"Economic and political policies undercut women's economic roles as farmers and merchants, abrogated their land rights, pushed them out of the public sector of the economy, and lowered their jural status," writes Leacock. This meant that "women's position relative to men deteriorated sharply with colonialism." Patterns of employment changed. Women were encouraged to stay at home. They became more and more dependent on their husbands' wages.

There were similar declines among the Tsimshian, a community of fishers and hunters living on the northwest coast of British Columbia, according to the gender scholar Jo-Anne Fiske at the University of Lethbridge, Alberta, in Canada. Fiske believes that it's unlikely the Tsimshian distinguished between domestic and public spheres until the region was colonized. After that, women were pushed away from the crafts that had given them income and independence. Trade with Europeans, particularly in valuable furs, became dominated by men. "Widows suffered the greatest hardships," she writes. They lost prestige because, without paid work, "they could no longer maintain traditional claims to lineage resources."

The historian David Veevers confirms that English overseas corporations, hugely powerful during Empire, governed with a gendered fist. "From the Levant to Virginia, from Massachusetts to Sumatra," he writes, "the patriarchal order of gender was circulated and transplanted from one global region to another."

Researchers are only just beginning to unpack the effects that the spread of this gendered order has had on people globally over the last few centuries. The pressure to recreate ideal households in the European image, and to only ever engage in what was seen as the right kind of sexual behavior, the Cornell University historian Durba Ghosh has written, "proved to be restrictive for native and indigenous women, moving them away from meaningful participation in political and familial affairs, such as decisions about family property and labour." In the name of "modernizing" women, colonialism placed them within ever-tighter gendered straitjackets, slowly disenfranchising them, and moving property, income, and authority into the hands of men.

Indigenous women in the United States in the twentieth century arguably ended up with far less power than their ancestors in places like Seneca Falls had enjoyed in 1590. They lost status not only within their own societies, but their societies also lost status because of colonization. Thousands of children were sent to boarding schools designed to assimilate them into white, Christian society, while stripping them of their own cultures and languages. "My mother died while surviving civilization," the Native American journalist Mary Annette Pember has written about her mother, Bernice, who was sent to one such school in Wisconsin and suffered the psychological effects throughout her adult life. The nuns in charge would force her to do countless hours of heavy manual labor while telling her that she was a "dirty Indian." Reports have only recently revealed the extent of brutal abuse that went on in these institutions across North America.

The pain of this injustice runs deep. "Whatever they take away from our communities is to benefit themselves," I'm told by the Navajo scholar Jennifer Nez Denetdale. For all the resistance that her community has put up against cultural change, a great deal still has to be consciously remembered and reclaimed. "The imposition of settler colonialism has vastly transformed who we are today and how we practice Indigenous knowledge."

Today, what has become a mainly male and Christian leadership in the Navajo Nation is working to bolster the same brand of heterosexual patriarchy seen elsewhere in the United States, says Denetdale. As recently as 1998, a woman was discouraged from running for president of the Navajo Nation. LeNora Fulton was told by both the men and the women in her community that women shouldn't be leaders.

■   ■   ■

In the museum next to the Wesleyan Chapel in Seneca Falls, one of the few mentions of Haudenosaunee women can be found in three new banners, none of which details the ways in which the women were failed by those who could have helped them. There's barely any explanation of the atrocities they experienced under settler colonialism. Even here, in the town at the very heart of the story of women's rights in the United States, narratives remain incomplete. The history of suffrage that's glossed over, the one that's messier than the triumphalist version, proves what few want to admit: patriarchal ideas are carried within states and institutions to which women have also been committed, from which they have also drawn benefits, and which they have also defended.

This history also goes to show that the emergence of patriarchy could never have been a single global catastrophic event at a point in time so long ago that we have no record of it anymore. How could it be when there are people today who can recall how it was imposed on their own communities within their own lifetimes? There are matrilineal societies that are resisting its encroachment even now.

So, when Friedrich Engels described the "world historical defeat of the female sex," he was talking about the patriarchy he recognized not globally but in Europe, where he lived, a place where men held extraordinary power at almost every layer of life and had done for as long as anyone could remember. European patriarchy was being exported in the nineteenth century to other places. And here at least, the central dilemma remained: How did *any* society first come to organize itself around the principle of male domination? How could people ever have landed on such a remarkably skewed system of gendered oppression? If patriarchy wasn't some biological or divine inevitability, then what was it?

The ghosts of Johann Jakob Bachofen, Lewis Henry Morgan, and Friedrich Engels haunted this question long after their deaths. Their theory of shared matriarchal origins, which claimed that people everywhere were once led by women before the patriarchs seized power, never disappeared. On the contrary, it lived on in Western feminist and socialist literature for decades, waiting for more solid historical support.

Finally, in the 1960s, archaeologists thought they had found it.

CHAPTER 3

Genesis

A dusty road dotted with pistachio trees takes me from the ancient Turkish metropolis of Konya, home to the shrine of the Sufi poet Rumi, to the ruins of Çatalhöyük—once described as the first city in the world.

This is a place that defies understanding. Most of the settlement was long ago buried under a bump in the otherwise flat, arid plains of Southern Anatolia. What little of it has been uncovered reveals a society in which nothing follows the rules as we might expect them to be. The edge of the archaeological site disappears abruptly into multiple levels stretching cavernously into the ground. Houses in Çatalhöyük—meaning "a fork in the road," because that's all this was just before it was excavated—were built like boxes jammed together, back-to-back and side-to-side. There were flat roofs and no windows or doors. People came and went by ladder through openings in their ceilings, walking on the tops of buildings instead of between them. Dwellings were built upon old dwellings in layers.

What makes Çatalhöyük special is that it was occupied after the end of the Old Stone Age from at least 7400 BCE, in a period of time called the Neolithic, before humans are known to have begun writing. This means it was occupied almost five thousand years before the first pyramids went up in Egypt and more than four thousand years before Stonehenge was built in Britain. It is possibly even older than the Harappan civilization of the Indus Valley. Çatalhöyük is near the Fertile Crescent, the part of the Middle East that nourished some of the world's first farming communities. The land looks dry now, but there would have been wetlands here once, lush with fish and birds. People would have collected berries and grazed their goats nearby. There were clay and reeds to help them build their homes. But as unimaginably early as it is in human history, Çatalhöyük still teems with social and artistic complexity.

Thousands of people called this their home. Walls were plastered regularly and striking artwork created on the fresh surfaces. Vivid red frescoes show tiny stick figures hunting oversized animals. There are headless bodies preyed on by looming vultures with wide wings. Bull heads are embedded in the walls, their horns protruding like the interior of some American cowboy ranch.

"It was perceived as being in the middle of nowhere, this huge mound with this really rich material culture from nine thousand years ago," I'm told by Ruth Tringham, a professor of anthropology at the University of California, Berkeley, whose work has focused on the archaeology of Neolithic Europe. Almost as soon as excavations began, in May 1961, Çatalhöyük became a focal point for those who wanted to understand how humans organized themselves in one of the planet's oldest known settlements. In 1997, Tringham headed up part of a team that continued work on the site, helping to piece together what life might have been like for those who lived here.

It wasn't just the buildings or frescoes that fascinated archaeologists. Focus fell on something much smaller, an object not much bigger than my hand. Now in pride of place in its own glass case at the Museum of Anatolian Civilizations in Ankara, this treasure is known as the "Seated Woman of Çatalhöyük."

Experts believe there may have been a cult of ancestor worship at Çatalhöyük. The remains of dead ancestors were kept in the same homes in which people lived, under platforms in their floors. Skulls were sometimes removed, even plastered and painted, then passed around between people. Hundreds of small figurines have been found in this settlement, some of them clearly representing humans, others looking like animals or more ambiguously anthropomorphic. But the haul of sculptures at many Neolithic sites from this region and even further afield is unmistakably heavy with what look to be curved female forms. The museum has dozens of them, clusters of tiny Barbara Hepworth–like clay shapes. One has the torso of a pregnant woman on one side and the protruding ribcage of a skeleton on her back. None of these finds, though, is quite as remarkable as the Seated Woman.

When I see her, I understand the fascination. Her head has had to be reconstructed because it was missing when she was found, but it hardly matters when the rest of her body says so much. She has been described as a fertility symbol by a few scholars. To me at least, she doesn't look pregnant, nor particularly provocative. She is voluptuous, with naked rolls of flesh spilling around her like waterfalls. There are deep indentations to mark her knees and bellybutton. These feel like the signs of a body that has lived for a long time, an older woman weathered by age, perhaps. But it's her posture that truly stands out. Her back is perfectly straight. On either side of her hips beneath resting hands are what seem to be two big cats, maybe leopards, looking straight ahead.

The most intriguing aspect of the Seated Woman of Çatalhöyük is not her gloriously abundant body, then. It's her pose in command of two creatures. In a society obviously preoccupied with animals, hunting, and death, she looks arrestingly authoritative. Maybe even—depending on your perspective—matriarchal.

■   ■   ■

Not long after excavations began there in the 1960s, Çatalhöyük turned into a site of pilgrimage for New Age devotees and goddess-worshippers, inspired by the female figurines unearthed here. American and European visitors eagerly descended on the ruins in the belief they had found proof of egalitarian societies in the ancient past, ones that celebrated femininity and venerated different forms of what they called the "Great Goddess." These visitors had discovered, to their minds at least, a window onto a prehistoric city that put women first. The nineteenth-century myth of a shared matriarchal past was on its way to being revived.

Goddess tours of Anatolia continue to make obligatory stops at Çatalhöyük. These days, many of them are organized by Reşit Ergener, a Turkish economics professor who became curious about the history of goddesses after meeting American women who visited this region in the 1980s. He went on to publish *Anatolia, Land of Mother Goddess*, a book exploring legends such as that of the mother goddess Cybele, worshipped in these parts thousands of years ago. Ergener started running his own tours in 1990.

"I was enchanted," he tells me. "Why I got interested in it so much, I think it's my personal history, my life. I have grown up with strong women in my childhood. My grandmother, my mother, my sister, all very strong women."

There's no doubt that people in this area have traditionally worshipped goddesses. Evidence of them is everywhere, particularly from antiquity on. Cybele is seen in classical Greek and Roman literature. But the bigger question is whether these deities are any reflection of social relations among real, everyday people in the past. And it's here that the history becomes contested. Just because a society has female deities or produces scores of female figurines doesn't mean it's necessarily dominated by women.

It was the late British Dutch archaeologist James Mellaart who was the first to ignite the matriarchal legends that continue to swirl around Çatalhöyük to this day. When he and his team discovered female figurines in their early excavations in the early 1960s, Mellaart immediately built a narrative around them that nurtured old myths of the kind promoted by the anthropologist Johann Jakob Bachofen and the philosopher Friedrich Engels. As far as Mellaart was concerned, Çatalhöyük provided hard archaeological evidence for their theory that the earliest human societies placed women at their center, worshipping goddesses and following matrilineal systems of inheritance.

In an already impressive career, "Çatalhöyük was Mellaart's most important find," an obituary would later note. It secured his legacy. And he probably knew that it would. This settlement is as complex as it is old. Almost at a stroke, it overturned earlier assumptions about Neolithic people living relatively basic lives. Mellaart went further, arguing that Çatalhöyük was too big and sophisticated to be a village of farmers. He chalked it up as a city, immediately raising its historical significance.

Anthropologist Ruth Tringham tells me that in the 1960s it felt as though every book on architecture opened with a mention of Çatalhöyük as the world's first city. Having elevated it to this status, Mellaart argued that some of the buildings were too elaborately decorated to have been everyday homes. They looked to him more like temples or holy shrines. "This, for him, was going to make his name. He was just enormously excited by these materials," adds Tringham. Mellaart interpreted artwork as a goddess giving birth to a bull or ram. Another image, he suggested, showed a goddess with a vulture.

"The supreme deity was the Great Goddess," he concluded.

Mellaart had anointed the site with the veneer of the sacred, shuffling it up another notch in historical value. "Immediately you've got these very exciting words like 'shrine' and a 'temple' and 'goddess,' and you've got all of this going on," recalls Tringham. "They became buzzwords for this as some sort of religious center." Word spread, attracting feverish interest from across the globe. "It was thought of as some sort of mecca for the goddess. . . . It was very famous. It was made famous because of the goddess." Tringham says that as recently as the 1990s, when her team was working at Çatalhöyük, worshippers would still turn up every so often to pay homage and meditate. "We treated them very respectfully and let them do their dances and their rituals," she tells me, with a wry smile.

It was no surprise that the crowds came. Accounts of Mellaart's findings were enthralling. In a piece for *Scientific American* in 1964, he recalled with pride the day he first started work there. "Ten days later the first Neolithic paintings ever found on man-made walls were exposed, and it was clear that Çatal Hüyük [an alternative spelling] was no ordinary site." Mellaart described it as a "community with an extensive economic development, specialized crafts, a rich religious life, a surprising attainment in art and an impressive social organization."

A photo of the Seated Woman of Çatalhöyük accompanying the article was unambiguously labeled in capitals: "STATUE OF GODDESS."

Discoveries came thick and fast. In the 1990s it would take Tringham and her colleagues as long as seven years to uncover a single house at Çatalhöyük. By contrast, Mellaart unearthed more than a hundred buildings in just three seasons in the 1960s, she says. "He would excavate really quickly." His aim wasn't to get the fine-grained detail but the big picture. "He just wanted to know the pattern of the settlement." For that, he needed to have a bird's-eye view of as much of the site as possible.

This febrile period of archaeological activity would burn out as quickly as it began. Mellaart's excavations ended soon after 1965. He was banned from the site by the Turkish government following a scandal about missing artifacts and dodgy forgeries. After his death, in 2012, rumors intensified that he might have exaggerated his findings, possibly even inventing evidence to support his theories. But whatever the state of his reputation by the end, his work at Çatalhöyük did reveal genuine finds that helped to rewrite the past. The site revolutionized how researchers thought about Neolithic people. That period of time could no longer be seen as simple and primitive—not if there were Stone Age settlements as rich and complex as this one.

His impact, though, went beyond archaeology. An entire narrative about women's history had formed around Çatalhöyük. Mellaart's support for the theory of a matriarchal prehistory shaped how people in the second half of the twentieth century would come to think about gender and power at humanity's roots.

An article in *Feminist Studies* in 1978 by the American historian Anne Llewellyn Barstow helped catapult Mellaart's work to the attention of writers and thinkers outside his field. Barstow included snippets of conversations she had had with him. His findings, she explained, pushed back the origins of institutional religion and urban civilization by three millennia. Women were front and center in this new history. "Mellaart makes a case for an impressive female status in this Neolithic society," she wrote. There were no signs that Çatalhöyük had ever been attacked, nor that people there had been massacred or died violently in large numbers, at least not from the evidence of what had been excavated so far. Barstow took this to mean that these Neolithic communities with their "female cults" were notably more peaceful than societies that followed.

For all this excitement, though, other experts felt a growing sense of unease. Stories were developing a little too fast. The case for the nineteenth-century matriarchal myth was already considered tenuous. It wasn't clear that the findings at Çatalhöyük alone were enough to resurrect it.

Nobody could really know if the Seated Woman depicted a goddess, was a fertility symbol, a literal representation of a real person, or something else altogether. When I ask the tour guide Reşit Ergener what he sees in the Seated Woman, he answers with a laugh. "Personally, my grandmother!"— and that's arguably as good as any other explanation. Even the experts can't be sure why the residents of Çatalhöyük sometimes disinterred their dead to remove their skulls and pass them around. They may never understand why bull horns were plastered into walls and benches inside people's homes. The best researchers can do is to make educated guesses about what people in the past may have been thinking based on their artwork or burial patterns. "It's very rare that we can interpret a piece of archaeological data absolutely," warns Ruth Tringham. Scholars have to be humble about what they don't know. "It gets worse and worse the further back you get into prehistory. Where I work, we have no written sources, and even written sources are ambiguous."

The power to decode meaning with limited data sits in the hands of the person with the most intimate understanding of the site: the archaeologist. In this case, that archaeologist was James Mellaart. Once he had his lens fixed in the direction of the goddess, everything else was expected to slot into that same account of the past, forming what felt like a consistent narrative. The matriarchal myth was this way given flesh and bones.

There was always grumbling skepticism. But there were also plenty of others eager to breathe more life into his version of history. A crop of best-selling books in the 1970s and '80s would turn the belief in a female-centered, goddess-worshipping prehistory into a larger movement. By then, feminists and scholars alike were too invested in it for it not to be true.

■   ■   ■

Before the gods, the story went, there were the goddesses.

In her popular 1976 book *The Paradise Papers*, the art historian and sculptor Merlin Stone traced parallels between the violent suppression of women's "rites" in the past and the loss of women's "rights" into the present. She wrote that the "Great Goddess—the Divine Ancestress" had been worshipped from the beginning of the Neolithic from 7000 BCE until "the closing of the last Goddess temples" in roughly 500 CE. "There were records of such Goddesses in Sumer, Babylon, Egypt, Africa, Australia and China." In her bestseller *The Chalice and the Blade*, first published in 1987, the social scientist Riane Eisler also looked to distant history for evidence of the "cataclysmic turning point" that marked, in Friedrich Engels's famous words, "the world historical defeat of the female sex."

Belief in a matriarchal past began to blossom in some feminist circles in the second half of the twentieth century, just as it had in the second half of the nineteenth. The extraordinary (if at times a little too extraordinary) accounts relayed by writers like Stone and Eisler would find a ready audience among women looking for historical precursors in their fight for equal rights. The American activist Gloria Steinem was among those quick to reinforce the myth. "Once upon a time, the many cultures of this world were all part of the gynocratic age," she wrote. Echoing the New York ethnologist Lewis Henry Morgan, Steinem added that the reason men had been at the periphery of these societies was because paternity hadn't yet been discovered. Women were worshipped and considered superior because of their capacity to give birth.

Digging deep into archaeology and anthropology, sifting through the scattered evidence of humanity's past, Stone, Eisler, and Steinem were among a cadre of popular thinkers promoting the case that universal female power was no pipe dream. It was a real, tangible part of human prehistory. Books and articles like theirs featured ancient female figurines prominently, including the Seated Woman of Çatalhöyük but also other striking examples from ancient Crete, Egypt, and Greece. The debates of the previous century had returned as Western feminists sought once more to figure out how and why male domination in their cultures had come about.

The answer had to lie in deep time, they thought. And finally, there appeared to be solid scientific evidence.

Another archaeologist would join this chorus. Where James Mellaart had uncovered the extraordinary example of Çatalhöyük, the broader set of evidence tying everything together would be provided by an equally iconoclastic and controversial researcher named Marija Gimbutas. Born in Lithuania in 1921, later moving to California—a region that came to sit at the heart of New Age thinking in the West—she had spent decades researching the Neolithic cultures of the Danube Valley in southeastern Europe from around 6000 BCE. Gimbutas called this time and place "Old Europe." She married her archaeological findings to evidence from European myth and languages, revealing what looked like a cultural pattern focused around mothers and the worship of female deities.

Gimbutas had been raised on the rich folklore of Lithuania, on its fantastical tales of women with supernatural powers. There was the "Baba Yaga," for instance, considered a witch in Russian folklore, whom Gimbutas described as a Slavic goddess of death and regeneration. In Celtic cultures, she wrote, women enjoyed a relatively high status and were known for fighting in battles. In many of the stories she collected, goddesses, witches, or otherwise supernatural women were described as transforming into animals such as vultures, crows, or goats. The "Andre Mari," which Basque folklore saw as a prophetess, generally took on the form of a bird.

The lingering remnants of a long-lost past coalesced before her eyes. Her books were stuffed with illustrations of round-bottomed female figurines etched with spirals and zigzags, shapes that she believed were symbols of femininity. Both the mythological and material evidence seemed to point in the direction of a prehistory in which life had been different for women and the brutality of patriarchy didn't yet exist. These observations would turn Gimbutas into the intellectual driving force behind the burgeoning goddess movement.

Gimbutas's last book, *The Living Goddesses*, was published in 2001, seven years after her death. Finished by Miriam Robbins Dexter, a linguist with a strong interest in archaeology and mythology who was teaching at the University of California, Los Angeles, at the time, it documented the archaeological and mythological data that Gimbutas had amassed over her career for what she was convinced were the original matrilineal societies of Europe.

"She used to say she wasn't a feminist," says Dexter, who had known Gimbutas from the late 1960s all the way up to her death. "Marija, until the

1970s, was doing very traditional archaeological work." She wasn't driven by anything other than the evidence, Dexter adds. "What shaped her work was one step in front of the other, as it did mine, and just finding these things that surprised her."

Gimbutas didn't see the societies of "Old Europe" as necessarily matriarchal but certainly viewed them as egalitarian with "feminine" cores. It was "the feminine force that pervaded existence," she wrote. "The mother and the mother-daughter images are present throughout Old Europe, while the father image, so prevalent in later times, is missing." These interpretations were quickly taken up and spread to the masses. In *The Chalice and the Blade*, Riane Eisler wrote, "The finds of female figurines and other archaeological records attesting to a gynocentric (or Goddess-based) religion in Neolithic times are so numerous that just cataloging them would fill several volumes."

It was a history that was bound to appeal to feminists. But as Dexter says, this was never about politics for Gimbutas. It was only about the facts as she saw them. That her work became wildly popular came almost as a surprise. "A friend of mine organized a book signing," Dexter recalls. "She hired this two-storey church that was so full, people were sitting in the aisles. Marija had no idea that people liked her work that much, because she was focused on her work, not on what people liked or disliked."

In 1990, by which time Gimbutas had contracted cancer, her ideas had become so fashionable that the *New York Times* ran the headline "Idyllic Theory of Goddesses Creates Storm." It presented sixty-eight-year-old Gimbutas as a heroine to women's rights activists, lending what had until recently been unverified myths and intangible theories the "stamp of science and the reassurance of history." Her publisher told the newspaper that Gimbutas had shown people "that what feminists wished were true is in fact true."

■　　■　　■

Goddesses were only one half of the new grand narrative of women's history. If Old Europe was egalitarian, peaceful, and centered on the divine feminine, when did everything change? When did we get to the patriarchies we have now?

It was here that archaeologist Marija Gimbutas channeled the ghost of Friedrich Engels and his claim that there had long ago been a historical defeat of women. There had indeed been a catastrophic turning point, she argued. And she dated it to between three thousand and six thousand years ago when the peaceful societies of Old Europe were violently overrun by invaders from the Russian steppes north of the Black Sea. These incomers valued war and battle above anything else, Gimbutas said. When they came, it was nothing less than a cultural takeover. This was the big moment that Engels had theorized about, the one that marked the start of male domination.

Gimbutas described the incomers from the steppes as belonging to the "Kurgan" culture, after the Russian word for their mound-like graves in which the dead might be buried alongside their weapons. Archaeological evidence suggested that they were nomadic, riding horses and later chariots. They also kept livestock. While peacefulness and the creation of beautiful pottery had been a feature of Old Europe, these people instead formed a destructive "ruling warrior caste," Gimbutas wrote. Matrilineal patterns of inheritance and family veneration were replaced by patrilineal ones, with women relegated to subordinate roles.

The Kurgans, her theory went, spread all the way to India, Iran, and Chinese Turkestan to the east and, in the other direction, all the way through Europe to Britain and Ireland. Their presence could be detected in the common language roots shared by all these regions. Linguists since at least the end of the eighteenth century have recognized that the languages spoken by billions of people across this vast stretch of the world—including Spanish, French, English, Persian, Hindi, and German—do have words and grammar in common. They've been termed the "Indo-European" family. As Miriam Robbins Dexter explains, they are believed to have a single source, a lost language whose traces can be seen in India's ancient Sanskrit as well as in old Anatolian and Germanic tongues.

According to Gimbutas, the Kurgans didn't just export their language from the steppes into Europe and Asia; they also brought their patriarchal cultures, assimilating or destroying those they met along the way. She saw evidence of this shift among Mycenaeans, early ancient Greeks who flourished around 1600 BCE. Mycenaeans had a galaxy of goddesses and produced thousands of female figurines, Gimbutas wrote, but they were also at the cusp of a social transformation. She argued that this was brought about by the arrival of Indo-European speakers from the Eurasian steppes. By around 500 BCE, roughly coincident with classical Greece as we recognize it now in literature and art, that cataclysmic shift was complete. Its outcome could be seen in ancient Greek legends. Male gods such as Jupiter and Zeus became the heads of the heavenly pantheon. "Zeus, the chief male deity, was descended from the typical Indo-European warrior-god," she explained.

Goddesses didn't disappear entirely, but they did morph into more patriarchal versions of themselves. "Greek goddesses . . . now served male deities"
as wives and daughters, Gimbutas wrote. They were retained by ancient Greek
cultures but faded into shadows of their former selves. Now they would be
subservient to powerful male gods, she argued, eroticized and sometimes
rendered weaker. "The Indo-European female figures were very naturalistic,
weakly personified," Dexter tells me. By contrast, "the indigenous figures
were very often Great Goddesses. Aphrodite, Artemis, Athena were among
the Great Goddesses. Every Great Goddess in Indo-European culture was
indigenous and had great powers that one could see were eroded with time."

The heavens reflected what was happening on the ground. As the goddesses were pushed to one side by the gods, everyday women were losing
their authority to men. In ancient Athens, real-life upper-class Greek women
would come to be secluded within the home and all but banished from public
and intellectual life. "In Greek mythology, Zeus rapes hundreds of goddesses
and nymphs, Poseidon rapes Demeter, and Hades rapes Persephone," wrote
Gimbutas. "These rapes in the divine sphere may have reflected the brutal
treatment of Old European mortal women during the transition from pre-
patriarchy to patriarchy."

The author Merlin Stone took up this religious theme in *The Paradise
Papers* in 1976, arguing that the growth of monotheistic faiths such as Judaism
and Christianity saw goddesses condemned as pagan idols, associated with
nature worship, witchcraft, and sexual permissiveness. In the Bible's book of
Genesis, which some historians believe was written from roughly 900 BCE,
Stone saw an allegory. When Eve was punished for her transgression in the
Garden of Eden, she was told that "your desire shall be for your husband and
he shall rule over you." This statement reflected how violently actual women
may have been treated as patriarchal attitudes hardened around them.

Seen this way, the historical account provided by Gimbutas and others
does appear to make some sense. There are facts that fit together. If there's a
problem with it, it's that it feels a little too neat. Social change is rarely this
simple, as we know from our own time. There's little room in the story that
Gimbutas, Eisler, and Stone paint for the possibility that people resisted or
fought back, the way that matrilineal societies did against colonial impositions
on their gender norms in Asia in the nineteenth and twentieth centuries. Was
violence really the only tool by which patriarchy spread? And if it was achieved
with violence, why did it take thousands of years? Was control not exercised

in other more subtle ways? And did women play no part in it at all? Were they only ever the victims, and men only ever the perpetrators?

The grand narrative of women's defeat couldn't have been more dramatic if it had been written by a novelist: gentle, artistic, goddess-worshipping communities brutally replaced by a militaristic culture that worshipped male gods and was ruled by patriarchs. The anthropologist Ruth Tringham, who worked at Çatalhöyük, is among many who have been openly skeptical. She has criticized both James Mellaart and Marija Gimbutas for building up tales using evidence that, to her mind, is ambiguous at best. Tringham rarely uses or refers to Gimbutas's work anymore, she tells me.

But Tringham also doesn't believe that Gimbutas was intentionally stringing anyone along. "She really believed it." What Gimbutas developed wasn't simply archaeological theory. It was an entire history that claimed to explain in the grandest terms possible how patriarchy emerged in Europe and beyond. "She took the Çatalhöyük material and transformed it," says Tringham. "What she did was a much more powerful thing than Mellaart ever did, which was to place the matrifocal and goddess-centered society of what she called Old Europe and show it didn't just change; it was replaced."

■   ■   ■

"I find thinking in mythological terms has helped people," the late literature professor and mythologist Joseph Campbell once said. "Myths and dreams come from the same place; they come from realizations of some kind that have then to find expression in symbolic form."

According to Cynthia Eller, a scholar of religions at Claremont Graduate University in California, just because a myth has less scientific or material basis in evidence doesn't mean it has no value at all. A myth can still be a lens through which we view our hopes and dreams. Her book *The Myth of Matri-archal Prehistory* explores the phenomenon of modern-day goddess worship among Western women in predominantly Christian countries. Eller doesn't believe there were matriarchal, goddess-worshipping societies in Neolithic times. But she does accept that having the space to imagine a female-centered past, however unlikely it is that it existed, has its uses.

"I think it's one reaction to misogyny, and not one that I want to cast aside," she tells me. "I think for women who've grown up in male-dominated or patriarchal societies, just the ability to picture a vibrant alternative is really exciting." It helps sets new boundaries for what we think is possible, in the same way that established religions offer inspiring allegories that are equally unsubstantiated in fact. We value the lessons, the feelings they provoke in us, even if we know they may not be literally true.

The matriarchal myth is a modern one. It's possible to trace where it came from, which makes it easier to debunk than some other myths. Yet it still has the power to inspire. "There are people who embrace that story for its inspirational value, and I really think it's great. In that vein, it's great, especially if you're living in a small patriarchal box, to say the options here are so wide and could be so different," says Eller. "It's proven to have enormous value for a lot of feminists. It gave them a lot of hope. It gave them this whole sense of having a precedent."

This need for a historical precursor, for material proof on which to base belief in an alternative society, may be one reason why the myth of a shared matriarchal past persists into the present. Perhaps it speaks to just how difficult it is for some to picture a fairer future. Having this history be true would be the easy answer to sexists who say that women can't be leaders or that gender equality is impossible. It is one reason why suffragists like Matilda Joslyn Gage were so excited about matrilineal societies in the nineteenth century. But for Eller, as reassuring as the myth might be, there's still something troubling about treating it as unequivocally real when the evidence for it is either ambiguous or, as some academics have claimed when it comes to the work of Marija Gimbutas, virtually absent.

"My problem is that you can't pretend this is history and then make your plans on how the world should change based on this flawed history," says Eller.

The women who are keeping the idea of a female-centered, goddess-worshipping prehistory alive, she adds, have their own reasons for doing so. While some are happy to accept that it may not be factual, says Eller, "for those who have adopted this story for political reasons because they want to refashion the world in some way, it's harder for them to let go of the notion of its historicity. If you take out the historicity piece for them, you're taking out the linchpin." If a matriarchal prehistory didn't really exist, their faith that women really could hold power in the future starts to feel shakier.

Another troubling aspect of the myth is how enmeshed it has become with a particular brand of beliefs about gender. The focus of so much Western goddess-worshipping literature, Eller explains, is on women as nurturers who are more connected to nature and on men as the destroyers of nature—and by extension, the destroyers of women. Men and women are framed as opposites or as possibly complementing each other, but never as varied individuals who might possess overlapping traits. Western goddess-worshipping myths leave little room for bloodthirsty, violent goddesses like Kali, the Hindu deity. Instead, the strength of female-led societies is pinned on women having virtues that men don't, and on men having violent natures that women don't.

In *The Chalice and the Blade*, for instance, Riane Eisler pits the female "chalice" against the male "blade," the feminine representing the bountiful cup-like "source of life, the generative, nurturing, and creative powers of nature." She describes prehistoric goddess-worshipping societies as peace-loving, anti-warfare, and harmonious, implying that society today would be better off with women in charge because women inherently foster peace and equality. Eisler at one point even suggests that the male-dominated invaders from the steppes who Marija Gimbutas described would have enslaved both women and "gentler, more 'effeminate' men." Her story rests on a narrow suite of gender stereotypes.

"I do think that's had a big impact on the kind of myths and stories that have appealed to Western feminists. They are partly based in that, the very rigidity of that binary," suggests Eller. Nineteenth-century American women's rights activists such as Matilda Joslyn Gage and Elizabeth Cady Stanton, she writes, also had an "analytical reliance on differences between women and men" that assumed femininity "was simply *better* than masculinity. Female domination was the morally preferable alternative to be followed in creating a new social order."

For the American gender theorist Judith Butler, beliefs in a matriarchal prehistory have too often overlooked the true complexity of gender difference in favor of simplistic, reductive accounts of women and their experiences. These beliefs squeeze women all over the world into one version of what women are and strain uncomfortably when it becomes clear that individuals don't always fit these definitions. What this kind of gender essentialism does, as other feminist scholars have also been at pains to point out, is ignore that women are also capable of cruelty and violence. Men, too, can be nurturing and creative. The "feminist recourse to an imaginary past needs to be cautious," argues Butler. The qualities we define as "masculine" and "feminine" are shaped by social and cultural forces. There's no basis for assuming that what sound suspiciously like nineteenth-century Western beliefs about gender were held by people living in completely different societies thousands of years ago.

But then, every feminist wave brings along its own notions of "female specialness," notes Eller. This is understandable in societies in which women have been undervalued. It's a way of regaining a sense of pride and self-belief. For some, this is the lexicon of female empowerment. The cracks appear when this "specialness" proves to be another straitjacket, distancing women from what are considered to be "masculine" traits and defining "femininity" in tight, prescriptive ways. Behind the "Mother Goddess," after all, is the archetype of the selfless, nurturing woman whose primary role is to reproduce and care for others—a set of expectations that doesn't fit all women and has proven a burden to many.

■ ■ ■

Skepticism around Marija Gimbutas kept mounting. The more her work trended among women's rights activists, goddess worshippers, and New Age devotees, the more her reputation suffered among fellow academics.

There was a suspicion that her research rested on a hope rather than on reality. Lynn Meskell, an archaeologist and anthropologist at Stanford University who studied the Çatalhöyük figurines, wrote that Gimbutas had built her theories around what her readers wanted to be true. They were "idealistic creations reflecting the contemporary search for a social utopia," betraying an underlying wish to find a past in which patriarchy didn't exist. People were interested in prehistoric goddesses not just for academic reasons, she suggested, but out of "a desire to remedy the results of millennia of misogyny and marginalization."

Meskell's critique of Gimbutas was more generous than some others. In Gimbutas's final years, then after her death, more and more critics piled on, dismissing her theories as little more than fairy tales for feminists. "A lot of people who truly didn't understand sort of jumped on the anti-Marija bandwagon," I'm told by her former colleague Miriam Robbins Dexter, who has remained loyal to Gimbutas despite decades of stinging attacks. "A lot of people are still writing that, still making fun of her, still making fun of all of us who write about ancient female figures."

The biggest problem for Gimbutas was her generously broad reading of the archaeological and mythological data. The goddess "personified every phase of life, death, and regeneration," she wrote in *The Living Goddesses*. In symbols for water, she found a connection between moisture and the life-giving powers of the goddess. In grain seeds excavated in ruins, she saw new life growing in the womb. In a bull's head and horns, she saw a uterus and fallopian tubes. In a triangular marking, she saw a woman's vulva. She saw the goddess in phallus-shaped stones, too, interpreting them as the binding of a male force to the goddess. The feminist historian Carol Patrice Christ once observed that Gimbutas saw the goddess "as bird and chevron, as the letter V, as water, stream, zigzags, and the letter M, as meanders and water bird, as breasts and eyes, as mouth and beak, as spinner, metalworker, and music maker, as ram, as net, as the power of three, as vulva and birthgiver, as deer and bear, as snake." She could have gone on.

While some admired Gimbutas for her interpretations, for others, they only made it harder to take her seriously. One male American archaeologist describes her work to me as a series of "coffee table books" designed for mass consumption rather than genuine scholarship. The tour guide and author Reşit Ergener admits that, despite being enchanted by accounts of goddesses in Anatolia, even he feels there's a limit. "There were lots of goddesses," he tells me. But "there are those who see the goddess in *anything. Anything* old, *anything* historical, that must be the goddess."

For some, the pushback against Gimbutas began to take a more bitter tone. In one notably caustic article published in 1999, the classics professor Bruce Thornton at California State University described her work as being full of "fanciful interpretations and leaps beyond the evidence . . . a shaky edifice of question-begging, special pleading, unexamined assumptions, and circular reasoning." He took aim at goddess worshippers but also at feminists and women's studies scholars more generally for entertaining theories that he believed were "religious at best and anti-rationalist at worst." Thornton ended by stating that the Enlightenment tradition of liberalism and rationalism had in his opinion improved women's lives, and that to turn on this in favor of prehistoric goddess myths, or to claim that a mythical past had been better for women, demonstrated "hypocrisy and ingratitude."

Marija Gimbutas wasn't just wrong, he suggested. She was *ungrateful.*

It was easy to forget that Gimbutas wasn't the first scholar to enter into this kind of speculation about a matriarchal past. It was in fact James Mellaart who had deliberately reignited the matriarchal myth in the 1960s. Long before him, it had been Johann Jakob Bachofen, Lewis Henry Morgan, and Friedrich

Engels. And throughout the history of archaeology and anthropology, men in these fields have made countless assumptions about prehistory being rigidly patriarchal, some of which are equally unsubstantiated. Yet nobody has ever been quite the easy target of ridicule that Gimbutas has been.

When I ask Miriam Robbins Dexter what motivated Gimbutas's many critics, she answers that for a small number of them it was simply anxiety over the implications of what she wrote. "It was fear, fear of the divine feminine," she says. "They can't believe there was any kind of religion that was not male centered." The challenge Gimbutas posed went far beyond whether a V-shaped marking on a piece of old pottery really did refer to a woman's pubic triangle. She forced academics to take seriously the possibility that societies in Europe might have venerated women as well as men, that male domination might not have been a fact from the start.

Academics have long taken for granted that men must always have had more power than women from the beginning, writes Mara Lynn Keller, a professor of religion and women's spirituality at the California Institute of Integral Studies. "Gimbutas fundamentally challenged the established view that European culture has always been male-dominant and that 'history' but not 'prehistory' was civilized." By the standards of art, aesthetics, and gender balance, she argues, "Old Europe" could in fact be considered "a true civiliza-tion," as Gimbutas put it, in ways that societies today are perhaps not. But this isn't how Western thinkers have been trained to picture progress and modernity. The conventional view is that things are better now than they were then.

The legacy that Gimbutas leaves behind remains disputed from many sides. But experts today do accept that she at least brought to the fore alterna-tives to explain archaeological evidence from the perspective of women—in a field in which gender has been regularly overlooked. Whatever the true meaning of the female figurines she studied, even if they didn't represent goddesses at all but ordinary people, the objects do demand that we address the question of gender in prehistory. Women can't be dismissed as passive or powerless as long as the Seated Woman of Çatalhöyük sits so authoritatively in her own glass case in the Museum of Anatolian Civilizations in Ankara, unashamed of her age and her body, her steady hands resting upon the two creatures flanking her.

We will be forever asking who this person was.

■   ■   ■

Like so many visitors to Çatalhöyük, I'm drawn to find meaning in this place, to get the remains to speak to me. It's a struggle. I start—as others do—by relating what I see to the cultures I already know. Are the bull horns in their walls hunting trophies? Did these people leave their dead out for their flesh to be eaten by birds of prey for the same reason that Parsi communities do in India? Did they worship their ancestors in the same traditional ways that are seen in Mexico? After a while, it becomes clear just how difficult it is to decipher a society that predates every other one I know by many thousands of years. I may find occasional parallels, but they could have nothing to do with each other.

Witnessing history at this level, walking among the debris of people's homes, staring at their broken possessions, grand narratives begin to melt away. All I can know is that these were everyday folk, trying to make sense of the world like the rest of us are. At a stretch, I might dare to imagine what occupied their dreams.

Feminist archaeology, an approach that emerged in the 1980s as archaeologists began to recognize the need to think about gender more subtly, was a turning point in anthropologist Ruth Tringham's career. Until then, she had thought about prehistoric people only as "faceless blobs doing things." They had no stories, no backgrounds, no individuality. Archaeology was dominated by big historical narratives. But as some feminists began to ask who these people actually were, looking into their life trajectories, new ways of thinking about the past began to bubble to the surface. Tringham has become less interested in the overarching landscapes of the kind painted by James Mellaart and Marija Gimbutas, and more interested in these finer-grained portraits.

"It was the feminist axis which really legitimized thinking about archaeology and prehistory at the very small scale," she explains.

"For me, it was being able to think about people, the actors of prehistory, the residents of the building I was excavating as actual sort of living people with hearts and minds." It was about stepping into their shoes. "They could be one of any number of genders, any number of ages; they would be all different. The households would be made up of real people, imagined real people, who were all very varied."

Simple objects and dwellings can this way be read in a multitude of ways. "Archaeology doesn't give you a true picture; it gives you a picture that you have to interpret," she tells me. "The way you interpret something is really about how broad is your imagination. . . . Where is your imagination coming from? What are the sources for building a scenario?" For instance, do you see a pot for storing food? Or do you see a precious urn? "Once you get into things like people, social behavior, social relations, then you have to be able to entertain different kinds of scenarios, different kinds of interpretations, at the same time."

The further we travel into the past, the more open our minds need to be. In her analysis of figurines belonging to the Halaf cultures of Anatolia and northern Mesopotamia around the fifth millennium BCE, the historian Ellen Belcher at the City University of New York has questioned whether female figurines were even designed to represent femaleness at all. Halaf figurines are famous for their exaggerated body parts, particularly the hips, breasts, and genitals. But Belcher notes that the mammary glands and pubic hair on these figurines, features which are shared by humans in general, not just by women, might not be there to signify sex at all. They might simply have marked out who was human in societies that lived closely with animals.

Belcher found that more than half the figurines she analyzed were of unknown or unexpressed sexual difference. "Figurines provide evidence of a much more nuanced approach to sexual difference, which at times, can be androgynous, as in breasts placed on both male and female representations, or overly distinct, as in the representation of over proportioned and adorned breasts or pudenda," she writes. It becomes clear that "gender was represented on a spectrum from ambiguous to overt."

The enormous diversity in female figurines is routinely airbrushed away under the label "goddess" or "fertility" symbol, as though all these objects were made for the same reason. We actually know very little about what purpose these figurines might have served in the Neolithic or who made them. They could have been anything, from toys and ornaments to markers of status or place. Perhaps they were many things at once. Belcher observes that figurines are sometimes known to have been roughly handled and then dumped in what appears to be the trash. They're not always valuable or sacred.

"Recent research suggests that past gender ideologies were far more diverse and complex, offering many models of feminine power, not only nurturing and mothering but also destructive or simply ambiguous," writes the anthropologist Kelley Hays-Gilpin. For her, there has been an uncritical acceptance of binary thinking around sex and gender when it comes to studying the past. "The fact that the majority of figurines in many times and places, including the European Ice Age, show no evidence of sexual features at all (and a few are surely male) suggests that projecting a present-day essential or ideal of the feminine onto the past on the basis of these data is misguided."

It's possible to see the way these modern-day beliefs have been projected onto the past at the archaeological museums in the Anatolian cities of Konya and Ankara. Vaguely anthropomorphic objects are labeled definitively "male" or definitively "female." It's hard to know how these judgment calls were made or why curators felt compelled to make them in the first place. In one room, I see lifelike mannequins showing Neolithic men smelting ore to extract metal. In another, there's a model of a woman grinding down grain into flour. But we have no proof that jobs like these, both equally labor intensive, were divided up this way by gender. There are obvious biases in the academic literature, too. At least one male scholar has described the Seated Woman of Çatalhöyük as "obese." It's not just matriarchal myths that weigh heavily on our understanding of prehistory. It's also our stereotypes.

Putting our assumptions aside is almost impossible. We're all constrained by our biases. Feminist archaeology may be slower work, but it is more intimate than the sweeping approach that experts used to take in the past. It requires the archaeologist to let go of certainty and embrace ambiguity. It accepts that even in a village with a strong culture of its own, individuals might have lived in different ways, just as people do now. It forces us to ask whether the social norms we take as given today might not have been the same ten thousand years ago.

■　■　■

Ironically, given his instinct that this was a female-centered, goddess-worshipping community, it was the archaeologist James Mellaart who first noticed the lack of gendered patterns in diet, health, and burial at Çatalhöyük when he started carrying out excavations here in the 1960s. This was important because differences in how men and women live or how they're treated can usually be spotted through this kind of data. If one group has higher status than another, you would expect to find them eating finer food and more of it, to look stronger and more robust, and enjoy more elaborate burials. But that's not what archaeologists have seen at Çatalhöyük.

One reasonable conclusion is that the settlement was neither female dominated nor male dominated. It may be that gender just wasn't a big concern for the people living here.

"The hard scientific evidence is that if you look at the diets of men and women obtained from bones, from graves, they are more or less identical," I'm told by the Stanford University archaeologist Ian Hodder, who led the Çatalhöyük Research Project until 2018, working alongside other researchers, including Ruth Tringham. He knows the settlement perhaps better than anyone alive. In an article for *Scientific American* in 2004, Hodder stated that there was "little indication that the sexes had specialized tasks or that daily life was highly gendered." For him, this pointed to a society in which sex didn't matter very much when it came to social roles. In another paper published roughly a decade later, Hodder was even more sure that theirs was "an aggressively egalitarian community," at least for some of the time.

"Most sites that archaeologists dig, you find that men and women, because they have different lives, they have different food and they end up with different diets," he says. "But at Çatalhöyük you don't see that at all. They have identical diets." Other biological measurements from human remains show the same lack of difference. For instance, Hodder's team found that both men and women had soot on their ribs, most probably from indoor ovens and a lack of ventilation in their small box-like houses. This indicated that men didn't spend more time outdoors than women did. What's more, although the men were taller than the women on average, the size difference between them was slight. Wear on their bones, another sign of people doing different types of jobs, was also more or less the same.

The one difference that researchers did notice was in the number of beads people were buried with, Hodder says. "Women tend to have more beads than men do. But everything else is the same."

Diane Bolger, an archaeologist at the University of Edinburgh, has argued that we need to rethink our belief that male and female roles in prehistoric societies were separately defined at all. As the case of Çatalhöyük shows, "when gender roles are investigated rather than assumed, the result is very likely to contradict simple, binary models." It becomes less obvious that their social systems were gendered in the way modern-day societies are.

This isn't how experts in this area usually work, though. "With funerary evidence, with skeletal analysis, you always start with 'Is it male or is it female or is it indeterminate?'" I'm told by the archaeologist Karina Croucher at the University of Bradford, whose work focuses on death and burials. "If you do away with that and start looking at other attributes, does it throw up different patterns? We don't know because no one's done it. We always start with male and female." This is a persistent habit. "It's partly to do with who does the excavating. It is still almost a colonial pursuit a lot of the time," she says. And European colonial beliefs were rooted firmly in a binary hierarchy between women and men.

"It comes down to our need to pigeonhole. And when we break out of that need to pigeonhole, things start to begin making much more sense in the archaeological record," adds Croucher.

Among the other unexpected things that researchers have learned from studying Çatalhöyük's human remains is that people who lived together in the same houses weren't always related to one another. "It's actually rare for parents to raise their own children," says Hodder. "Children weren't brought up with their biological parents. They were farmed out or fostered out. So, the whole community was one great family, where all the biological children are all mixed up." Some experts have suggested that maybe they had a more fluid understanding of kin relationships that wasn't simply about blood ties. Homes might have been grouped by the tasks they did, like growing crops or taking care of animals, or for religious or cultural reasons. "It's mind-bogglingly complicated," says Hodder. "How you situated yourself as an individual within all that was extremely diverse."

Ruth Tringham adds that Çatalhöyük may not even have been a city as James Mellaart originally proposed. The evidence points instead to thousands of residents living together in the same community, while at the same time operating independently as farmers and hunter-gatherers. "Mellaart couldn't imagine it was a regular village. He couldn't imagine it," she says. "In the sixties, not many people expected that hunter-gatherers could have as rich a cognitive practice and social relations that in fact they had, so they jumped to the conclusion that was most familiar." But as big and elaborate as Çatalhöyük was, it still resembled a village in many ways. This proves, perhaps, that there's no single way to forge a complex society. "People will create beautiful homes even if they're just small-time farmers."

This doesn't mean that people lived in perfect harmony. There may not be proof of gendered hierarchies, but there is some evidence of tension and violence among the people who lived here. Theirs was a society in constant dialogue with itself. "I think what we see at Çatalhöyük is that the motive for change is internal conflict and contradictions and problems that emerge," explains Hodder. "We can see through the sequence that pressures build up, tensions build up, density builds up, and there's wear and tear on the bodies and bad things are happening, and that leads to a resolution, and they go off in a slightly different direction." He's come to think that this was a community that afforded households great leeway in how they lived. Nothing was static.

The extent of social diversity in the past is something that archaeologists have only started to appreciate over the last twenty years, he adds. While at Çatalhöyük and at some other ancient sites in Anatolia, excavations have unearthed an abundance of female figurines, that's not true of other Neolithic sites even relatively nearby. When I visit Göbekli Tepe to the east of Çatalhöyük near the border with Syria, I see enormous monolithic stones with animals beautifully carved into them—and only one obvious depiction of a woman (and even that seems to have been scrawled hastily, like graffiti). Some experts have suggested, based on the phallic shape of the stones, that this might have been a gathering place for men and boys. Göbekli Tepe is some two thousand years older than Çatalhöyük. And if it proves anything, it's that there are no apparent rules for how people lived in prehistory.

As far as Hodder is concerned, the famous figurine of the Seated Woman of Çatalhöyük isn't a goddess. He sees instead, as I do, "a powerful image of a woman post-childbirth. She's got great sagging breasts, and sagging stomach and sagging bottom. I mean, this is a very proud and mature woman." The figurine doesn't look like other fertility symbols either. "It's not about reproduction and sex and things. There's no mothering going on, and there's no 'goddessing' going on."

The fact that new homes were built on top of old ones at Çatalhöyük allows archaeologists to see changes over time. And this does indicate that the settlement may have transitioned from being an ungendered society to one in which older women were important as symbols or representatives of their houses, he adds. If this is true, the Seated Woman may have been a respected figure in her household. Perhaps also in her wider community.

Whether or not she really was a goddess also depends on how Neolithic people in Çatalhöyük thought about deities in the first place. This isn't an easy question. "There's a Western, Christian understanding of what a religious function looks like," says Cynthia Eller. Someone raised in a rigidly male, monotheistic tradition might assume that the only possible religious alternative is a monotheistic goddess. "They imagine that if you have a female figurine, you have a goddess, and that the goddess controls everything and that she's awesome and gracious and gave birth to the entire universe." But this is actually "a real reach from what we know about religions that worship goddesses—which is most religions."

In Hinduism, for instance, there are multiple gods and goddesses. But many Hindus also venerate objects and real people, including politicians and movie stars. There's a mutability about faith and usually less separation between the sacred and the secular than there is in other traditions. My own middle name, Devi, literally means "goddess." The word is often used in India in reference to everyday women as a sign of respect. If the Seated Woman wasn't a goddess, she could well have been a "devi" in that same sense of the word.

But again, I find myself projecting my own cultural experiences onto what I see.

There are only a few undisputed truths about Çatalhöyük. It's hard to escape the likelihood that the settlement wasn't rigidly patriarchal. But neither was it noticeably matriarchal. In one grave, a woman was buried clutching someone else's skull close to her body. Archaeologists assume that heads pulled out for special treatment in this way were likely to have come from people who were important to the community. Those they've uncovered so far come equally from men and women. "So, there's no sense that women were somehow excluded from the political process," Hodder tells me. There's no clear evidence from burials, either, that ancestral lineage was traced through only one sex. This means Çatalhöyük may have been neither matrilineal nor patrilineal.

"My view is that they were very much gender blind, that gender was probably incredibly fluid and transformative and noncategorical," Hodder concludes, his choice of language perhaps also reflecting the politics of his time. "Most of the time they were working together, cooking together, working in the fields together; they're making tools together. We just don't find strong categorical differences."

. . .

The anthropologist Kathryn Rountree was watching archaeologists at work at Çatalhöyük in 2003 when she spotted something amusing.

The members of one team had just uncovered a small female figurine carved delicately out of pale green stone. At the time and at least in public, scientific experts generally dismissed as nonsense the theory that Neolithic communities were matriarchal or that they necessarily worshipped goddesses. Serious academics believed themselves too rational and objective to fall for these myths. Yet Rountree noticed that when researchers found this precious figurine, they immediately began referring to her as the "Mother Goddess." One scientist looked at the piece under a microscope and "exclaimed, without a detectable hint of irony, 'I have touched the Goddess!'"

Perhaps the myths will always precede the truth about Çatalhöyük. Maybe, whether or not they admit it, it was the promise of the goddess that attracted some archaeologists to this settlement in the first place.

As I get ready to leave the dry, flat Konya plains, my mind drifts back to Marija Gimbutas. Before she died in 1994, Gimbutas did something that few women archaeologists have been able to do before or since. She unapologetically wrote her own grand narrative. Taking the evidence as she interpreted it from female figurines, folklore, and linguistics, she built a bold, sweeping history. To the end, she clung to her belief that Europe and parts of Asia had once been home to female-centered, goddess-worshipping cultures before being turned upside down by the arrival of violent, warrior cultures from the Eurasian steppes between five thousand and six thousand years ago. These "Kurgan" or early Indo-European speaking incomers were for her and her followers the original patriarchs.

Gimbutas's theories may have been flung to the margins of serious archaeology, ridiculed by her former colleagues, but when I ask Miriam Robbins Dexter how Gimbutas felt about her critics when she was alive, she tells me that they didn't bother her too much. "She didn't take things terribly personally. She wasn't terribly hurt," Dexter says.

"She said they will change their mind in twenty years. That's all she said."

Standing on the unexcavated parts of Çatalhöyük, knowing how much more there is under my feet to be discovered, is at once frustrating and exhilarating. Few places in the world have proven quite so challenging to our beliefs about human nature. The way this settlement was organized unsettles everything we thought we knew about the past. There's no single pattern that appears to define social relations in the Neolithic. Neither male domination nor female domination seem to have been the rule.

So, a piece in the puzzle of patriarchy remains missing. As blind to gender as this society was nine millennia ago, we know that this broader region of the world became increasingly dominated by elite, powerful men as it entered the Bronze Age thousands of years later. Rules for women across all classes became more restrictive. Work gradually started to be divided up by gender. Social inequalities and class hierarchies emerged. Patriliny and patrilocality eventually became the norm. We still don't know the circumstances that brought about these changes.

•   ▪   ▪

Relatively recently, though, new evidence has come along to potentially crack this mystery. And it's here that the story takes a surprising turn. These new scientific findings happen to tally with parts of the grand theory that Marija Gimbutas originally proposed. Roughly two decades after her death, this has forced some of her former critics to revisit her work. While there remains no proof that prehistory was matriarchal or goddess-worshipping, some have had to admit that when it came to the spread of patriarchal practices and social structures, Gimbutas may have hit on something after all.

Minds have changed—just as she predicted they would.

CHAPTER 4

Destruction

T his murder had been committed before the eyes of entire society," I'm told by the Turkish activist Fidan Ataselim, one of the founders of the women's rights group We Will Stop Femicide Platform.

It happened in August of 2019, roughly fifty kilometers from the capital Ankara. Thirty-eight-year-old Emine Bulut had gone to meet her ex-husband in a café. The two fell into an argument. He stabbed her in the neck before escaping in a taxi. What happened next was caught on camera and shared across social media, sending shockwaves across Turkey. For once, people couldn't look away.

Bulut cried out, "I don't want to die!"

We Will Stop Femicide Platform estimates that at the time of her death, 245 women had already been killed in Turkey that year, most of them by their partners or other relatives. That number would rise to 474 by the end of the year. At her ex-husband's trial, at which he received a life sentence, protestors shouted Bulut's dying words outside the courthouse: "We don't want to die!" Her ten-year-old daughter could be seen in the footage tenderly willing her mother to live.

Like most countries, Turkey is caught between its liberal and conservative forces. The twentieth century saw a raft of reforms as the Turkish republic sought to break with the Ottoman Empire's old traditions. These included measures to emancipate women. In 1934, women secured the right to vote before women in France or Switzerland. An airport in Istanbul is named for the world's first female combat pilot, Sabiha Gökçen, born in 1913. But there has been mounting backlash recently. As more women work, divorce their husbands, and step outside traditional gender roles, explains Ataselim, men see "all their privileges and means of domination are gone."

In 2016, President Recep Tayyip Erdoğan announced that a woman who prioritized her career over motherhood and housekeeping was like half a person. "You cannot put women and men on an equal footing," he had already said a couple of years earlier. "It is against nature." The year after Emine Bulut was murdered, his government warned that it might pull out of the Istanbul Convention, an international agreement aimed at bringing in stronger protections against domestic violence and gender-based discrimination. The following year, Turkey became the first country to withdraw from it.

"Turkey is a patriarchal society like other countries of the world. Patriarchy continues to maintain itself as a very deep-rooted system," Ataselim continues. Her fellow campaigner Melek Önder tells me the same. "Maybe we have a long way to go," she says, "but it has always been like this historically."

When violence against women is widespread, when hard-won rights look so precarious, when the grip of male power seems intractable, it may well feel as though it has been this way forever. Political leaders routinely invoke "tradition" and "nature" when clamping down on women's rights. This is how it's always been, they claim. But history tells a different story. This is the same country, after all, as the settlement of Çatalhöyük, where thousands of years ago people likely lived and worked side by side regardless of gender. The norms that a society follows must be built.

Women's rights and freedoms weren't missing in deep time. Just like in the present, they had to have been destroyed.

■ ■ ■

"History is protean," wrote the late American historian David Lowenthal. "What it is, what people think it should be, and how it is told and heard vary with time, place, and person."

Accounts that explain the emergence of what we now call patriarchy have often been painted in broad strokes. Everyone wants the answer to be clear-cut. "History no less than memory conflates, exaggerates, abridges," Lowenthal explained. What is "crucial or unique is made to stand out." Some experts believe, for instance, that the single turning point for gender inequality was agriculture. Many think that it was when humans started to keep property. Others place the blame squarely on religion. There are a few, even now, who remain attached to the notion that men were just always dominant by nature. Grand, sweeping narratives run like threads through the work of some of the world's most famous historians, philosophers, and scientists.

Marija Gimbutas was no exception.

Her followers were captivated by her bold theory of peaceful, female-centered, goddess-worshipping societies in Old Europe replaced by violent patriarchal hordes who came in from the vast grasslands to the north of the Caspian and Black Seas, in the territory that now stretches from Ukraine to Mongolia. Critics felt differently. "Initially, I was quite skeptical of Marija Gimbutas's position," admits the veteran British archaeologist Colin Renfrew. "She did get a bit over-elaborate."

Since then, Renfrew has changed his mind. "I think more recently a lot of her ideas have turned out very well." That's not to say her grand narrative was correct in every way. But fragments of it have held up to scrutiny, he tells me. "Broadly, I think what she said now seems rather persuasive and much of it makes good sense today." Compelling evidence has come along to support at least parts of her theory, leading others to also wonder if Gimbutas wasn't quite the fringe thinker she had been painted out to be.

This turnaround came about not through any exciting new archaeological finds but because of a series of breakthroughs in biology. Back in 1984, scientists at the University of California, Berkeley, had managed to retrieve and reproduce short bits of DNA taken from a 140-year-old museum exhibit of a quagga, an extinct South African horse with zebra-like stripes on the front half of its body. Their research proved that with considerable effort it was logistically possible to study the complete sets of genes of long-dead specimens.

The remains of other extinct creatures went on to be mined in the same way. Before long, scientists moved onto humans. Their efforts started in the middle of the 1990s with Neanderthals, a form of human estimated to have disappeared around 40,000 years ago. Then, in 2005, a team of researchers that included Colin Renfrew reported that they had teased out genetic material from Neolithic farmers who had lived 7,500 years ago.

"It's a complete disruption of prehistory," I'm told by the Danish archaeologist Kristian Kristiansen, based at the University of Gothenburg in Sweden. He was among the first to hitch his wagon to this trend, immediately publishing papers in collaboration with geneticists. The worlds of biology and archaeology collided, he explains. And this brought radical new insights into history.

"It's a revolution," he says.

Genes may sound like an iron-clad source of evidence, one that can't be disputed, but there's plenty of room for mistakes. Genetic data needs to be skillfully interpreted against what researchers already know from history, archaeology, and other sources. Kristiansen believes, though, that scientists can use ancient DNA to paint a picture of human migration from prehistory into the present. The way they've done this is by comparing the DNA of skeletons at various points in time with each other. They can also compare these samples to the DNA of living people. This way they can start to find out, for instance, whether Neolithic farmers living in Europe thousands of years ago are related to some modern-day people of European heritage, the same way that DNA tests can gauge whether family members are blood relations.

"Of course, DNA doesn't tell you about language, but it does tell you about a population, dynamics, and migration," Renfrew tells me. "I very much follow the DNA evidence."

It's this biological approach that has revived interest in Marija Gimbutas and her theory about the rise of patriarchy. Following in the footsteps of the early twentieth-century Australian archaeologist Vere Gordon Childe, Gimbutas had argued that early Indo-European-speaking people, belonging to what she called the "Kurgan" culture, might have migrated thousands of years ago from the grassy Eurasian Steppe toward the west into "Old Europe." For her, this marked the start of the region's enormous cultural transition into male domination and away from goddess worship. The problem was that nobody could be sure whether this migration ever actually took place. For decades, it was a topic of fevered debate among archaeologists.

Now, remnants of ancient DNA point to the likelihood that it did happen. People thought to have geographical roots in the steppes, speaking some early form of Indo-European language, probably did move in large numbers into parts of Europe during the end of the Neolithic and into the early Bronze Age, around 4,500 years ago. This is roughly the same time that Stonehenge was being finished in Britain. These dates aren't as early as Gimbutas predicted, but they do support aspects of her theory.

"I think the DNA evidence now does indicate a significant movement from the east," says Renfrew. "Exactly where the movement originated is still a matter for discussion, but I think it's clear there was a movement from the east that brought Indo-European speech into Europe and so to western Europe."

Genetic evidence also points to the possibility that these people from the east mixed with the farmers and hunter-gatherers they met along the way, and then began to outnumber the local populations. In a large study published in the scientific journal *Nature* in 2015, researchers claimed that many present-day people with heritage in Europe—particularly those with family roots in Germany and Britain—share some ancestry with these early migrants. Geneticists have spotted similar links among living people who have family heritage in India, although the movement into South Asia is likely to have happened much later, between roughly 1500 and 1200 BCE, according to some estimates. "In general, it does back up to a good degree what Marija Gimbutas herself advocated," says Renfrew.

Experts have begun to ask themselves what else she might have got right. In his 2018 book *Who We Are and How We Got Here*, the Harvard University geneticist David Reich, a high-profile figure in the field of ancient DNA studies, wrote that the migrants originating from the Eurasian Steppe had "a strikingly male-centered culture that celebrated violence," almost exactly as Gimbutas had written. He suggested they might have been responsible for cutting down swathes of forest in northern Europe to make way for grasslands on which to graze their animals, transforming the landscape to resemble the one they left behind. In essence, he argued, they had tried to recast Europe in the image of their grassy plains. Other geneticists have termed the movement of people during this time as a "massive migration."

This remains a matter of debate. "It's probably better to think of it as a process rather than as a migration, so over several centuries, I would say. It wasn't suddenly lots of people rushing in, I think. It was more a change of economy," says Renfrew, displaying a little more caution. Yet the apparent scale of the movement revealed by the data has surprised him. "It wasn't melding; it was a displacement."

It's even plausible, he adds, that Gimbutas was right all along about the people who lived in "Old Europe" being more female centered and worshipping goddesses before this "displacement" happened. "It's very difficult to know what people thought, but there's no doubt there was a rich repertoire of gods and goddesses, and mainly goddesses, in the cultures in southeast Europe at the time of Old Europe before 3500 BCE," he tells me. "That's what Marija emphasized when she emphasized the patriarchal nature, as she saw it, of the incoming new society."

For Miriam Robbins Dexter, who has always championed Gimbutas, this is the vindication she has been waiting for. "I have to say, it pleased me so much when the DNA evidence started coming out a few years ago," she says. "It's huge. For me, it's huge because we truly know who the Indo-Europeans were, where they lived before they expanded out, who expanded out, what were their attributes, what was their world view."

As far as Dexter is concerned, there's no doubt that these people were the patriarchal invaders that Gimbutas described. "The Indo-Europeans were warriors," she states.

Yet I can't help but recall David Lowenthal's warning about the temptation to exaggerate when it comes to writing the past. Even serious experts love a simple storyline. The further removed we are from the history being written, the greater the risk of dramatization, of reducing people to good and evil. "Because it is over, the past can be arranged and domesticated, given a coherence foreign to the chaotic, ever-shifting present," Lowenthal wrote. The dramatic myth of a matriarchal prehistory enchanted Western thinkers for nearly two centuries, despite there being little evidence for it. Is twenty-first-century science really providing proof of Friedrich Engels's "world historical defeat of the female sex"? Were these "invaders" from the steppes really the world's first patriarchs?

Or is the truth, as it often is, more complicated?

■   ■   ■

One of the darker realities of academic research into Indo-European history is that this field became popular in the nineteenth century because of efforts to prove the existence of what some believed to be an original "Aryan" race, superior to all others. It was an idea taken up later in Nazi Germany.

Germans were the true descendants of the Aryans, the Nazis believed, only they had been undermined by other ethnic groups living among them, sullying their supposed racial purity. The political attraction of this fabled past was that it offered a twisted narrative to help restore Germany's ethnic pride after its loss in the First World War. Fascists wanted to prove that things were better in a bygone era, before migration and cultural mixing. This story, once woven, came to form one of their justifications for the Holocaust.

Seventy-plus years on, Indo-European studies remain burdened by an unhealthy interest from far-right nationalists and white supremacists who have never quite let go of the Aryan myth. For populists all over the world, manipulating history continues to serve politically motivated goals. The belief that culture is somehow bound up in race, that entire populations are by their nature fundamentally different from others, has never gone away. There are plenty who still nurture the old prejudice that migrants have the power to damage a country's culture, to erode its ethnic authenticity.

This is the political backdrop to genetic research into ancient migration.

The Stanford archaeologist Ian Hodder, who led excavations at Çatal-höyük in Anatolia, accepts that there must have been some movement of people originating from the Eurasian Steppe thousands of years ago, as Marija Gimbutas always claimed there had been. "The evidence is unequivocal, really, that she was right." But he advises against slipping into assuming that one skeleton or the bones of a few people can somehow represent an entire population or its culture, as some scientists have since implied. Real societies, as we know, are always diverse.

"If you look at the map, they have a couple of samples here and there of ancient DNA," Hodder tells me. From this, it has been too easy to rush to quick conclusions—in this case, that Neolithic populations were naturally peaceful and female-focused while the incomers were all innately violent and male-focused. Only their arrival in large numbers, this story insinuates, could have transformed how societies were organized. "I mean, it's just terrible; it's just terrible, terrible," he says.

Racially tinged speculation of this kind is especially fraught in an age in which images of male migrants from Asia and Africa have been used to whip up nativist fears of foreigners in Europe. "These scholars paint a picture of groups of roving, predatory young men that were thought to be part of the social organisation of all Indo-European societies," the Cambridge University archaeologist Susanne Hakenbeck wrote in one withering critique in 2019. "We are being offered an appealingly simple narrative of a past shaped by virile young men going out to conquer a continent, given apparent legitimacy by the scientific method." It's a story that rests on the narrowest of racial and gender stereotypes: foreign men as predators and native women as prey.

What Hakenbeck found particularly disturbing was that she had seen this version of history being enthusiastically shared on far-right and white supremacist forums online, among men who enjoyed the idea of being descended from hyper-masculine bands of warring males.

It should be obvious that mass migration is never the only catalyst for cultural change. We know that the movement of even small numbers of people back and forth around the world can transport ideas, technologies, religions, and habits. European colonizations in the eighteenth and nineteenth centuries are examples of how gender norms can shift profoundly without entire populations being displaced. Encounters between Neolithic people in "Old Europe" and those from the Eurasian Steppe likely happened in many different ways. Given the enormous time spans involved here, it would take some stretch of the imagination to believe there was one sudden militaristic takeover. It's far more plausible that there was a slow diffusion of habits and practices over time, in which migration played only a part.

"I'm very suspicious of the assumption that just because you have a spread of genes you have a spread of culture. I just think that's wrong," Hodder tells me. "What we need is a return to careful consideration of those cultures and a reevaluation of the evidence to understand exactly how that migration occurred."

Martin Furholt, an archaeologist at the University of Oslo who researches social organization in prehistoric communities, has warned against brushing over the diverse, messy realities of everyday people's lives when we think about big social change. Prehistoric people living in what is now Europe, for instance, didn't give up hunting and gathering to quickly adopt agriculture and domestication. It took hundreds of years, and even then, their choices depended on their circumstances. Similarly, any "massive migration," as some geneticists have termed it, may well have involved people borrowing customs from each other over centuries, synthesizing their cultures, making strategic choices—even if there may have been murder and captive-taking at times. Societies, like individuals, are capable of a wide range of behaviors depending on the pressures they face.

We know this. Yet however unclear the evidence might be, writes Furholt, the story always seems to come back to a "constant clash" of cultures, in which men from one group exploit women from another.

There are plenty of reasons to be more cautious. For one, even if the "Kurgan" mound-burial societies from the steppes were on the warpath, that's no reason to assume that women weren't fighting as well. As the military historian Pamela Toler notes, "The horse-riding nomadic tribes of the Eurasian steppes may win the prize for being the earliest (and most consistent) cultures to allow women to openly fight alongside their male counterparts." Some of the earliest archaeological evidence of female warriors comes from a burial mound, thought to be roughly three thousand years old, of three armed women near Tbilisi in Georgia, writes Toler. One died with an arrow stuck in her skull.

There's a long habit in academia of assuming that only men have been hunters and warriors, that one sex alone is truly capable of violence. In 2018, archaeologists excavated a human skeleton in the Peruvian Andes thought to have belonged to a hunter living nine thousand years ago. The body was buried with twenty-four stone objects, including projectile points and a knife. It was reasonable to think this collection of items might have comprised a tool kit for hunting big game. But when this hunter turned out to be female, there was undisguised surprise. In a comment for *National Geographic*, the Arizona State University anthropologist Kim Hill betrayed his biases. "You can't just stop in the middle of stalking a deer in order to nurse a crying baby," he told the reporter—forgetting that all women aren't always pregnant or nursing.

Hill suggested that the hunting kit may instead have been symbolic or religious, rather than something used by the person it was buried with.

There was incredulity, too, after a high-status warrior grave in the Viking Age town of Birka, Sweden, dating from the middle of the tenth century CE, was found to belong to a woman. Genetic evidence in 2017 overturned long-standing assumptions that the grave must have belonged to a male warrior. In the early Middle Ages, "there were narratives about fierce female Vikings fighting alongside men," the researchers wrote. "Although, continuously reoccurring in art as well as in poetry, the women warriors have generally been dismissed as mythological phenomena." Now there was hard evidence that these stories may not have been myths at all.

Even after the warrior's sex was established, there were scholars who expressed doubts. Some asked whether the objects in the grave were just family heirlooms. Exasperated, the archaeologist who led the study, Charlotte Hedenstierna-Jonson at Uppsala University, found herself having to reassure reporters that this was "a real-life military leader, that happens to be a woman . . . someone who worked with tactics and strategy and could lead troops in battle." One explanation for why she held such a high-status leadership role could be that she was a member of the social elite. As the archaeologists Diane Bolger and Rita Wright have documented, there are many examples of societies in which "class and rank superseded gender." Another possibility is that warfare and leadership just weren't gendered in the same way they tend to be these days.

Pontus Skoglund, an expert in ancient DNA working at the Francis Crick Institute in London, admits that geneticists tend to lack a critical perspective when it comes to gender, not least because the field is dominated by men. But he adds that some archaeologists, too, suffer the same problems. "As ancient DNA started to become a thing, the first archaeologists who jumped on board were quite positivistic about biology, and so they have been the ones that have shaped perhaps the interpretation," Skoglund tells me. It's possible that some spotted an opportunity to make waves using this new technology. "I'm not saying that geneticists are innocent, naïve people, but that's an element."

In 2017, researchers at Stanford University and Uppsala University published a paper looking at the DNA of prehistoric people who had lived in Europe. They suggested that there was something unusual about the migration patterns of those who entered the region from the steppes and spread during the late Neolithic and early Bronze Age. "We estimate a dramatic male bias," the authors wrote. They believed there may have been between five to fourteen males migrating for every one female who moved with them. In other words, most of the people who made this journey appeared to have been boys and men.

They were "males, males, young males," the archaeologist Kristian Kristiansen tells me, flatly.

If this imbalance existed, Kristiansen suggests it may have nudged them into behaving in ways they might not have otherwise. "Such differences in sex-specific migration patterns are suggestive of fundamentally different types of interactions between invading and local populations," the authors of the 2017 study wrote. Their implication was that the migrants didn't have enough women of their own, so they were forced to look for wives and sexual partners elsewhere. In Kristiansen's opinion, this contributed to the brutal practice of taking Neolithic women as they settled in new territories, violently if necessary. It's an interpretation that prompted one piece about his work to carry the provocative, almost cartoonish, headline "Steppe Migrant Thugs Pacified by Stone Age Farming Women."

In a paper that Kristiansen and his colleagues published in the journal *Antiquity* the same year, they portrayed the incomers originating from the Eurasian Steppe as nothing less than a "social and demographic force." What may have driven these men from their homelands to new pastures, they argued, was that they were younger siblings, so they weren't in a position to inherit from their fathers in the same way as their older brothers were. They had nothing to lose.

They "elected the battle-axe as the most prominent male symbol," the paper continued. Even more speculatively, they asked whether these "youthful war-bands were led by a senior male" and maybe given names such as "Black Youth" or the names of dogs and wolves as part of their initiation rituals.

According to the American anthropologist David Anthony, who studies the social life of early Indo-European speakers in the steppes and beyond, these boys and men wore dogs' teeth as pendants. They not only "remade" the genetic makeup of Bronze Age Europe but, in his view, possibly also the "the linguistic and social and economic structures of European societies." Anthony describes them to me as nomads. They were among the first people in the world to commit to mobile lives with wagons and horses, he says. Just being physically higher up, he adds, would already have given them a sense of power over others on the ground.

They sustained themselves by keeping cattle. As well as being a source of meat and dairy, livestock "supported a new division of society between high-status and ordinary people, a social hierarchy that had not existed when daily sustenance was based on fishing and hunting," writes Anthony. Those with more cattle and horses may have been further up the social pecking order. Based on what he can glean from early Indo-European vocabularies, he believes they also recognized the authority of chiefs and had a male god, a "Sky Father." They seem to have had a fascination, too, with "binary doublings," illustrated in one human-origin story that begins with twin brothers. Their worldview, he concludes, centered around their cattle and their sons.

"Gimbutas has been proven right in her main thesis," Kristiansen tells me. Fundamentally, he agrees with her that the earlier Neolithic societies were very differently organized from the steppe societies. "Gimbutas was painting it too black and white, and there was too little nuance, too little understanding of the process," he says. "But she was a pioneer in a way. So, when you are a pioneer, you start off painting it black and white."

Between them, Kristiansen and Anthony have taken the portrait of patriarchal invaders sketched by Gimbutas and filled it in vivid Technicolor. They offer a terrifying picture of a foreign society focused around male power. The imagery throughout their work is of violence, imperialism, the military, and gendered stereotypes. It sounds as though these people were almost coordinated in their conquests. Indeed, Kristiansen tells me he suspects that these battle-axe-wielding groups of men and boys were among the world's first warrior societies. They adopted warfare as an institution, he claims. Small surprise that an article about his research in *New Scientist* magazine in 2019 asked if they might have been "the most murderous people in history."

When I ask Kristiansen if he believes that modern-day patriarchy is a product of this period of ancient history, when migrants from the Eurasian Steppe moved into Europe and parts of South Asia, he replies with an unqualified yes. "I do think so," he says. For him, there's an obvious line between the ancient past and the present.

"I think there is a *longue durée* here."

. . .

Again, I have to stop myself from getting swept away by the dramatic story-lines offered by those I speak to. The lives of everyday people in the past are unlikely to have been quite as one-dimensional as the grand narratives are. This is real life, after all.

The problem with some of the academic literature on the Neolithic and the early Bronze Age is that we know from our own experiences in the present that social change rarely happens suddenly or without resistance. Even if encounters between people were at moments coercive or violent, would there not have been a degree of struggle or negotiation? Wouldn't people have at least tried to cling to their traditions and fought to maintain their family ties? Could some women have chosen to live with the new arrivals because they promised a better way of life or a higher status than they had in their own communities? And what about the women who migrated from the steppes with their fathers, brothers, sons, and partners? What role did they play? Did they also wield their battle-axes?

When I press him on this, Kristian Kristiansen admits that events were perhaps not quite as simple or linear as even some of his accounts have suggested they might have been. "Inequality can unfold in many different ways," he tells me. "There are forces against inequality and there are forces towards inequality, so it's not a straight line. We don't have a straight evolutionary line. We have ups and downs." There may be those who push for more power for themselves, who would like society to be structured in a particular way that advantages them or their ideologies. "But there are also levelling mechanisms."

For instance, says Kristiansen, if you look at the burials in cemeteries he has studied in Germany from around the middle of the third millennium BCE, "women are treated completely equal to the men." This suggests that they didn't necessarily have a lower social status than the men they were buried with. Both he and David Anthony add that that while women were sometimes brought in from far away as wives, some of their children (younger sons in particular) were sent back to live with the families they left behind. This kind of "fosterage," as they describe it, could only plausibly have happened if strong links were maintained between families. "The relationships with the wife's family were still important as a source of allies, friendships, loans, that sort of thing," Kristiansen tells me. This raises questions about just how brutal or catastrophic the encounters between communities could really have been.

What is too easily left out from the big, essentializing narratives of history are the counterbalancing forces of resistance. Changes in how societies were organized must have been challenged, the same way they are now. But this pushback or slow negotiation is hard to spot in the archaeological record. Only in the margins can we see the forms it might have taken, revealing a possibility that the move toward more patriarchal systems was more piece-meal, possibly even precarious.

"There were nuances," agrees the British archaeologist Karina Croucher. The archaeological record reveals humans constantly trying different ways of living, shifting priorities depending on the environmental or social pres-sures they were under. Sometimes gender appears to be salient. At other times, according to Croucher, "there's not much evidence that gender as we understand it was a big concern." People might behave differently if they're at war, for instance, or if there's a shortage of resources.

It's undeniable that social changes were already happening in parts of Europe and Asia long before early Indo-European speakers originating from the steppes moved in large numbers into these parts of the world. Neolithic communities may have been dwindling before any large-scale migration 4,500 years ago. They were facing environmental pressures such as climate change and disease, for instance. We also know that Neolithic societies in Europe weren't always as peaceful as Marija Gimbutas imagined them to be. Two Neolithic mass graves with more than a hundred bodies were discovered in Germany and Austria in the 1980s. They were treated as exceptions at the time, but it's since become clear that they weren't. In 2015, researchers reported that skeletons in another mass grave in Germany dating to roughly 7,000 years ago had fractured skulls and shin bones. Almost half the victims were children.

Some of the most compelling evidence of all lies in the genetic data. The Y chromosome, found in biologically male DNA, is a reliable way of track-ing inheritance through the male line. Through this kind of Y chromosome analysis, the geneticist David Reich has observed that around "20 to 40 per-cent of Indian men and around 30 to 50 percent of eastern European men" may share common descent from just *one* man who lived roughly 4,800 to

6,800 years ago. It's an ancestral legacy so lopsided that at least 10 percent of men alive today who have family heritage in the broad region extending from South Asia to Scandinavia have this male ancestor in common.

As the dates prove, this skewed pattern of inheritance along the father's line couldn't have begun with the descendants of Eurasian Steppe migrants 4,500 years ago. It started much earlier. Genetic analysis reveals that there was already a severe bottleneck in the diversity of male Y chromosomes many centuries before—not just in Europe but also parts of Asia and Africa. Scientific estimates date this contraction to between five thousand and seven thousand years ago.

Studying mitochondrial DNA, passed through the female line, geneticists can see that living people today share a far broader diversity of female ancestors than they do male ancestors. One potential explanation, offered by Stanford University researchers in 2018, is that this could have been caused by widespread changes in social structure. Competition between warring clans may have killed off lots of men, for instance, leaving fewer to survive to have children. Women from defeated clans weren't killed, the researchers implied, but kept as wives, concubines, or slaves. Another plausible explanation is that a small elite of men had lots of women as sexual partners, while other men had fewer or none. This is perhaps why we don't see a corresponding lack of genetic diversity on the female line. Women in these societies were still having children and passing on their genes over generations into the present.

If some version of this is true, it means that patterns of power could have been shifting well in advance of any large-scale movement of people hailing from the Eurasian Steppe. Neolithic societies, for whatever reason, may have already been showing symptoms of social stress and inequality. A relatively small number of men were having more children than most, or at least having more children who survived and went on to have children of their own for generations. This echelon of men became only narrower when the so-called "invaders" moved in from the steppes 4,500 years ago. And again, there are lots of reasons why this could have happened. According to Kristiansen, one is that Neolithic people may just have been weaker at that time. "Neolithic peoples were eating a lot more muesli and bread," he claims. By contrast, the incomers with cattle "were taller and quite healthy because they had a diet of meat and milk products."

Whatever the reason, fewer men continued having more children than most other men. In the process, says Kristiansen, "Neolithic male lines go extinct within a few hundred years." But the underlying pattern stretches over millennia, before and after. The question for us today is whether this can tell us anything about the rise of male domination.

■   ■   ■

They "razed the bartering yurts and ravished the tall-hatted women" of their enemies, reads a translated passage from *The Secret History of the Mongols*, the earliest known work of Mongolian literature, written not long after the death in 1227 of Chinggis Khan, popularly known in English as Genghis Khan.

We know so little about the details of individual lives in prehistory, the social changes people saw, or how they felt about the world. We don't know about their families, their struggles, their successes and failures. One of the few ways we can hope to fill that chasm is by searching for faint echoes of older cultures in more recent ones from which we do have written records. *The Secret History of the Mongols* is one such document. Between its deliberate mythology and hero worship is a portrait of an empire so ruthless and power-ful that Mongol invaders treated men, women, and children as pawns in their battles and strategic alliances. Through the course of the story, charting the life of Genghis Khan from birth to death, countless thousands of people are killed, captured, taken as slaves, and given as gifts to others.

The Mongols, similar to the early Indo-European speakers who moved out of the Eurasian Steppe, were nomads who expanded outwards from grasslands in the east. They kept yaks and camels, and were possibly the first to ride warhorses, writes the historian Frank McLynn in his 2015 biography of Genghis Khan. Unlike those living in the Stone Age, though, we have vivid details from multiple sources about Mongol society, its families, and its leaders. Under Genghis Khan, the Mongol Empire became the largest the world has ever seen in terms of territory. Mongol armies could ride six hundred miles in nine days, explains McLynn, giving themselves an immedi-ate advantage over others. Their lands would come to stretch across Asia as far as the Adriatic Sea.

And according to some scientists, the descendants of this empire are found almost everywhere today. In 2003, an international team of biologists from China, Mongolia, and countries in Europe revealed a Y-chromosome lineage so common across a huge stretch of Asia that it was shared by roughly 8 percent of all the men in the region. This region is so big that this 8 percent comprises roughly one in two hundred of all men in the world. By tracing their genetic signal back to its source, the scientists reasoned that they were descended from a single male ancestor who may have lived in Mongolia around a thousand years ago. Their best guess was that this man was Genghis Khan. He did, after all, according to one tally by McLynn, have twenty-three official wives, sixteen regular concubines, and hundreds of less regular concubines.

His sons are also likely to have fathered more children than average. After crushing one rival tribal group, for instance, Genghis Khan is known to have taken one of the nieces of the defeated leader as a wife for himself and given another of the nieces to his son. It was common to capture people and keep them as slaves, workers, or concubines. His sons, their sons, and so on inherited his social prestige as well as his genes, becoming powerful leaders and claiming more women of their own over generations.

Powerful men don't always have more children (celibate religious leaders are one example). But if having lots of children reflects a certain kind of elite male authority, perhaps genetic analysis can at least offer a means of tracing people in history who had a disproportionate degree of control over others—men who might be considered the patriarchs of their time. In 2006, researchers at Trinity College, Dublin, for instance, discovered a Y chromosome connection among millions of men linked to a single person who may have lived in Ireland around 500 CE. In medieval Ireland, "the siring of offspring was related to power and prestige," they wrote. One man who might have been at the root of this particularly big family line, they suggested, was Lord Turlough O'Donnell, who died in 1423. He had no fewer than eighteen sons with ten different women, resulting in fifty-nine grandsons.

Power and wealth are transmitted through sons if a society tends to be patrilineal. And this means that genetic data can also be used to gauge how far back patriliny might go. According to Kristian Kristiansen, evidence for it is seen not just in Europe's genetic record but also in its archaeological record stretching to at least the end of the Neolithic. A study he co-authored in 2019, looking at the genetic relationships between people buried in two cemeteries roughly seventeen kilometers apart in southern Germany, dating to the middle of the third millennium BCE, suggested that the women buried there weren't related to the others in the community but that the men were closely related to each other. "We can show that for the males in the household, there is a patrilineal, patrilocal kinship—where the males, they stay, at least those males that are household elders or leaders," he says.

The anthropologist David Anthony adds that linguists who have reconstructed early Indo-European vocabularies have found a kaleidoscope of terms
to describe relationships on the father's and husband's side of the family, but
very few to describe the mother's or wife's side. A woman's birth family didn't
seem to matter so much. "It's a very male-dominated social structure," he
says. "Number one, it's patrilineal. So, your responsibilities, rights, and duties are inherited through your father." Daughters, on the other hand, would
generally leave home and join their husband's social group.

One of the most valuable pieces of written evidence in an Indo-European
language to have survived this time is the Rig Veda, a sacred Hindu text
thought to have been compiled around 1500 BCE, around the same time
that Indo-European speakers are believed to have entered what is now India
from the north. It's notoriously difficult to decode how actual families lived
from ancient scriptures because these texts often describe ideals rather than
reality, and people rarely follow them to the letter. But for Anthony, the Rig
Veda does betray a preoccupation with men. "It's a remarkable document,
and it's very, very male oriented," he says. One prayer, for example, asks for
good cattle, horses, and male children.

That said, it would be a mistake to assume that just because a society
values sons, it must have all the hallmarks of "patriarchy" as we recognize it
today. The Mongols, for instance, were patrilineal and valued sons but showed
tremendous latitude in how they thought about gender.

"Mongol women were a particular source of fascination to foreign observ-
ers," writes Frank McLynn. They were described as fat and ugly, he states,
as indistinguishable from the men, even as unisex or androgynous. Yet there
was grudging respect for them, including a "particular admiration for the
way they could give birth standing up and then carry on with their work as
if nothing had happened." Both men and women had to be able to do every
kind of work, and they worked hard. "Men, women and children were all
expected to be expert with horses," McLynn adds. Foreigners noticed that
women "could ride horses as well as the men, they were expert drivers of
carts, talented archers."

In the Mongol Empire, then, the rules around gender and power weren't
the same as they were in other patrilineal societies, before or after. There
was no rigid division of labor, there were no separate domestic spheres in
which women were confined, and women weren't seen as necessarily weak
or inferior. Even patrilocality wasn't set in stone. As McLynn notes, on the

steppes, sons-in-law would sometimes live with the bride's family if they were poor. Sons as well as daughters could be used as pawns by their parents to make desirable marriages with wealthier families.

"Cynics have even been heard to say," writes McLynn, "that Genghis's code was more liberal than Napoleon's, as the French emperor abolished divorce for women." Under Genghis Khan, men and women could both divorce by mutual consent.

So, there was never one single form of "patriarchal" society, which was somehow introduced to Europe and Asia at the end of the Neolithic, before sweeping across the rest of the world. Rather than a moment when everything changed, or a "world historical defeat of the female sex," as Friedrich Engels put it, the picture that emerges from the evidence is that even in places where the balance of power was becoming gendered, the way it was gendered was still being negotiated. Patrilineal societies were writing their rules over time, sometimes for thousands of years.

The cultural historian Bruno De Nicola notes that as well as sons, the Mongol Empire valued the high-ranking women who bore those sons. A woman's rights to property and her economic standing went up when she got married, and up again if she gave birth to a son and heir. If *The Secret History of the Mongols* is anything to go by, Genghis Khan's mother was an enormous influence in his life. She commanded considerable power and respect. The wives of rulers or male members of the royal family administered property, cattle, horses, and people. Within this sphere of influence, the most powerful women could be in charge of thousands of people. They would drive their own carts as they moved from place to place. Social status could easily matter more to an individual's life than their gender.

Marriage as a means of political alliance also gave women greater importance because they quite literally embodied the links between Mongol kingdoms. As the empire grew under Genghis Khan, certain high-status women became more involved in politics, occasionally seizing the reins of power altogether if circumstances allowed—for example, if a husband died and the sons were too young to assume control. "This model of politically active and outspoken women among the Mongol royal family would be exported beyond the context of pre-Imperial Mongolia and into the Mongol Empire," writes De Nicola.

"Marco Polo observed that women were constantly involved in trading activities, selling and buying all that they and their dependants needed," he continues. There are also references to women taking part in military actions. Among them was a daughter of Genghis Khan, who in one legendary account "defeated every man brave enough to fight against her."

■   ■   ■

Since the nineteenth century at least, Western scholars have looked upon history as a set of relentless binaries. Men are violent and cruel. Women are nurturing and peaceful. People either worship a goddess or they worship a god. Societies are either female-centered or they must be male-centered. They are completely matriarchal or they are completely patriarchal. Ethnic groups are by nature creative or they are inherently destructive.

This way of thinking has long played out in the accounts of those who have tried to explain the origins of patriarchy. It remains embedded in the imaginations of scientists and historians to this day. But the more fine-grained evidence we have for how people really lived in the past, the more these binaries break down. One example is the way that Marija Gimbutas wrote about Minoan and Mycenaean civilizations, which immediately preceded the rise of classical Greece. For her, these two civilizations represented the cusp of the big shift toward male domination in Europe.

Minoans living on the island of Crete from around 3000 BCE until roughly 1100 BCE had artistic cultures rich in pottery and bronze, grand architectural palaces and cities, and one of the continent's earliest writing systems. Female forms feature heavily in some of the most famous excavated examples of Minoan art, among them a figurine of what has been called the "Snake Goddess," a strident female figure, bare-breasted but otherwise ornately clothed, holding up two snakes in her outstretched arms. The neighboring Mycenaeans on mainland Greece, on the other hand, were relatively more patriarchal and warlike, according to historians. Their people were sometimes buried alongside their swords and spears. And they spoke an early form of Greek, which is known to be related to the Indo-European family of languages. Their culture flourished a little later, from around 1600 to 1100 BCE, but they overlapped for a while with the Minoans.

Based on her analysis of these two adjacent cultures, Gimbutas had argued that the Minoans must have been one of the matriarchal, peaceful, goddess-worshipping societies of that region. "The Minoan goddess or goddesses continued Old European traditions," she wrote in her final book, *The Living*

Goddesses. Among the Mycenaeans, by contrast, Gimbutas saw a mix of both Old European and Indo-European culture, one that "glorified war" but at the same time "produced thousands of goddess figurines." For her, the Mycenaeans therefore looked like a society transitioning into patriarchy, from one binary social condition to another.

Eventually, she argued, "the male element came to dominate almost completely." Their differences, according to Gimbutas, weren't accidental. They were to her mind two fundamentally different populations. She claimed that the Mycenaeans may have been the descendants of tribes that followed the cultures of the Eurasian Steppe people to the east.

On this count, she turned out to be wrong. When an international team of researchers that included geneticists at Harvard University carried out DNA analysis on ancient human remains from this region, publishing their results in 2017, they found that "Minoans and Mycenaeans were genetically similar." They spoke different languages and had their own distinct cultures as far as anyone could tell, but the two were closely related to each other, with recently shared ancestors. So closely related, in fact, that they would have physically looked alike, with mostly dark hair and dark eyes.

What the researchers did find in their 2017 study, though, was evidence of a small element of extra ancestry among the Mycenaeans related to hunter-gatherers from eastern Europe and Siberia. Although it was hard for them to know when or how this emerged, it's possible that visitors from the east may have exposed Mycenaeans to the language they spoke, or that they had encountered it during travel or interaction, before it was more widely adopted. So, the cultural differences between the Minoans and Mycenaeans weren't carried on entirely genetic winds. New social and political ideas may have been brought in the same way they often are, by people meeting each other and learning new ways.

Marija Gimbutas wasn't right about everything. But where she was correct in her analysis was that between the Neolithic and the Bronze Age, gender relations changed profoundly. Ancient Greek society would become deeply skewed in favor of men. Its literature, philosophy, science, and art would reflect a civilization more hierarchical than had arguably ever been seen before. Whatever brought about this social shift—whether it was cultural interaction, proselytization, forceful coercion, environmental change, social disruption seeded by a small number of people, or some combination of factors—a certain form of gendered oppression was gradually established in Europe and parts of Asia. The already powerful would further consolidate their power.

Older, wealthier free men would eventually come to rule over their households, elite men would come to rule over their states, and powerful gods would rule over them all, the same way that the English political theorist Robert Filmer would go on to describe in his *Patriarcha* in the seventeenth century. After the start of classical antiquity in this part of the world, around 800 BCE, male domination would become the social norm. It would weed its way into people's minds, warping how they thought about themselves—and about human nature itself.

CHAPTER 5

Restriction

W hen *does* gender become salient?"
It was one of the last questions I asked Ian Hodder, the archaeologist
who led the most recent excavations of the Neolithic settlement of Çatalhöyük in Southern Anatolia. What I wanted to know was if there really had
been a single moment in history, a turning point when everything changed
for women. As I found out, there was no simple answer.

I think about this when I reach the sunlit ruins of Pompeii, south of
Naples. This ancient Roman city was so eerily preserved under volcanic ash
and pumice after Mount Vesuvius erupted in 79 CE that I can almost imagine
myself living here now. Voices from the past reach out through the excavated
walls. There's ancient graffiti in one spot that says someone hung out with his
girlfriend here. Someone else has taken the trouble to note that he defecated
there. The ruins in Anatolia had been like a rabbit warren. I couldn't make
sense of them. But I find a comforting intimacy in Pompeii's streets, with its
regular pavements, shops, and houses. This feels more like my own time.

Hodder's observations of the archaeological evidence at Çatalhöyük had
led him to believe that gender couldn't have been particularly important to
the people who lived in that settlement more than nine thousand years ago.
There weren't big differences in how women and men lived, or in how they
were buried. There didn't seem to be much evidence of a strict hierarchy,
at least not from what had been excavated so far. But as we both knew, even
if gender didn't matter then, it would certainly matter later. In roughly six
thousand years, around the start of classical antiquity, societies in this broad
region looked very different.

Later still, by the time Pompeii was at its height, deep social inequalities
of all kinds had set in. Ancient Rome and Athens, the centers of power and

intellectual life in this part of the world, relied on slave labor. A person's existence was shaped by whether or not they were free, where they were born, which family they belonged to, their class, their wealth. It was shaped by gender, too, in different ways depending on which other social buckets the person had already been sifted into. Those in power had developed stiflingly narrow cultural beliefs about male and female natures, inviting deep suspicion of those who didn't fit in.

It dawns on me, uncomfortably, that one of the many things that are familiar about Pompeii is this inequality. The gender-free egalitarianism of a settlement like Çatalhöyük is more distant from the reality of our own lives today than the rigidly gendered, deeply sexist societies of antiquity.

That unsettling similarity is no accident. It's not just because Pompeii is only two thousand years old instead of nine thousand. It's more than the lifelike statues, the poetry and plays, the gossipy personal letters, the court documents and legal rulings that make it easy to relate to classical life. It's also because present-day Europeans have built their beliefs about the roots of "Western Civilization" around this particular place and time. For centuries, they've looked up to the ancient Greeks and Romans, worshipped their playwrights and philosophers, drawn life lessons from their writings, and erected neoclassical columns to mimic theirs. Unlike Çatalhöyük, which was practically empty when I visited, Pompeii is heaving with visitors. People seem to be obsessed with it. And that's in no small part because they were raised to believe that this was the source of their modern, advanced society. We live in the shadow of these ancients. Their world is still being remade in ours.

"In Britain, the study of the classics served to define the colonial ruling class," writes Nancy Sorkin Rabinowitz of New York's Hamilton College, whose work spans Greek literature and intersectional feminism. Indeed, I was among those students who had learned to revere the classics. Everyone at my upwardly mobile state grammar school in London in the nineties was taught Latin. Marilyn Katz, a professor emerita of classical studies at Wesleyan University, Connecticut, writes that "the study of ancient Greek and Latin was from its early days implicated in the moral and social grooming of the young (white) men of America for their roles as the country's economic and political elite."

But the study of the classics wasn't just about knowing history. "Classics became a discipline devoted not just to studying the past but to preserving it," writes Katz.

When those in power looked to ancient Greece and Rome, they were searching for validation of the unequal societies they were choosing to build. They borrowed from ancient art and architecture, but they also deliberately borrowed the prejudices of that era. Rabinowitz explains that in the late eighteenth and nineteenth centuries, Western Europeans looked to antiquity to affirm their racialized and gendered beliefs. "These men did not simply discover a pre-existing Greece [. . .]," she writes, "they invented it to meet their needs."

The historian David Lowenthal observed that Americans go to Europe to feel at home in time. Europeans, it could be said, go to Pompeii, Rome, and Athens. We feel at home here. And yet we also know that cities like these were brutally unequal. Ancient Athens, home to the great philosophers Plato, Aristotle, and Socrates, might even be considered the worst place in human history to have been a woman.

■   ■   ■

"Athens was in many ways an unusual city," notes the classicist Sue Blundell in her book *Women in Ancient Greece*.

If the written evidence is anything to go by, ancient Athens was a city-state racked with the tension of maintaining a warped social order around patrilineal systems of inheritance and myths of male superiority. There were benefits to being an Athenian citizen, but the price of belonging was a pressure to follow the rules. An Athenian woman couldn't own property. She could rely on legal protection only through her father, husband, or other male relatives. The idea of separate public and private spheres comes from this era, from the Greek *polis* meaning the city-state, and *oikos* meaning the family and the household. The boundary between these two spheres would come to define a woman's place.

We know from ancient Greek literature that the ideal, respectable woman was hidden away, quiet, and submissive. The philosopher Aristotle, writing in the fourth century BCE, took as a natural fact that some people were destined to be slaves and others free, adding that when it came to sex, too, "the relation of male to female is by nature a relation of superior to inferior and ruler to ruled." For the state, a woman's primary value lay in giving birth to new citizens to sustain and defend the population. But men, too, had conventions they were expected to follow when it came to mixing with women outside their own households, as well as standards of courage and restraint to live up to.

Aristotle was on the relatively moderate end of sexism. Other Greek texts seethe with a misogynistic suspicion of women so strong that you can almost see the frothing at the mouth. In describing the myth of Pandora, the first human woman created by the Greek gods, the poet Hesiod, who lived around 700 BCE, wrote in *Theogony* that from "her has sprung the race of womankind. The deadly race and tribes of womankind . . . with a nature to do evil." It was a woman-hating theme he returned to often.

And this, we assume, is how the ancients thought.

But we flatten out the past. We take what we want from it. And those in power have taken just a narrow slice. In truth, ancient Greek and Roman cultures spanned such an enormously long period of time that, much like our own, they couldn't have been static. The status of women was shifting all the time.

By studying homes in Greece's archaic period between 800 BCE and 480 BCE, the archaeologist Ian Morris at Stanford University has argued that gender ideologies didn't start out as fixed as they would later become. Earlier on, houses were usually one-roomed in open settlements, which couldn't have allowed for men and women to segregate, let alone for women to be hidden away. Homes started to subdivide into rooms after roughly 750 BCE, explains Morris, and presumably even then only for the wealthy, who could afford larger houses, with slaves to do the outdoor labor of the women who were kept indoors. The domesticated woman in ancient Athens, as much as in nineteenth-century America, was an ideal that only the wealthiest could afford to meet.

Just because we attach certain assumptions to the domesticated housewife in our own time, though, staying at home may not have meant then quite what it means now. For periods of Greek history, the aristocratic wife of a male Athenian citizen could actually exercise significant power from running her household, the *oikos*.

"She managed everything that went on inside," I'm told by Sarah Pomeroy, a classics professor at the City University of New York and the author of the pioneering 1975 book on women in antiquity, *Goddesses, Whores, Wives, and Slaves*. This was no small thing in a society in which the *oikos* could be a busy, almost industrial center of production. These women managed their slaves. They beat their slave girls. Within their homes, the people beneath them manufactured textiles and food, from field to table if necessary. The *oikos* and *polis* weren't separate worlds; they relied on each other.

But society never stood still. Over time, the balance of political power shifted from the *oikos* further into the *polis*. In ancient Athens, one of the big drivers for this was ironically the introduction of democracy around the fifth century BCE (the model for our own democracies many centuries later). "When democracy flourished in Athens, then women were most oppressed," says Pomeroy. Political participation was restricted to adult male citizens (another feature adopted by modern democracies), benefiting the lower-class male citizen but undermining the upper-class woman in her *oikos*. "It was democracy that oppressed not only women but slaves and non-citizens," adds Pomeroy. "It just elevated the male citizen above everybody else who lived in Athens."

Yet, even as suffocating a place as ancient Athens became for a while, the city didn't stay this way. Later in its history, the Greek world expanded and came into greater contact with cultures that had different values. "Greeks are now rubbing shoulders with the Assyrians, the Persians, and the Egyptians, many of whom have far more liberal attitudes about their women," I'm told by Stephanie Budin, an expert on women in the ancient world who earned her PhD from the University of Pennsylvania. When this contact happened, the pressure on some of Athens' women eased.

"And the next thing you know, women have more status and freedoms in society."

When we recognize the realities of everyday people's lives over time, we can start to see just how precarious gender norms were. We can appreciate how much these norms varied between classes, between the slaves and the free, the foreign and the native-born, the old and the young. They emerged gradually, sometimes fitfully, and could go in any direction.

As misogynistic as writers could be in ancient Greece, for instance, they frowned upon the physical abuse of wives by their husbands, at least judging from the literature. The historian Leslie Dossey at Loyola University Chicago has found that even late in antiquity, "Greek authors continued to consider it shameful for a husband to beat his wife." The philosopher Plutarch saw behavior of this kind as betraying a lack of proper male self-control, humiliating him rather than her. "When a Greek man loses control of himself to such an extent, he can expect the outside community to intervene on his wife's behalf," writes Dossey. A wife could bring her husband to court for it.

In ancient Rome, on the other hand, in which women had relatively more rights and freedoms, and certainly tended to be more seen and heard, wife-beating was considered acceptable. Roman wives were expected to put up with physical punishment to correct their behavior in the same way that slaves and children might have to. A wife was advised to "temper her husband's anger with proper submission" to avoid her humiliation, Dossey explains. Unlike in ancient Athens, the shame was hers, not his. In the early days of the Roman Republic, a husband even had the right to kill his wife for adultery.

If antiquity has been compressed and these nuances ignored, it's at least in part because of our own biases. The classicist Marilyn Katz has observed that experts in her field long betrayed a tolerance verging on sympathy for Greek sexism. As recently as the 1970s, male academics referred to "a healthy strain of misogyny," she writes, and "a quite normal measure of husbandly jealousy." Female subordination and male dominance were taken as biological rules, which meant the sexism of antiquity was accepted as universal. Even now, it's difficult to know whether we're looking at the past as it was or as these experts have filtered it for decades through their own prejudices. Historians have only recently started to question, for instance, whether gender categories meant the same to people in antiquity as they do now. They're just beginning to shed the racism that allowed them to talk about Greek women being kept in "Oriental" seclusion.

But then, readings of the past have always been political. In scouring the classics for what they could use in the present, those in power never had much of an incentive to notice anything that might challenge their hierarchies. History is a powerful tool for those who want to define human nature. In 1762, the philosopher Jean-Jacques Rousseau described ancient Greek women, hidden from public life and devoted to their households, as the wisest, most beautiful, and charming in history. "This is the mode of life prescribed for women alike by nature and reason," he wrote.

As Rousseau proved, the big trap of looking to the ancient world to understand gender relations is that it can give the illusion of seeing human nature at its most basic—because it was so long ago. If women two thousand years ago were dominated by men and they're still dominated by them now, this argument goes, then this must be normal. But there was nothing normal about the social inequalities of ancient Athens. Elite male power wasn't achieved easily. One group didn't automatically dominate and the other did not simply submit. It was established slowly, through constant, considered effort, sometimes using violence or the threat of it, but more often by layer upon layer of social norms, laws, and edicts. Hesiod's spitting anger only proves how much effort it took to convince people that women might be inferior to men.

Honor and shame, expectation and guilt, patriotism and loyalty, all had to be wrapped around a state's expectation of how people should behave. Gender boundaries had to be defined and policed. None of this could have happened without sweat.

. . .

The story of humanity is one of constant movement. We can see that in patterns of migration, back and forth, transporting new ideas and technologies. But it's also the story of people trying to get other people to do what they want.

The world's earliest states, entities that these days feel reassuringly solid but once had to be built from scratch, were caught on the horns of this dilemma. The problem they had was convincing people to stay within their boundaries, to not wander off because they didn't like the conditions, I'm told by the American anthropologist James Scott, who has devoted his career to understanding how the first states emerged and the factors that helped them grow. Without a population, states had no power. And this made people the most valuable commodity of all.

Part of Scott's research has focused on ancient Mesopotamia, a region in the valleys straddled by the Euphrates and Tigris rivers, part of the Fertile Crescent, described by historians as a cradle of human civilization. This area maps onto parts of modern-day Turkey, Syria, Iraq, and Kuwait. Some three millennia before the Golden Age of Athens, Sumerians built what are thought to be among the world's first "proper" cities here. They developed one of the world's first written languages, tiny dash-like markings known as cuneiform. Sumerians were followed by the Akkadian Empire, Babylonians, Hittites, and Assyrians, eventually overlapping for a time with ancient Greeks.

As Scott explains, life could be more secure and predictable for people living within these early states than it might have been for those on the outside. But in other ways, it could be bleaker. Compared with relatively looser hunting, foraging, and gathering communities, diets might be narrower, more reliant on grains that could be stored in large quantities and divided up between people into fixed units. Young men might be expected to go to war at any time, facing the risk of death. Young women might face pressure to have as many children as possible.

"The problem of these early states was population," Scott says. "How to collect that population under conditions of unfreedom, and how to hold them there and get them to produce the surplus that's needed for the elites that run the state, the priestly caste, the artisans, and the aristocracy and royalty." Population—maintaining its size and controlling it—is crucial to understanding the rise of inequality and patriarchal power.

Usually, though, the focus has been on property. Friedrich Engels and other nineteenth-century philosophers thought that men established their power over women around the same time that humans started to take up agriculture. This was when people started accumulating land, cattle, and other things they could own. Elites and the upper castes began to take control of larger amounts of wealth. And it was this, Engels argued, that prompted men to look for ways to make sure their children were their own, so what they had would be passed down to legitimate heirs. This drove them to take control of women's sexual freedom. According to this version of history, when men started doing agricultural labor, women's work also became more confined to the home. And that was how separate gendered spheres of public and private life emerged.

These days, however, archaeologists and anthropologists don't see agriculture as the sharp turning point for gender relations that Engels and others believed it to be. "I think the old idea that as soon as you get farming, you get property, and therefore you get control of women as property, I think that idea . . . is wrong, clearly wrong," I'm told by the archaeologist Ian Hodder. "I think we have to accept that these societies were egalitarian and were relatively gender-blind for a long period after early agriculture."

The switch to farming wasn't a sudden leap but a long, gradual process of cultivation, explains Hodder, in which people had close relationships with wild plants and animals, and were tending but not necessarily planting, sowing, or domesticating them. Some communities carried on hunting and gathering depending on the seasons or the climate. Others might have tried domestication for a while but changed their minds if it didn't work for them. Seen from this point of view, the famous Seated Woman of Çatalhöyük, the figurine flanked by two animals that look like they're resting comfortably under her outstretched hands, could be interpreted as a sign of that evolving relationship between humans and the natural world—one in which some were starting to take firmer control of their environments, bending them more tightly to their wills.

There's no doubt that women played a role in plant and animal domestication. It makes little sense to start with the assumption that they didn't. The economic historian Walter Scheidel at Stanford University notes that there are several drawings of women working in fields, reaping corn ears in Egypt at the time of the pharaohs. Women in other cultures, including Hittites, ancient Persians, and Indians, were known to have tended animals, he adds. Rebecca Futo Kennedy, an associate professor in classical studies at Denison University in Ohio, tells me that there are lots of stories of young women working as shepherds and goatherds in ancient Greek and Roman literature.

Poorer women and enslaved women, as well as children, have been expected to work outdoors throughout history, and this is a tradition that continues to this day. On reporting trips in the last decade, I've interviewed women farmers and manual laborers in India and Kenya, sometimes working with infants strapped to their backs in slings. United Nations data shows that women make up almost half the agricultural workforce in low-income countries today and are nearly half of the world's small-scale livestock managers. The idea that women are physically incapable of agricultural labor isn't borne out by the facts. The activist and scholar Angela Davis has written of slavery in the United States: "Since women, no less than men, were viewed as profitable labor-units, they might as well have been genderless as far as the slaveholders were concerned." Pregnant women and those with infants were still expected to work. Under slavery, she explains, women were the social equals of men. Scheidel adds that female slaves did heavy agricultural work such as hauling logs and ploughing with teams of mules and oxen.

In response, some researchers have argued that maybe it wasn't agriculture in general that changed the status of women but a particular type of agriculture—the kind that uses a plough. Hoe cultivation, done by hand, tends to be seen in more egalitarian communities, according to some studies. Farming with ploughs, which uses domesticated animals and needs relatively more upper-body strength, is often seen in more male-dominated communities. But again, this isn't a blanket rule. And given that not all men are physically stronger than all women, and an individual's physical strength varies over their lifetime, neither can it be expected to be.

Women have worked outdoors in some plough societies. Scheidel quotes one traveler to Europe's Basque Country in the nineteenth century, who noticed that women "showed themselves quite as good as the men at working in the fields; they harnessed the oxen, and led them. . . . They drove the cart to the market, or the plough along the furrow." The lives of everyday folk in rural areas, he suggests, have rarely matched up to the cultural ideals or assumptions of wealthier people in the cities.

It's difficult, then, to pin gender inequality firmly to the emergence of agriculture or property ownership. If there were changes in the balance of power between people in prehistory because of these factors, they must have been subtle, because they left no deafening trace in the archaeological record. Where we really can start to spot a shift in gender relations, the first shoots of overarching male authority, is with the rise of the first states. The moment gender becomes salient is when it becomes an organizing principle, when entire populations are categorized in ways that deliberately ignore their everyday realities and force them to live in ways they may not otherwise choose.

It's when the category a person belongs to overrides the way society thinks about the individual.

■   ■   ■

Administrative tablets from the Sumerian city of Uruk nearly five thousand years ago are "lists, lists, lists," writes James Scott.

What leaps out among artifacts from ancient Mesopotamia is how meticulous those in charge were about keeping track of humans, goods, and property. Uruk and its hinterlands, the location of the legendary *Epic of Gilgamesh*, written from around 2100 BCE, may have at one point been home to as many as ninety thousand people. In a complex, hierarchical state like this, ruled over by a small number of elites and administrators who needed to keep a close grip on the population, record keeping was crucial. Lists were one of their tools of control.

"Person power is the key to power in general," Scott tells me. "You needed units of aggregation, units of discipline, units of taxation."

Keeping a population growing was best served by creating conditions in which as many women as possible were having as many babies as they could, raising those children to be useful to the state as workers, warriors, and breeders. Ancient Mesopotamian cities became concerned with taking censuses, including gender as a category alongside age and location, so they could measure their human resources and collect taxes more efficiently. Categories were needed for hierarchies to function, for leaders to know how many people they had, and how to allocate work and rations between them. People had to be given social codes to follow so the state would keep ticking efficiently without falling apart. It was like a machine in a sense, every part designed for a particular function.

Rules didn't come automatically. The meaning and significance attached to gender developed over time, and not always consistently. Akkadian myths suggest that neither boys nor girls were considered better than the other. Sumerian texts had separate terms to refer to different stages of life, most of which weren't gendered. But there are also signs that a youthful "masculinity" was beginning to be attached to warfare and battles. This wasn't confined to men, though. It's also seen in reference to a goddess.

The very earliest written examples we have of Indo-European languages, belonging to a branch spoken across ancient Anatolia, including Hittite, don't appear to have had a grammatically separate feminine gender, I'm told by the linguist Alwin Kloekhorst at the University of Leiden. The feminine gender would have been added to the other Indo-European languages at some point. It's definitely there in these languages from 3300 BCE, he explains, but not before 4000 BCE. This doesn't mean that sex or gender were irrelevant more than six thousand years ago, only that grammar later came to reflect a distinction between women and men that must have mattered at the time it changed. Hittite kingdoms many centuries later were ruled predominantly by men. "The queen is always the one underneath the king. It's clearly a gendered society," explains Kloekhorst. They did have gendered nouns, he adds, but they continued using one pronoun for "he" and "she," which was a nonbinary "they."

Once codes were created and meaning given to categories, they had to be policed for fear of transgression. And that's exactly what's seen over time in the historical data. Laws around marriage, divorce, and adultery in Mesopotamia become harsher for women as time passes. Their freedoms and privileges are slowly eaten away. At the same time, over centuries, working women gradually disappear from the records. If there's attention on what women are doing, it's increasingly on their loyalty as wives, mothers, and citizens.

The late historian and feminist Gerda Lerner, author of the 1986 book *The Creation of Patriarchy*, spent eight years researching how the status of women deteriorated through the long history of Mesopotamia. Her conclusion was that this is the time and place where "female subordination within the family becomes institutionalized and codified in law." In her view, it happened along these lines: First, there were people in charge of administration and record keeping in the temples. These "temple elites" were joined by parallel "military elites," who became chieftains and eventually pushed priests into the background of political life. These chieftains became kings. The strongest of these kings consolidated their domains into kingdoms and nation-states.

Every stage, she wrote, "went in the direction of strengthening male dominance in public life."

But there's one problem with this account: If there was more power to be had over time, why were *men* the ones to claim it? Was it only men who made up the temple elites, military elites, monarchs, and chiefs from the beginning? Why didn't *women* grab any power at any stage?

The easiest explanation might be that there was an incipient natural male dominance and female subservience in these societies that asserted itself more forcefully over generations. Lerner fell back on this reasoning to some extent, employing stereotypes of men as power hungry, physically stronger, and domineering, and women as naturally weaker, in need of protection. Her argument was that women accepted subordination as the price to pay for keeping themselves and their children safe. In one especially unsettling phrase she writes that men came to learn that "women would endure enslavement." Like so many before her, resting underneath Lerner's version of history was the suspicion that women's oppression might be built into our natures, that it was a fact long before states came along to institutionalize it.

But we know that powerful women did exist during that time. Lerner herself observed that upper-class women in ancient Mesopotamia enjoyed "positions of significant economic, legal, and judicial power." Royal documents from one city north of Sumer showed that women owned property, were involved in business, and worked as scribes. Male kings were common in ancient Sumer, but there was at least one notable independent female king. The third dynasty of Kish is listed as having been founded around 2500 BCE by Kubaba, a woman who previously worked as a tavern keeper. Her position, as far as we are aware, wasn't the result of a relationship to a powerful man as a sister, wife, or a daughter. She ruled in her own right. And she was so successful that legend had it that she reigned for a century.

It's clear that women were neither powerless nor uninterested in power.

Nor did they hesitate to turn to violence in defense of the causes they believed in. When researching her book *Women Warriors*, historian Pamela Toler set out to collect stories of women in battle. She recalls that "the main thing that struck me when I looked at women warriors across cultures rather than in isolation is how many examples there are and how lightly they sit on our collective awareness." These women weren't rare exceptions. Famous female military leaders have been recognized on almost every continent for thousands of years, from the first-century British queen Boudica to the seventh-century Chinese princess Pingyang. According to legend, the Hausa queen Amina of Zazzau, in what is now Nigeria, is said to have led armies to war for more than thirty years in the sixteenth century. The walls she built to protect her cities, some of which survive, are still named after her.

Equally importantly, women warriors don't just come from the ranks of queens and princesses. Whenever ordinary women have been given the opportunity to fight in battle, they've taken it. Toler notes that in the twentieth century, thousands of women joined the revolutionary guerrilla armies of Africa, Asia, and Latin America, "making up perhaps as much as 30 percent of these forces." Starting in 2014, she adds, between seven thousand and ten thousand Kurdish women joined the battle against the Islamist radical group ISIS in the Middle East. Women have also gone to the lengths of disguising themselves as men to be able to fight alongside them. Among the most famous is Deborah Sampson, who fought in the American Revolution in the eighteenth century under the name Robert Shurtleff. Even after her identity was uncovered following an injury, she was given a full military pension in recognition of her heroism.

■   ■   ■

We know from our own societies that people come in all shapes and sizes, that individuals have all sorts of traits and interests, that gender manifests in multiple ways. Yet we look to the archaeological record to do something magical. We expect it to show us worlds in which every single person followed strictly defined social patterns and never deviated from them.

In this imagined world, everyone is easily classified. Every woman is incapable of fighting in battle or of being a ruler, and every man is born a warrior. Each person in the past is extruded through the same narrow caricatures. We ourselves become guilty of blindly accepting the gender codes and hierarchies that those in power in the earliest states tried so hard to naturalize.

In 1998, the Assyriologist Julia Assante showed how easy it was for modern-day researchers to build these caricatures when she questioned the translation of the Mesopotamian word *harimtu*, the plural of which is *harimatu*. *Harimtu* had been assumed by scholars from the nineteenth century onward to refer to a sacred prostitute who was attached to the temples. Experts at the time often claimed that every woman in antiquity fell into one of two categories, each based on her sexual availability to men. She was either a loyal, faithful daughter or wife, or she was a prostitute attached to no particular man. These *harimatu*, then, automatically fell into that second category. But Assante noticed that there was no evidence in Mesopotamian texts that any *harimtu* actually sold sex.

Maybe, she wondered, they weren't prostitutes at all.

Assante's reasoning and evidence are completely sound, I'm told by Stephanie Budin, who catalogued the history of misconceptions like this in her book *The Myth of Sacred Prostitution in Antiquity*. Yet she adds that there has been fierce resistance among fellow historians to rewriting the meaning of *harimtu*. "There is a phenomenal amount of sexism involved in it."

When the literature is read more objectively, without the baggage of assumption, the *harimatu* sound more like single, independent women, explains Budin. "They don't have a father; they don't have a husband. They are basically free to do as they want." These are women who happen to live free of society's patriarchal bonds. She notes that women in this period also worked as tavern owners, doctors, cooks, and entertainers. Letters sent by women weavers to their menfolk at an Assyrian trading colony in eastern Turkey from around 1900 BCE show one admonishing her husband for not getting her the full price for the textiles she had shipped out to him.

There should be no shame in sex work. Equally, though, it strains plausibility that every woman who left her home to support herself or her family in ancient Mesopotamia or at any other time was a sex worker. It is "as if there were no space for women to inhabit in between the well-to-do citizen wife and the woman who sells sex for financial support," writes the classicist Rebecca Futo Kennedy, who has fought for her field to more fully appreciate the real lives of working women in antiquity. Her work is informed by her own family's experiences. Kennedy's grandmother was a working-class immigrant who became a barmaid after her husband died and left her with three children to support.

The job of tavern keeper, which women in Mesopotamia were known to have commonly held (although this has sometimes been translated to "alewife"), was certainly unlikely to have meant then what it means today. Both men and women drank fermented drinks like beer. It was a clean source of fluid. Ration lists show that women and men were both given beer on a daily basis, according to Julia Assante, with the average intake estimated at roughly four or five liters a day. Wives went to taverns alone or with their husbands, she adds. So, taverns couldn't just have been places of entertainment or debauchery. They would have been necessary stops for all sorts of people.

"Usually, we are finding women have more rights and prerogatives than is generally understood in popular culture," Budin explains. "The ability of women to own their own money, run their own businesses, or take part in family businesses is far better attested now than has been previously appreciated." Only over many hundreds of years did their lives become constricted, choked by the steady drip-feed of gendered codes and laws. Separate tracks appeared for men and women, depending on their social class, each track moving steadily away from the other as the centuries rolled by.

There are signs that the rules didn't always sit easily as they were introduced. A state can impose laws, but this doesn't mean that families are happy to follow them. In parts of Mesopotamia, there was a recognition that categories might need to be sidestepped on occasion because they couldn't fully capture people's needs. Budin tells me that there were cases in certain cities where men designated their daughters or wives as "men" so they could give them inheritance rights. "A dying father can literally say in his last will and testament that I am making your mother a father of the household, or I am making my daughters sons, and they get to inherit like sons," she says. A woman's legal gender was changed to give her a different status within her family. This not only proves the practical limitations of gender categories but also people's willingness to look beyond them.

What's odd is how hard so many scholars even today try to dismiss evidence of working, independent women or powerful women rulers and warriors in the ancient record. It is almost as though history doesn't make sense to them unless women are powerless and invisible.

In 2008, Kathleen McCaffrey, a graduate student of ancient Near Eastern studies at the University of California, Berkeley, noticed experts tying themselves in knots trying to explain why the bodies of women discovered in the ancient Sumerian city of Ur had been buried with royal objects or with weapons. At times, explained McCaffrey, the integrity of hard archaeological data was being questioned because it didn't align with gendered expectations. Researchers seemed more willing to believe that their data might be wrong than to entertain the possibility that their assumptions might be. When they found patterns of evidence that reinforced their gendered expectations, they accepted them without question. The same proof wasn't demanded of royal objects found in male graves, McCaffrey explained, because "common sense" didn't require it.

McCaffrey's conclusion was that "common sense" wasn't a good guide when it came to interpreting gender in the ancient past. "Common sense dictates that a royal seal in a woman's grave is a man's possession out of context; thus, intuition places the burden of proof entirely on the side of proving that the seal belongs to the women," she wrote. If Sumerian females were buried *like* kings, a parsimonious explanation might be that they *were* kings, she wrote. Maybe the problem wasn't with the buried women but with the way in which the word "king" had been interpreted by modern-day archaeologists and historians.

The result of the bias, she concluded, was to crowd out "women who are not wives and men who are not warriors."

If the old notion about all males being naturally dominant over all females is put to one side for a moment, what else could explain the changing pattern of gender relations in a region like ancient Mesopotamia? One answer might be that power was sweepingly taken away from all women—and that categorization by the state was the tool by which women were both classed and systematically disenfranchised. By gradually introducing broad rules and laws, an entire group of people in all their individual complexity could be effectively pushed to the margins and suppressed. We have plenty of historical parallels for this, in the practice of racial segregation in the American South, in India's caste system, and in the aristocracies of Europe. Gendered rules not only forced people into narrow social roles to better serve the state; they could also allow elite men to grab power, rights, and property from the women with whom these things were previously shared.

Gender is the foundation of patriarchy, according to the psychologist Carol Gilligan and the psychoanalyst Naomi Snider. Categorizing is an exercise in stereotyping. It irons out differences, defining people by their few shared qualities, or by how they might be useful. Dividing people into groups in this way, even when it's arbitrary, pushes us to look for differences between them. And this is what makes it such a powerful psychological tool. Divisions can quickly become laden with social significance. The hierarchical binary commands, they write, that "a man, in order to be a man, must not be a woman or like a woman, and vice versa."

James Scott has similarly written about how members of dominant groups learn to act with authority and self-assurance once their dominant position is made clear. "For hereditary ruling groups the training has typically begun at birth; the aristocrat learns to act like an aristocrat, the Brahmin like a Brahmin, the man like a man."

Military states, for example, might group all young men together because of their perceived collective capacity to fight, regardless of each individual's actual capacity. In the *Iliad*, attributed to the ancient Greek poet Homer,

Prince Hector tells his wife, Andromache: "War is the concern of all men." Not *some* men, but *all* men. For young women, their function might be seen as reproductive, to have babies and to raise loyal citizens to work and fight in wars. Or depending on the culture or their class, it might be a particular form of work. Scott notes that one of the first documented slave institutions seen in Mesopotamia was a textile workshop powered by thousands of women. In ancient Greece, too, weaving was hugely important and usually seen as women's work.

In real life, not all women want to weave or to stay at home and have babies. Not all men want to go to battle and risk their lives. But the elites didn't care about the individual. It was in the interest of these early states for each person to live within the boundaries of expectation. The machinery of power depended on it.

The inevitable tension this created can be seen in a speech in 17 BCE by the man who would become the first Roman emperor, Augustus. Witnessing what he thought was moral decay in Rome, he feared that the city-state might disintegrate. "If we could survive without a wife, citizens of Rome, all of us would do without that nuisance," he declared to the Senate. "But since nature has so decreed that we cannot manage comfortably with them, nor live in any way without them, we must plan for our lasting preservation rather than for our temporary pleasure." Augustus brought in laws encouraging people to marry, stay faithful, and have more children. His words suggest that he was doing this in service of nature. But why would anyone have to legislate for what comes naturally?

The laws could only have been in service of the state.

■　　■　　■

At its most basic, the ancient Greek household, the *oikos*, can be seen as a system for keeping people in a condition of unfreedom.

By classical antiquity, those in power had tweaked their rules and laws to the point where everyone knew their place. From the slaves at the bottom of the social hierarchy, all the way up to children and wives who were subordinate to their fathers and husbands, each was inducted into the social codes of the state. The everyday female citizen's purpose was to give birth to and raise more citizens, and the purpose of the everyday male citizen was to defend the state. Part of the way ancient Athens achieved compliance was by instilling a sense of loyalty to the city. The personal needed to be assimilated into the wider group, sacrificed to serve a larger ideal.

We can see echoes of this in later history, and indeed all the way into the present. After 1206, Mongol leader Genghis Khan brought in compulsory military service for boys and men aged fifteen to seventy, according to the historian Frank McLynn. He organized people, including women and children, into political and military units in which everyone was required to show loyalty to the Mongol Empire. Sons could be recruited and taken away at age fifteen to be inducted into these social norms, deliberately erasing any signs of other values they might have had or folk customs they might have followed. Many countries today still have mandatory military service or conscription at times of war. In 2015, North Korea, which already has the longest period of national service for men in the world, extended compulsory service to women.

In ancient Athens, family values were nothing short of a form of psychological control. People were made to believe that female freedom would threaten the integrity of the state. Girls were eventually controlled to the point where they "were being married off at the age of thirteen or fourteen to make certain that they couldn't experience any freedoms or naughty behavior," I'm told by Stephanie Budin. "That one woman in a hundred who leaves her husband for her lover or is caught having an affair is going to stir up so much paranoia and panic. That entire *oikos* is thrown into calamity."

The effect of marrying off girls so early to older men is that wives and husbands must have seemed utterly different from each other in their behavior and temperament. A child might be expected to run a busy household for an adult who was as much as ten or fifteen years older than her. These paternalistic relationships fed the impression that women were foolish and immature, and men were rational and wise—when, in fact, it was just their age differences that made it appear that way. We live with these stereotypes to this day.

Gender also became associated with virtues like honor, courage, and loyalty. There was anxiety around those who didn't follow the rules or live up to society's values. Ancient Greek writers often warned of unruly women, especially the ones jostling for personal advantage, who refused to sit back and submit to lives of self-sacrifice or loyalty to the state. The poet Hesiod wrote about an attractive woman looking to take over a man's property: "She is after your barn," he cautioned. The sixth-century BCE poet Theognis of Megara wrote that a woman wouldn't refuse to marry a bad man if he were wealthy, "for she would rather be wealthy than good."

Women *metics*, foreign residents who paid taxes to the city but didn't have citizenship, became the frequent targets of lawsuits and defamation, I'm told by the classicist Rebecca Futo Kennedy. These women were usually more independent and more likely to work for a living. "One of the most damning stereotypes used to discredit *metics* in Athens was their love of money and possessions over city," she writes. They were portrayed as sexually deviant, as risks to the state. Their self-interest was seen as undermining social harmony.

The picture that emerges from between the lines of these ancient Greek records is a society desperately trying to keep its house in order for fear that everything would fall apart. Sarah Pomeroy explains in *Goddesses, Whores, Wives, and Slaves* that even the most misogynistic of writers in ancient Athens betrayed an anxiety that the uneven power balance between men and women might be unstable. In Greek legend, the wife of King Agamemnon, Clytemnestra, takes a lover and then kills her husband, only to find herself stabbed to death by her son in revenge. In the myth of the Amazons, a tribe of powerful warrior women fight men as equals in battle but are ultimately defeated. The scholar of Greek literature Froma Zeitlin uses the term "Amazon complex" to describe the societal panic that women might reject male subordination and try to become the dominant sex.

That complex, palpable paranoia is seen throughout the literature. Greek plays are replete with fictional women audaciously trying to subvert the patriarchal order. In *Assemblywomen*, a satirical play by Aristophanes, women take over the government of Athens. This was a recurrent theme for the playwright. "Three of the eleven extant comedies of Aristophanes show women in successful opposition to men. A secluded wife like Phaedra may yearn for adultery; a wife like Creusa may have borne an illegitimate son before her current marriage; a good wife like Deianira can murder her husband," writes Pomeroy. "These were the nightmares of the victors: that some day the vanquished would arise and treat their ex-masters as they themselves had been treated."

These nightmares are seen in other cultures across the world that have an unequal social order. The rituals around caste and class hierarchies can be remarkably elaborate. Nothing demonstrates the insecurity of Europe's monarchies quite as much as their need for pomp and ceremony. In India, there are countless subtle rules for how people from different castes should behave with one another. The ethnologists and gender scholars Dev Nathan, Govind Kelkar, and Yu Xiaogang have noted that in some of Asia's more patriarchal communities, there's a belief that women are witches or sources of evil. "The idea that women had some power which was subsequently stolen from them by men, and then carefully guarded by them, is quite frequently seen," they write. In one part of northeastern Thailand, the weapon used by people to overcome evil spirits is a wooden penis.

Fighting off its own insecurity, ancient Athens constantly found itself on the back foot. For all the effort ancient Greek poets and playwrights put into portraying female inferiority and subordination as natural, in insisting that the social order of Athens was perfectly normal, nothing undercut them quite so much as the fact that societies outside Athens didn't follow the same rules.

Ancient Egypt, for instance, had a completely different way of thinking about gender and power. "We have this rich cache of papyri, and a lot of them are letters written by women or contracts made by women. There are contracts for property, there are wills," says Rebecca Futo Kennedy, referring to documents found in Egypt dating to Hellenistic times, after the conquests of Alexander the Great in the fourth century BCE. "They actually have access to what we would call finance and legitimate forms of power." Kennedy explains that there was a tradition of women being authorities in their own households, and that this may have trickled up to the top, making it possible for people to imagine and accept women in power. While male pharaohs were common, there were renowned female rulers as well, including Cleopatra and Nefertiti.

"The status of women in ancient Egypt is probably the highest in the Mediterranean world," I'm told by the Egyptologist Faiza Haikal at the American University in Cairo, the first woman to be named president of the International Association of Egyptologists. "Certainly, higher than the Greek or the Roman, because the Egyptian woman was very independent. She could work, she could adopt anybody, she could inherit, she could run her own business. . . . She had practically all the rights of men." There were literate women, women working as doctors and midwives, musicians, and priestesses.

"There are many ways to be a woman in the ancient world," agrees Bethany Hucks, a doctoral student in Egyptology and archaeology at Heidelberg University. The Egyptian goddess Isis was one of the most popular deities in the ancient world, and far from one-dimensional. Religious cults in antiquity often gave women, including lower-status women, opportunities to have a public presence, enjoy genuine authority, and behave beyond social norms. Our view from the twenty-first century may give the impression of a linear trajectory from archaic times toward modern-day patriarchy, but, as Hucks explains, "there was a chance there in the ancient Mediterranean for things to become much more equitable."

. ■ ■

"They are exercising; they're doing what are technically manly activities. They're running, jumping, throwing," I'm told by Andrew Bayliss, a historian at the University of Birmingham and an expert on Sparta—a city-state infamous in ancient Greece for the visibility of its women in contrast to the relatively cloistered lives of high-class women in neighboring Athens.

Sparta forced the question of where the natural boundaries of gender behavior lay. Athenians couldn't help but remark on the physical differences between Spartan women and their own. They were sturdier and more tanned from outdoor exercise. They would have eaten a lot more than other Greek women, notes Bayliss. In *Lysistrata*, an Athenian comedy by Aristophanes, women organize a sex strike to stop the Peloponnesian War between Athens and Sparta. There's a scene in which a Spartan woman named Lampito appears. "The Athenians start commenting on her appearance, and they talk about how brown she is, they talk about how muscular she is, and she says that she could throttle a bull, she's so strong."

Athenian literature often painted Sparta as a weird or unusual place. The Greek philosopher Aristotle was especially hostile, moaning about Spartan men being too beholden to their women. He suggested that Sparta was a "gynecocracy," meaning it was run by women.

What's odd is that even recently there have been academics who have referred to Sparta as the "East" and Athens as the "West," says Bayliss. They're almost echoing Aristotle, implying that Sparta was more foreign. But of course, it was only ever foreign from an Athenian point of view. To the rest of the world, Athens must have looked equally unusual. "We kind of think of the Athenian way of doing things as normal, and because they cast the Spartans as the polar opposite of them, that creates the impression that Spartan women are totally abnormal," explains Bayliss. In truth, he says, "Athens is probably an extreme and Sparta an extreme at the other end."

Spartan society was more focused on warfare than some others, which meant women were expected to manage property while men were away fighting. It's this particular social backdrop that may have helped create different expectations for how women and men should act. At one stage in Spartan history, women owned two-fifths of the land. Older widows could amass so much personal wealth that they might not have had to remarry when their husbands died. "Wealthy Spartan women would also have been able to provide financial assistance to poorer male relatives, which could have given some women even more influence over their men," writes Bayliss.

This isn't to say that Sparta didn't have its own restrictive ideas about what was socially appropriate, only that what it saw as appropriate wasn't the same as it was in Athens.

The everyday lives of young Spartans, while still bound by patrilineal Greek values, were influenced by the relatively more militaristic direction of its society. It was also a society unafraid to go its own way, explains Bayliss. Spartans thought it was important for women to be strong and healthy to bear children who would be useful citizens, in the same way that men were expected to be strong and healthy to fight wars. "Spartan women married comparatively later. An Athenian girl might have been married at fourteen, and a Spartan girl is more likely eighteen, nineteen," he adds. Unmarried girls wore their hair uncovered and sported shorter dresses that, while more revealing, were designed to let them move about more easily and to exercise.

Another noticeable difference between Athens and Sparta in the historical record is that Spartan women weren't just seen; they were heard. Among the most popular parts of Greek literature describing Spartan life are laconic sayings. These are pithy statements that can be as witty or profound as they are frugal. The word "laconic" comes from Laconia, the region of Greece in which Sparta was located. When one Spartan was told that the arrows of a powerful opposing army would darken the skies above them, he's said to have replied, "Good, we'll fight in the shade." And it wasn't just men who were known for these sharp one-liners. There are around forty preserved phrases like these that have been attributed to women.

"There are quite a few good ones," says Bayliss. A common theme is women criticizing their menfolk for not fighting bravely enough. That women expected their husbands and sons to go out and fight, even at the risk of death, shows just how invested they were in the military aims of the state. "The most graphic one is the mother who hitched up her dress and said, 'Do you plan to creep back in here where you emerged from?'" when her son had shown cowardice in battle. There are stories of girls mocking boys for their weakness, and of daughters and wives telling their fathers and husbands what to do.

Walter Penrose, a historian of gender and sexuality in the ancient world at San Diego State University, tells me that if these accounts aren't apocryphal, but reflect words that were genuinely spoken by real people at the time, Spartan women appear to have thought of themselves as courageous. This is important because neighboring Athenians saw courage as a firmly masculine quality, to be prized only in men. "The actions of daring women were attributed to *tolma*, or audacity, rather than to *andreia*, courage."

A cowardly man in Athens might be described as effeminate. In Sparta, courage wasn't gendered this way. "Spartan cowards were *not* compared to or called women, because Spartan women were not perceived as lacking in courage," Penrose explains. In both Sparta and the Peloponnese city of Argos, women were in fact lauded for their courage. "Courageous actions of women, which were deemed 'masculine,' 'audacious,' and hence 'unnatural' by Athenians, were praised by other Greeks," he writes.

This wasn't because courageous women were unusual but because every culture in the world has its own way of negotiating gender. In ancient Eurasia, says Penrose, there is archaeological evidence "of women buried with weapons among ancient Scythians, Sauromatians, and Thracians." These real women warriors, if that's what they were, may have been the inspiration for the Greek legends of warrior Amazons. "Clearly, women fought in these societies. Through trade and colonization, Greeks had contact with various warrior women of differing ethnicities, but seem to have subsumed all or many of them under the idea of the Amazons," he adds. "Perhaps this is because the Greeks did not understand a society where women fought or had power."

What might seem like deep-rooted Athenian beliefs about gender, then, "never really quite matched up to the set of facts that they had."

The contradictions and paradoxes in the literature bothered Penrose from the moment that he began researching gender diversity in antiquity. Some ancient Greek philosophers see intelligence as masculine, for instance, but in history and myth there are women who are clearly intelligent. There are exceptions to all the rules, yet a constant, almost desperate insistence that the rules are natural. In the end, Penrose landed on the conclusion that the male and female binary that appears to have been so immutable a part of Greek society, based on the literature that has come down to us, has actually been overstated.

"I think there is a tension there, and that's why I was leery of a binary, because it's so much more complicated than that."

The Princeton University classicist Brooke Holmes has similarly written that "we shouldn't lose sight of the fact that gender seems to have operated in highly reductive ways in ancient texts and lives, reinforcing polarities of thought and laying constraints on how individuals expressed their interests, talents, desires, fears and hopes, as well as how they saw each other." Between the lines, in the anxiety and paranoia, is where we can start to see how difficult it must have been in real life for people to stay contained within the state's rigid classifications.

■　　■　　■

There's an ancient Greek medical text *On Regimen*, attributed to the fifth-century BCE physician Hippocrates (the one doctors remember these days when they take their Hippocratic oath), which says that a baby's character is decided in the womb by a battle between its mother's seeds and its father's seeds. Each of these seeds, Walter Penrose explains, can lean toward the feminine or masculine regardless of which parent it comes from, meaning that mothers can make male-leaning seeds and fathers can produce female-leaning ones. So, for instance, a "masculine" female baby could be the result of the father's female-leaning seed overcoming the mother's male-leaning seed, but still mingling with it. And there are, of course, other combinations.

If this sounds complicated, it is.

The fact that it is so complicated tells us something. It proves that the ancient Greeks had no choice but to acknowledge that not everyone automatically aligned with society's gender expectations from birth. The fact of "feminine" men and "masculine" women, people whose qualities didn't match their stereotypes, had to be explained. This is what *On Regimen* was attempting to do.

"It took me a while to come to the conclusion that it is a political text. There's a politics going on there," Penrose tells me. The author of *On Regimen* wasn't just trying to explain reality but was writing for an audience that had to navigate a rigidly gendered society. "The reason he's spelling all this out is so that the parents can work on their regimen, their diet and their exercise, so that they don't wind up with a child like this," one who defies gender expectations. Athenians were known to be viciously intolerant of people who didn't conform. There are accounts of intersex people in ancient Greece and Rome being killed, sometimes as babies, for fear that they represented cosmic instabilities or signs of bad things to come. This medical text, then, reflected a desire for people to fit into strict gender protocols amid an uneasy recognition that not everyone would.

"It's the tension between the ideology and the reality," says Penrose.

This observation sits within a wider body of scholarship that has for decades questioned how we think about women and men in classical antiquity. In their anthology *Sex and Difference in Ancient Greece and Rome*, the classicists Mark Golden and Peter Toohey describe just how complex this question really is. Inspired by the French philosopher Michel Foucault's writings on sexuality in the 1970s, some experts have asked if the sexual act of penetration, for example, might be seen as "the main means of defining gender. Men penetrated, women were penetrated. As a result, not all males were men," Golden and Toohey write. Subordinate males who were penetrated, including slaves and boys, could see a change in their status as men.

"The word 'women' is hardly unproblematic either," writes Nancy Sorkin Rabinowitz. As she explains, "Ancient people not only had different words but used the words they did have for female human beings in different ways." Romans saw women who were more sexually active, rather than passive, as more manly, for example.

These uncertainties have never been resolved. There remain cultural differences in how societies think about what makes a person a man or a woman. A case in point is the way in which the Roman Catholic Church and the Islamic Republic of Iran today treat sexual reassignment surgery for transgender people. Both are rigidly patriarchal and view men and women as having clearly defined social roles, but while the Catholic Church regards being transgender as a kind of mental instability requiring psychological treatment, the Islamic Republic sees it as a physical issue that should be corrected with surgery. The Iranian state even subsidizes sexual reassignment operations in the belief that this will bring a person's body and mind into correct alignment with each other. Transgender men and women in Iran, after these operations, are expected to meet the moral and social obligations consistent with their gender. For transgender women, this includes wearing a veil in public. For the Catholic Church, on the other hand, a postoperative transgender man is still a woman.

"The idea that biology is destiny—or, better still, destiny is biology—has been a staple of Western thought for centuries," writes the professor of sociology Oyeronke Oyewumi, based at Stony Brook University, New York, referring in particular to the Greek philosopher Aristotle. This idea has cast a long shadow over the world, particularly in the countries that were colonized by Europeans. Oyewumi explains that in the Yorùbá language in Nigeria, traditionally there were no separate personal pronouns for men and women. This is because "gender was not an organizing principle." Until the British Empire stretched into Nigeria, age and seniority were seen to matter most to a person's status. This is what makes it difficult to know which rulers were men and which were women from historical records, writes Oyewumi. In Yorùbá society, "social relations derive their legitimacy from social facts, not from biology."

But even within the history of Western thought, including in ancient Greece, there was always equivocation around the legitimate basis for social relations between women and men. Around 380 BCE, the philosopher Plato wrote in *The Republic* that an ideal society would have capable women as its ruling guardians alongside capable men. He argued that everyone should have the same education and training, even if the sight of "naked old wrinkled women showing their agility" in the gymnasium made men uncomfortable.

"All is habit," Plato commented. We can get used to anything.

Before him, Greek myths of gods and goddesses breached norms of masculinity and femininity, sometimes playing with the idea of the androgynous, transgender, and intersex. There's the story of Hermaphroditus, the beautiful son of the deities Hermes and Aphrodite, who was merged with a female nymph and became a dual-sexed person. The goddess Athena had qualities that Athenians associated firmly with men, including heroism and intelligence. She was the goddess of war, worshipped for her military strength and wisdom. The god Dionysus was sometimes depicted as an older man with a beard, while at other times he looked youthful, with long hair and the pale skin usually associated with higher-status women who were kept indoors.

"Athena and Dionysus are not merely symbolic of how those who may not fit so well into the social structures can still be recognised," write the classicist Alison Surtees and the gender scholar Jennifer Dyer, "but rather they represent the fluidity that lies under the pretence of stability that is continually celebrated and must be continually reaffirmed as divine, natural, ideal and normal."

While ancient Greeks were clearly fascinated with life beyond their gender norms, there was at the same time a sense that the social, economic, and political stability of the state depended on erasing this complexity. This is perhaps what stood in the way of realizing a more equal society. Judith Fletcher, a historian at Wilfrid Laurier University in Ontario whose work focuses on the culture of classical Athens, writes about the untamed, powerful "wildness" that young women on the cusp of adulthood between virginity and marriage were thought to possess, a "potency which must be incorporated within the state if the state is to survive." The state couldn't function without its suffocatingly narrow set of social rules, ensuring that citizens behaved in a way that maintained the population, its productivity, and the dominance of the elites.

Only in the heavens could anyone live beyond the walls of social expectation. Only the immortals had the freedom to be themselves.

CHAPTER 6

Alienation

There are some childhood experiences that haunt us forever. One of mine was as a teenager, when I caught a whispered call between my mother and the daughter of an old friend of hers from India.

Trisha (I've changed her name and some personal details to protect her identity) had been through an arranged wedding to a British man of Indian heritage who lived with his elderly parents in London. Theirs was a small terraced home, nothing special. But for Trisha, confident and beautiful, from a relatively modest family that had never left India, the prospect of life in Britain felt trimmed in glitter. As it did for my own parents once.

From what I could piece together by eavesdropping, married life didn't live up to expectations. Her husband could be strict, but it was when he was away at work that her mother-in-law and father-in-law made her life truly intolerable. She was treated like a maid, told where she could and couldn't go. The situation wasn't severe enough to call the police, I guessed. But it must have been wretched, because Trisha wasn't supposed to be making these phone calls. They were snatched in the moments that nobody was watching her or planned in advance when she knew the family would be out. My mother reassured her, telling her calmly to stick it out for now, and call her again if things got too bad.

Months passed. Trisha gave birth to a baby. Her husband's parents eventually passed away. The calls to our home became less frequent. Her world gradually settled into something that made her happy.

Decades later, I still wonder why my mother never told her to leave.

Perhaps she did. Although even at the age that I was, I knew it wouldn't necessarily have made a difference. There was such shame shrouding the idea of a wife leaving her husband that it wasn't unheard of for parents to advise their daughters to stay even with violent partners. Neighbors would turn a blind eye. The authorities, too. It took until 2015 for the United Kingdom to outlaw coercive or controlling behavior, a form of abuse made famous by the case of Sally Challen, a British woman who killed her husband with a hammer after forty years of being humiliated by him. Jailed for life in 2011, she was set free following a retrial nine years later.

Trisha's wasn't the only story of its kind I caught on the grapevine as a child. There were dozens more among family and friends, in the newspapers, on television. The message that soaked into me was a fatalistic one, that once a girl was married, she belonged to her husband and his family. There's a saying in parts of India that girls are *paraya dhan*, which means looking after a daughter is like watering a plant for a neighbor—that neighbor being her future husband's family.

I'm still learning the rules. I remember my older relatives ribbing me on my wedding day for smiling too much. It was inappropriate to look happy. Symbolically, an Indian bride is leaving the safety and security of her childhood kin for the precarity of a new life with people who, in arranged marriages at least, may be little more than strangers. In my case, I was marrying a man whom I had loved for years, whose family were nothing but warm and welcoming. But my public behavior was still expected to play out a script—whether the role made sense to me or not.

Even in a family as progressive as mine, the social codes were like a fog. The domineering mother-in-law is a mainstay of Bollywood soap operas. The put-upon wife and daughter-in-law are universal tropes. To this day, it can be hard for an Indian woman to escape the stereotype of the good wife, the one who politely obeys her husband and his family. At worst, she's consigned to the bottom of the domestic hierarchy until she bears a child. Often, only when she has a son. Maybe that's why I didn't question what was happening to Trisha. I'm sure that's why my mother responded the way she did, with gentle words, instead of telling her to pack her bags.

I realize I had been brought up in a world in which I had learned to accept her suffering.

.   .   .

"It's happening all across different classes," I'm told by Fairuz Choudhury, who works at the Hopscotch Women's Centre in Camden, north London, which helps women facing domestic abuse or who want to escape economic reliance on their partners. Many of the staff have personal experience of the same issues as the women who reach out to them.

"Normally the calls that we receive are for women who have a language barrier. They don't have much of an education, they are financially dependent, and their marriage was arranged," explains Choudhury. Most are first-generation immigrants, usually from South Asia, but others have also moved to the city from parts of Africa, the Middle East, and South and Central America. A few are from wealthy, educated families or are in marriages that weren't forced or arranged. What ties their stories together isn't the women's social or ethnic background but their isolation. It's the isolation that compounds their helplessness.

"We find that the majority of the women want to do something with their lives. They come into this country and see a sea of opportunities. They want to learn the language, they want to go out and about, they want to earn money. But they're denied all of this," she continues.

"Those facing abuse could have very limited access to the outside world. If they're lucky, they may go to the school gates and come back," adds the head of the center, Benaifer Bhandari. At home, the workload can feel endless. "There will be a very high expectation of the tasks that fall within her remit, and they will be extensive, and particular to each family member. So, she'll be washing clothes in a particular way for each one because they want it done like that, or cooking in a particular way for each one. She will have sole responsibility for the children and everything to do with them. So, there'll be nothing of her responsibilities that will be shared, and she'll also have everybody else to take care of as well. Her days will be very long, and then on top of that, there may be emotional and physical abuse."

Domestic abuse is often framed as a problem perpetrated by one partner against another, most frequently by men against women. But as the staff at Hopscotch explain, the network of blame usually falls more broadly. "In the majority of the cases we are seeing, it's not only the male's fault," Choudhury tells me. "It's a collective kind of abuse done by everyone in the family." A husband may be cruel or controlling, but so might his parents, sisters, and brothers. Children will be inducted into these power hierarchies. Almost all the members of the family can bring their weight down to bear upon the brides who marry into them.

A study in the Indian state of Uttar Pradesh published in 2020 found that living with their mothers-in-law tends to restrict the mobility of young rural women, so severely at times that they can't visit their friends or family by themselves. They are more socially isolated in marriage. The cycle repeats itself over generations, harangued or abused daughters-in-law turning into domineering mothers-in-law. Women become the instruments of the same patriarchal forces that previously oppressed them.

In some of the worst cases, a woman will have nowhere else to go. Her childhood family may have all but washed their hands of her. "They say you have to deal with it, you can't come back, because of honor and shame," explains Choudhury. A family's reputation might suffer if she were to separate from her husband or get a divorce. Sisters and brothers might then find it harder to get married. "Families don't have much of an option because they know it's only going to get worse, not only for her but for other siblings."

In his novel *The White Tiger*, Aravind Adiga describes the crushing trap that a boy from a poor Indian village finds himself in when he goes away to work for a wealthy family as a chauffeur. He has no choice but to endure their exploitation and abuse because his own family would pay the price for his leaving. As he knows, they would be hunted down and killed. He imagines himself as a rooster in a coop waiting for slaughter. Adiga's metaphor for the suffocating effects of poverty in what is in essence a feudal society applies just as easily to the most restrictive of patriarchal families. There are webs of obligation to be paid by the young to the old, as well as by women to men, keeping the system functioning. Transgressors aren't seen to be breaking the contract for just themselves. They're breaking it for the community.

In modern-day Pakistan, which has some of the highest rates of intimate partner violence in the world, one of the biggest risk factors identified by researchers is witnessing violence in the family or neighborhood, which then normalizes violence in the home. The effects can be so insidious that, according to a report by the Overseas Development Institute, mothers who had themselves faced violence went on to support violent sons who were abusive toward their own wives.

The staff at the Hopscotch Women's Centre tell me that it's taken too long for some of the cases that come through their doors to be recognized as a form of human bondage. In recent years, they've begun to recognize that what's happening to these women bears a striking similarity to modern-day slavery. It has all the hallmarks.

"The woman would have to cook food and serve food, and she would be asked to eat at a later time. Even when she did join the others to have meals, she did not feel encouraged to help herself with a second serving of food. They're so terrified of their in-laws," Choudhury tells me.

"They're not getting paid. They don't have access to basic necessities. They don't even have mobile phones. I've had cases where even if they've brought mobile phones from back home, or they bought it with their own money that their father gave them, the mobile phones were taken away by the in-laws or by the husband and locked up. They were not allowed to call back to their homes. They were not allowed to go out without being accompanied by any other family members.

"In certain cases, they would be locked up in the house or in the flat when the other members would go out."

■   ■   ■

In *The Creation of Patriarchy*, the late historian Gerda Lerner argued that women must have been humanity's first slaves, originally kept by men for having sex and making babies. Women's oppression, we often hear, predates all other forms of oppression.

In truth, it's hard to find substantive evidence for this. As matrilineal and more egalitarian societies prove, women everywhere haven't always been treated the same way. But philosophers and theorists have drawn comparisons between the legal and social status of wives in patriarchal marriages and the practice of slavery. Friedrich Engels described the subjugation of women as a degrading form of servitude or bondage. In marriage, he said, a wife became "the slave" of her husband's lust. The French philosopher Simone de Beauvoir wrote in *The Second Sex* that "woman has always been man's dependent, if not his slave." Ram Mohan Roy, the Indian social reformer who campaigned against widow sacrifice and child marriage in the early nineteenth century, argued that a wife was "employed to do the work of a slave in the house."

Clearly, though, not every marriage feels like bondage. The reality of slavery is absolute. But in 2017, statistics released by the United Nations' International Labour Organization for the first time recognized forced marriage specifically as a form of slavery. The most recent figures estimate that of the more than forty million people living in modern slavery worldwide, at least fifteen million are in forced marriages. This means that a person somewhere in the world is being married against her will almost every two seconds.

Younger brides are particularly at risk. Statistics for those living in abusive or exploitative families are next to nonexistent, but according to UNICEF, 650 million girls and women alive today were driven into marriage as children.

The problem is slowly declining in South Asia but remains prevalent in parts of Africa and the Middle East. In Niger, three-quarters of girls are married before they turn eighteen.

Being wrenched from their homes after they marry is what condemns many of these women and girls to lives of abuse. It is alienation from their childhood families that make them vulnerable. But this is exactly what marriage in the most patriarchal societies demands. If there's one thing that historically patrilocal and patrilineal systems have in common, it's that brides are generally the ones being "given away" by their families—more precisely, by their fathers. It took until 2021 for mothers in England and Wales to see their names included on the marriage certificates of their children, after the government corrected what it called a "historic anomaly." That anomaly began with the principle that in wedlock a woman was effectively passing from her father's authority to her husband's. By custom, a bride's surname changes after the wedding to match her husband's. Her identity becomes incorporated into his.

It may be only symbolic for many women these days, but that act of exchange implies ownership. Dating back to the Middle Ages, the English common law principle of coverture stated that women no longer existed legally as individuals once they were married. A couple was treated as one person in law, and that person was in effect the husband. A wife couldn't own property. She had no rights over her own body. Her children didn't belong to her. Those under the age of twenty-one were described by William Blackstone, the great seventeenth-century expert on English law, as being firmly under "the empire of the father." Only when the Custody of Infants Act was passed in 1839 did mothers in England get the right to petition for child custody, following a campaign by the social reformer Caroline Norton, who had been denied access to her sons when she left her violent husband.

This doctrine of coverture was exported by the British to their colonies, becoming the basis for marriage laws in countries from India to the United States. In 2022, as part of efforts to overturn American rights to abortion access, the conservative Supreme Court justice Samuel Alito even turned to treatises by the seventeenth-century English jurist Sir Matthew Hale, who had been involved in the development of English common law. In his own time, Hale had defended marital rape.

While we know that marriage hasn't always oppressed all women in the same way that slavery fundamentally degrades the enslaved, parallels like these may point to how rules and norms around marriage developed over time in at least some societies. Perhaps it wasn't the subordination of women that originally provided the model for slavery and other forms of oppression. Maybe instead it was the practice of slavery that gradually came to inform institutions of marriage.

■ ■ ■

There's a passage in the Old Testament book of Deuteronomy that serves as a kind of instructional guide for men who have captured women during battle:

> If you notice among the captives a beautiful woman and are attracted to her, you may take her as your wife. Bring her into your home and have her shave her head, trim her nails and put aside the clothes she was wearing when captured. After she has lived in your house and mourned her father and mother for a full month, then you may go to her and be her husband and she shall be your wife.

The history of war, I'm told by the anthropologist James Scott, is very often the history of wars of capture. There are lots of motivations for going to battle, but one of the most common has been to seize property. Often, that property was people. "In a sense, wars of capture were especially wars of capture of women and young children," he explains. "Women, not just because they could then become slaves, but because of their reproductive services. Because they helped increase the population, which was the objective of the war in any case.

"It was about grabbing people, not about grabbing land."

Stretching into prehistory, the more powerful and wealthy have always seized men, women, and children to be used as slave labor, servants, soldiers, human sacrifices, commodities to be traded, or simply as symbols of honor and status. All genders have been put to work in every possible way. Children were the most easily taken and assimilated. Men were castrated to work as eunuchs in royal households throughout the ancient world. Young women were taken as wives and concubines.

In some cases, the taken were absorbed quickly, with a few documented stories of people—particularly those captured into some Native American tribes—actively choosing their new lives over their old ones, maybe because they preferred these societies or had become so enmeshed in them that they couldn't imagine anything else. Others would find themselves permanently marginalized and degraded. Some would be killed. But for all its different forms, there is historical evidence of captive taking all over the world, from small-scale hunter-gatherer societies all the way up to enormous empires, and right across Europe, Africa, Asia, and the Americas.

"I think that's the thing that surprised me the most," I'm told by the archaeologist Catherine Cameron at the University of Colorado Boulder, "how worldwide this seems to be." An expert on captive taking in prehistory, she explains that slaves and those captured in war were a fixture of everyday life in the past. For a few ancient states, their very socioeconomic survival depended on it. Forced labor formed the backbone needed to sustain large cities and wage battle, to help religious and cultural institutions grow.

Cameron estimates that captives may have made up to a third of the population of ancient Greece for a while, 10 to 20 percent of Roman Italy, 15 to 20 percent of many early Islamic states, and as much as 50 to 70 percent of Korea before the seventeenth century. In Scandinavia, a twelfth-century farm may have had typically three slaves, she writes. According to the Domesday Book, which surveyed the population of some of England's settlements in 1086, the proportion of slaves in the country may have been around 10 percent. The first United States census, in 1790, showed that for every one hundred free white people in the southern states, there were fifty-three people who were enslaved.

The historian Adam Hochschild has suggested that by the end of the eighteenth century more than three-quarters of the world's population may have been living under some form of human bondage, including indentured labor, serfdom, and slavery. Until fairly recently in human history, then, most people weren't "free" in the modern sense of the word. They took as given that their existence depended on others who had direct control over them, whether it was a feudal lord or master, a pharaoh, or a monarch.

"We think of power as owning things," Cameron tells me. But in the smaller societies she has studied, it wasn't land or property that those in power sought. It was humans, and especially younger women and children who might be more easily absorbed into society through marriage or force. "You own the people, and the people respect you. You walk around with your train of slaves and that demonstrates, every single day, how powerful you are."

It was common for armies in ancient states to kill enemy men and take women and children away, depending on their social or economic needs. Viking raiders are certainly known to have seized people in this way. A paper published in the *American Journal of Human Genetics* in 2000 confirmed what historians already suspected, that a large number of slaves captured from the British Isles, particularly from Ireland, and taken to Iceland more than a thousand years ago were women and girls. Biological data shows that the families formed between Viking men and their captives went on to help populate the country.

The brutal act of seizing entire groups of people in warlike raids, and then forcibly marrying the women and girls, continues to this day. Since 2014, thousands of schoolgirls have been abducted in Nigeria by the militant Islamist group Boko Haram, many of them raped and married to their captors. Also in 2014, Islamic State militants took captive thousands of Yazidi women, men, and children from northern Iraq, forcing some into religious conversion and marriage. Many went on to be bought and sold as slaves for years afterward.

The legacy of taking captives as wives also survives culturally in the modern-day ritual of bride abduction, seen across the Central Asian countries of Kyrgyzstan and Kazakhstan, in Armenia and Russia, and in parts of Ethiopia, Somalia, and Indonesia. In spring 2021, there were protests in front of the interior ministry of Kyrgyzstan after a twenty-seven-year-old, Aizada Kanatbekova, was found dead following a suspected case of bride abduction. Her body had been left in an abandoned car. The man assumed to have kidnapped her was also found dead, apparently having stabbed himself. Kyrgyzstan's president promised afterward that this should be "the last bride kidnapping in history."

Few expected it would be. Bride abduction has been illegal since 1994, but it's lightly policed. As many as one in five women and girls in Kyrgyzstan are abducted for marriage. What complicates enforcement of the law is that not all kidnappings are nonconsensual. Sometimes the tradition is used by couples who want to elope when their families don't approve. But even when it's used as a ruse, the custom rarely involves only the woman and her abductor. In Kyrgyzstan, it often includes the man's friends and relatives. Older women might urge the stolen woman to stay, convincing her to put on a symbolic white scarf to show that she accepts the groom.

Women abducted against their will in Kyrgyzstan do sometimes manage to escape. But the risk of leaving can be almost as high as staying. When a woman's virginity comes into question, as it does in these cases, it's harder for her to marry someone else. The boundary between choice and coercion becomes blurry. A study published by the University of Central Asia in 2016 showed that babies born to abducted brides in Kyrgyzstan tended to be significantly lighter than average, suggesting that the mothers had experienced physical and psychological trauma in the run-up to giving birth. Although Kyrgyzstan has higher rates of female employment than the global average, another study in 2021, published by Germany's Institute of Labour Economics, showed that Kyrgyz women who were kidnapped as brides also had a 10 percent lower likelihood of working.

Bride capture grays the line between slavery and marriage. It could be seen as an extreme and violent variant of patrilocality. Women don't just move to live with their husbands; they're forced to move. It's hard to imagine how this couldn't have an effect on gender dynamics in the societies throughout history that have taken wives this way. In prehistory and into antiquity, according to James Scott, "the women in these early societies, a huge proportion of them were not, if you like, from the dominant culture." In the *Odyssey*, the great epic attributed to the ancient Greek poet Homer, references to slavery are most often to women, probably because the men in their communities had already been killed in warfare or raids. Scott tells me that in ancient Rome, the name "Barbara" was used to refer to the wife of a Roman citizen who had origins as a slave—as in "barbarian." This word's roots, in turn, lie in a racist term in ancient Greece referring to a foreigner who couldn't speak Greek.

These wives may have seen their fathers and brothers, even their mothers and children, killed by the same people to whom they were now married. Not only were they foreigners in their new homes; they would also have been harboring the pain and anger of this trauma. Perhaps this could go some way to explaining the misogynistic suspicion of women that runs through the literature of ancient Athens. Male anxiety that women weren't loyal to their families or to the state, that they might someday revolt, may have been grounded in a genuine fear because so many of them were foreign captives.

"If you have some large proportion of your population that is foreign in some way, and they're mostly women, I suppose that could affect your perception of all women," suggests Catherine Cameron.

This raises the possibility that slavery and patrilocality might each have informed the other as societies began to draw up their rules around marriage. Patrilocality was a social system in which women would leave their families to be with their husbands, becoming outsiders in their new homes. At the same time, captive taking and slavery provided models for how to treat outsiders.

When we look at the historical literature of medieval Europe, says James Scott, a lot of it is about "how to tame your wife, with the same words you would use for taming a wild animal, and how in a sense you can corral their behavior within the confines of what an easily controlled domesticated animal might do." The fact that a wife would need to be "tamed" at all tells us something about her circumstances. The British socialist feminist Sheila Rowbotham has written that among peasant families in Russia before the Bolshevik revolution of 1917, "it was customary for the bride's father to give the groom a new whip so he could exercise his authority if he wished."

Peasant women, she adds, were often sold to the highest bidder.

■ ■ ■

"There is no known slaveholding society where the whip was not considered an indispensable instrument," writes the Harvard sociologist Orlando Patterson. Born and raised in Jamaica, where slave labor on plantations once sustained the sugar industry, Patterson has focused his lifelong research on the concept of freedom and the history of slavery—particularly on the devastating impact of enslavement on a person's sense of self. The body survives, he explains, but everything else is subsumed into nothingness. Slavery represents nothing less than "social death."

Of the factors essential to psychological well-being—the need to belong, to have control over one's life, to be able to trust others, and to see people as essentially good—slavery is an assault on all of them, Patterson writes. It takes away the basic social elements that someone needs to feel safe and well adjusted. And it replaces them with degradation of the most fundamental kind. There is little room left for human connection beyond that between the master and the slave.

"One of the first thing they do to captives immediately is change their identity, shave their heads, take away their clothes," I'm told by Catherine Cameron. They might be physically branded. Who they are has to be erased and rebuilt. And captives would have been painfully aware of this fact. Their best hope for survival might be to acquiesce and fit in, because those who resist would be the first killed. "If you're showing a desire to escape, an unwillingness to learn the language, an unwillingness to learn the traditions, some suspicion of the religion, any of those things, I think you would be looked upon as a very problematic person."

Yet, as we can see through history, the captive's origin was rarely forgotten. They were always the outsider. Patterson describes captives and slaves as the "enemies within," an internal threat, viewed as necessary yet never accepted as entirely trustworthy. That emotional distance was also crucial in allowing captors to dehumanize those they had taken. Once people were seen as socially distinct, they could be imagined as essentially different. Brutality toward them could almost be rationalized. In ancient Rome, slaves were categorized as legally dead—in other words, not human in the first place. In the United States, racist ideologies linked to slavery so pervasively degraded African Americans that, by the nineteenth century, white scientists and physicians came to assume that those with black skin felt pain less than those with white skin.

The very presence of captives in early captor societies could have transformed the way everyday people thought about violence and inequality, says Cameron. It made the gross mistreatment of fellow humans seem acceptable. Enslavement lowered the bar for depravity. It taught ordinary people how to separate and subjugate others, to normalize violence in their own homes and communities, to deny individuals their dignity and agency, and to extract their labor for free.

Women trafficked into prostitution today, writes Patterson, come "closest to the experience of traditional slaves in their commodification and sale, repeated physical and sexual assault, and isolation." The global trade in women has a racial element, too, just like the captive taking of the past. Nepalese women are trafficked into India; women from Eastern Europe and Africa are trafficked into Western Europe. These women may be given new names, see their passports taken away, be cut off from family and friends. Their identities are transformed piece by piece.

"Once broken and seasoned," continues Patterson, "they become totally dependent on their masters and willingly work for him (or her, the number of women pimps and madams being unusually high) for near to zero pay." Firsthand accounts from pimps reveal the thrill and sense of power they draw from degrading the women they keep, destroying them to the point of erasure, thriving from their dependency. One pimp told anthropologists that an "intense hatred" of his victims motivated his abuse. Patterson describes this trade in trafficked women as brutal as anything he has seen in historical records of slavery.

A woman is used up, he writes. Not just her body, but her "entire personhood."

At once a close relationship and an exploitative one, contemporary slavery has parallels with some of history's oldest slaveholding societies. In ancient Egypt, slavery "established an extreme form of personal intimacy through total submission. The good slave was one who completely lost his identity in the master, became one with him," explains Patterson. Honor and obedience were bound up in this attachment, the master drawing honor from the slave's obedience. This wasn't just a form of violent degradation. It was also a bond between two people.

■   ■   ■

In 1974, the sociologist Christine Delphy published a study looking at cultures of household consumption among poorer, rural households in France in which families didn't always have enough to eat. She recalled the story of a young peasant farmer who welcomed two women from the city to his home for tea. When they arrived, he opened a humble tin of pâté for them to share.

"His aunt, an old woman who kept house for him because his mother was ill, was there," wrote Delphy. The aunt acted on her own initiative in giving herself the least desirable part of the dish, the bit that everyone else at the table sniffed at. "On her bread she put only the fat."

When asked why she had taken the fat that nobody wanted, the aunt rationalized her choice by saying that she *liked* it.

Delphy was unconvinced. What caused the woman to carry out this act, she believed, was the deep-rooted conviction that she was there to serve the family, that her contribution to it was worth less than everyone else's. She had internalized the notion that she didn't deserve any more than the fat. This ideology of female sacrifice, even at the price of a person's own health and well-being, was one that Delphy observed right across France, in the cities as well as in the countryside. "The mistress of the house takes the smallest steak without thinking," she recounted. Even in metropolitan Paris, when there was a potato shortage, a woman queued to buy potatoes for her working husband. She and her children, she admitted, would eat cheaper pasta or rice.

But nothing encapsulated the subordinate status of wives more obviously than the fact that their domestic labor was unpaid. "They are excluded from the realm of exchange and consequently have no *value*," wrote Delphy. Even outside the home, women were more likely than men to work as volunteers.

This couldn't be explained by the nature of the work they were doing. It wasn't that cleaning, cooking, caring, or doing agricultural work were always unpaid. People could be hired to do these jobs, and these workers would expect to receive wages. It wasn't the case, either, that wives were getting nothing in return. It's just that what they were getting in return was so little.

The wife's job was to work, honor, and obey, concluded Delphy. What she got in return was upkeep.

This situation was so obviously exploitative that "when a farmer couldn't afford to hire a domestic worker he took a wife." Delphy's argument was that, rather than her work being worthless in monetary terms, it was a wife's relationship to production that gave her labor so little value. It was because she was a *wife* doing it, in the same way that if a slave were doing it, they wouldn't be paid either. In the family, and by extension in wider society, the product of her labor was seen to belong to her husband.

And this was reflected in the law. In England, the Married Women's Property Act was passed in 1870, finally allowing women to keep the money they earned or the property they inherited after they were married. But in France, even until 1907, a married woman would see whatever wages she earned go straight to her husband. As recently as 1965, a French husband could legally stop his wife from working. "My proposition is that marriage is the institution by which unpaid work is extorted from a particular category of the population, women-wives," Delphy stated. Marriage in the cases she had studied in France was nothing less than a legal contract that kept a wife in a form of human bondage.

The value to societies of the domestic labor performed for free is enormous. According to the American economist Nancy Folbre, the cost of replacing all the nonmarket work done in the United States, including the time given to supervising young children, would run to at least 44 percent of the country's gross domestic product. Yet it's not only taken for granted; until relatively recently in history, it was also legally demanded of wives. Before the middle of the nineteenth century, Folbre writes, the laws governing marriage in the United States gave husbands authority over their wives in exchange for only basic support. This was "stipulated as a minimum level of subsistence, not a specific share of family income." Efforts at the time to lobby for the legal rights of wives to half of their husbands' incomes failed.

But legislation isn't the whole story. What had struck Delphy wasn't just the unfairness of the way women were treated but also the elderly aunt's behavior when it came to the unwanted fat on that pâté. It's one thing to grudgingly put up with the unequal life that you're saddled with. It's quite another to convince yourself that this is what you deserve.

Submission has become woven into the concept of femininity, explains the Yale University philosopher Manon Garcia. As far back as the eighteenth century, she writes, the philosopher Jean-Jacques Rousseau painted women as "beings of opinion and not reason, of submission and not of freedom." He argued that they existed for others, not fully for themselves.

Folbre adds that there were many American states that passed laws around the early nineteenth century "stipulating wifely subordination, some of which remained legally enforceable until the 1970s." The ideology of female submissiveness lives on in some parts. As recently as 1998, "the convention of Southern Baptists, the largest Protestant denomination in the United States, declared that a wife should 'submit herself graciously' to her husband's leadership," in line with the New Testament exhortation that "wives should submit to their husbands in everything," she writes.

The principle that a wife should submit herself fully to her husband's authority persists in public attitudes around domestic violence and rape. Most countries began to accept marital rape as a crime only in the last few decades. There are some, including India, Afghanistan, Nigeria, and Saudi Arabia, which still don't. Laws in Saudi Arabia and Qatar require women to have a male guardian's permission before they can marry. According to a report by Human Rights Watch, family law in Qatar says that a wife "can be deemed 'disobedient' if she does not obtain her husband's permission before working, traveling, or if she leaves her home or refuses to have sex with him without a 'legitimate' reason."

In cultures in which extended families have tended to live nearby or under one roof, a wife's deference extends to her husband's parents. The late sociologist Fatima Mernissi found that in some of the Moroccan families she interviewed for her research in the 1970s, a husband was actively discouraged from loving his wife. As she explained, "his mother is the only woman a man is allowed to love at all." Mernissi saw mothers playing the decisive role in choosing their sons' brides. And they continued to play a big role after they married. Submission by daughters-in-law was expected.

In some of the more traditional households, it was the wife's duty to kiss her mother-in-law's hand daily and call her *Lalla*—meaning "mistress."

■   ■   ■

Writing about filial piety in ancient China, the American-born sinologist Donald Holzman was shocked by the lengths to which children would go to display devotion to their elders.

He recounted one legend in which a wife returned home late from fetching water. Her mother-in-law punished her for this infraction by temporarily banishing her from the house altogether. But instead of nursing a resentment as she might have done, the daughter-in-law used what little money she earned to send her mother-in-law anonymous gifts of food. Holzman was appalled, describing her selfless act of devotion as "grotesque." He couldn't understand how a story like this could ever have been passed down as a lesson in admirable behavior.

I have somewhat less trouble understanding it. The pull of filial and wifely duties can be incalculably strong in some Asian, African, and Middle Eastern societies, especially when compared to the individualism that's valued in the West. Escape is almost unthinkable. It would mean letting go of all the human connections that root you in the world, both physically and psychologically. But more than that, it would mean turning your back on the social order.

"Honor and power are intimately linked," writes the sociologist Orlando Patterson.

The webs of patriarchal obligation, as tightly woven as they can become, work in strange ways. They may be weighted with religion, tradition, or a duty to one's elders, loaded with guilt and shame. But they can also be couched in genuine concern for a child's place in a society that demands they conform for the sake of everyone else. Following the rules brings benefits, even if the rules themselves are ultimately unjust.

Complex dynamics like these play out in the persistence of female genital mutilation. Widespread in parts of Africa and the Middle East, this practice is believed to date at least as far back as the slave trade along the Red Sea, which saw female slaves sold as concubines. Then as now, it's designed to make sex either impossible or excruciatingly painful. The sole purpose is to secure a girl's virginity before marriage and sexual loyalty afterward. In a sense, then, it could be seen as a violent form of sexual bondage, tying a woman to her future husband. According to the World Health Organization, at least two hundred million women and girls alive today have undergone female genital mutilation, with another three million at risk every year. Yet it's often instigated by mothers and aunts.

Despite having experienced the physical and psychological agony of it for themselves, older women allow this to continue, sometimes even evading the law to get their daughters cut, because they believe they're preparing them for a world in which this is expected. Their fear is that girls won't find husbands inside their communities unless they go through this rite of passage. Surrender may be morally reprehensible, but when there are few other options, it can also feel pragmatic.

As the archaeologist Catherine Cameron tells me, for the girls and young women who were taken captive in the historical societies she has studied, survival and stability were often a matter of compromise. Safety could sometimes come in the form of marriage to their captors. If there was no hope of escape, at least as wives they might have a shot at changing their status. "The older you get, the more influence you get or the more power you get," she explains.

"A young fourteen-year-old girl dragged from another group has no power; she has nothing. She may be abused by the other women in the group, may be raped by the men, terrible things happening to her. But if she survives that, if she's taken by one man, that's some sort of stability." In the end, she's simply making the best of it. The more ties that are formed, the more secure her life becomes. "Children, that's another level of status. She can move up in status by having the man's child."

In the 1980s, Deniz Kandiyoti, a professor of development studies at SOAS University of London, coined the term "patriarchal bargain" to describe the ways in which women strategize within the constraints of systems dominated by more powerful and usually older men—those whom we might refer to as patriarchs. Kandiyoti showed how important it was to recognize that even when people are caged, there may be cages within their cages. Different forms of patriarchy call for different trade-offs, but they're all aimed at maximizing the benefits a person receives and reducing the costs they have to bear.

For a young bride marrying into a patrilineal, patrilocal family, this bargain plays out over a lifetime. The hardship she experiences now will eventually be replaced by the authority she will wield over her own daughters-in-law as a mother-in-law. Her "subordination to men is offset by the control older women attain over younger women," writes Kandiyoti.

This might explain why some older women end up applying pressure not just on younger women to live up to their gendered obligations but also on younger men to live up to theirs. Both women and men may be pressured into heterosexual marriage, and then also pushed to have children. The mothers of sons in patrilocal families also need to make sure that nobody breaks ranks by marrying the "wrong" person, splitting loyalties between partners and elders. Arranged or forced marriages have been one way of ensuring that the bargain works for older family members. This is one part women play in upholding patriarchal control.

In his memoirs, published in 2020, Nazir Afzal, the former chief crown prosecutor for North West England who has long campaigned against so-called honor crimes in Britain, describes the case of Surjit Athwal, a young customs officer who worked at London's Heathrow Airport. In an unhappy arranged marriage since she was sixteen, Athwal began an affair with another man. She eventually asked her husband for a divorce. Incensed by the suggestion, her mother-in-law ordered her murder. The family lured her to India, where she was strangled and dumped in a river by her husband's uncle.

Athwal's husband and his mother tried to cover up the crime. Both received life sentences after a campaign for justice by her brother, Jagdeesh. But what particularly disturbed Afzal about this case was that the mother-in-law showed so little remorse for the murder. When he saw her in prison, she threw insults at him in Punjabi. "She didn't care if she was going to be locked up in a jail for twenty-five years," he writes. As far as the mother-in-law was concerned, she was the hero. She had rescued her family's honor.

She had kept her end of the bargain.

The complexity of the patriarchal bargain multiplies when women find themselves negotiating between different patriarchal systems. In 2014, the call to #BringBackOurGirls trended across social media, prompting desperate efforts to rescue hundreds of schoolchildren kidnapped by Boko Haram in Nigeria. It was a campaign that united the globe, from Michelle Obama in the White House to Pope Francis at the Vatican. News reports emerged of girls who had likely died in captivity. There was the occasional story, too, of girls who successfully managed to escape. But there was one narrative that nobody expected: even when offered freedom, a small number of the abducted girls chose to stay with the men who had taken them.

Abduction and radicalization leave psychological scars. They confuse emotions, attaching captives to their captors in the same way that women trafficked into sexual slavery can be beaten into surrender. Some of the girls had given birth to children by these men and didn't want to abandon their families. They weren't always welcomed home by their parents either. But there was another factor at play here for a few. In an article published by the

BBC, one young woman told the journalist Adaobi Tricia Nwaubani that she enjoyed having the respect of others in the group as a Boko Haram wife. She had women working as slaves beneath her.

A psychologist who had been working with Boko Haram members to draw them out of radicalization explained that these girls had come from patriarchal communities in which, for the most part, they had never worked, had held no power, had no voice. All of a sudden, albeit as captives, they were in command of as many as thirty to a hundred other women who were at their beck and call. Their freedom began to seem relative. Staring at the prospect of going home, the psychologist said, they realized they would be "returning to societies where they are not going to be able to wield that kind of power."

■　　■　　■

Freedom is a concept that has become central to modern democracies. We staunchly defend it.

But, as Orlando Patterson has argued, most human relationships in reality reflect some degree of ownership of one person over another. We recognize freedom as something distinct, he suggests, only because so many people in history have had to live in the state of not having it at all. Even now, all of us are under someone's authority to a degree, whether it's our parents, our partners, our employers, or the state. It's the way this authority is exercised through the law and the eyes of society, the amount of agency we have in these relationships, and our ability to negotiate within them that determine how free we really are.

Around a thousand years ago, the bones of sixty-six women were dumped in the La Plata Valley of the American Southwest, in what is now northern New Mexico. In 2010, in an effort to figure out what had happened here, researchers at the University of Nevada published a study of their remains. Based on the patterns of trauma they could see on the skeletons, they con-cluded that these women were most probably captives who had been violently overpowered and struck with all kinds of everyday objects. Some of them had then been worked to the bone.

Not every woman in this community was treated this way. While the captives' bodies were found prostrate and sprawled, other women had been buried with more care and respect. The best guess on the part of the research-ers was that the captives were minorities with little or no status. They had never fully integrated into the society. And this made them victims of abuse from all sides. The captive women had labored to death, while higher status women living alongside them were doing less heavy work. In fact, they must also have benefited from their labor.

What the La Plata Valley case shows is that there's a territory between the slave and the wife, between the genuine captive and the free woman, in which status has always been negotiated. What tips the balance one way or the other are the independent resources we can command, and how much care and support we can expect from others. Our survival and well-being depend ultimately on human relationships. Security lies in knowing that we have somewhere to turn to if things go wrong, cushioning us from the hazards of the world.

The matrilineal communities of the Khasi Hills in Meghalaya, India, show how different women's lives can be when they don't have to leave their families after marriage and can instead stay near those who prioritize them. A study published in 2007 found that mothers in Khasi families helped their daughters make better quality choices about who to marry. These daughters were supported in resisting potential exploitation—and this could be measured physically. Women who lived with their mothers were "significantly taller" than those whose mothers lived elsewhere, which suggested that they were better fed and cared for. Khasi women who lived independently from both their husbands *and* their mothers happened to be the tallest of all.

The late anthropologist Ruby Rohrlich described the rise of the patrilineal family as involving the "subversion of kinship relationships," wresting women from the socioeconomic and religious solidarity of their own clans. Isolating brides within patrilocal families undermines the potential for sisterhood in every sense of the word. While brothers stay together in the same communities, sisters are sent off separately to marry, dropped into uncertain futures. If male-dominated institutions have grown as much as they have in more patriarchal societies, part of the reason must be that it's easier for men who are related to each other to foster trust and work together, to consolidate their power in fraternal solidarity. For wives isolated from everyone they've known since childhood, that kind of solidarity is impossible.

It's when we have nobody to turn to that we are at our most vulnerable. Orlando Patterson has described the experience of slavery as "natal alienation," an existence in which family ties of all kinds are rendered deliberately unstable and replaced by the bond between the master and the slave, the oppressor and the oppressed. "Because a slave was human, she wanted desperately to belong to her parents, her kinfolk, and through them to her ancestors; she wanted her children to belong to her, and she wanted those ties to be secure and strong," he writes. "But all ties were precarious."

Those ties are what we seek out. We're lost without them. The psychologist Carol Gilligan and the psychoanalyst Naomi Snider have argued that the effect of patriarchal systems has been to push men into believing that they are the only ones with a self. Women are forced to believe that they are selfless. At the extremes, men and women become emotionally detached from each other. Patriarchy persists, they suggest, "because it renders the loss of relationship irreparable."

This is what makes the concept of freedom, and also of women's liberation, as nuanced as it is. To be free, truly free with no ties to anyone at all, can be risky and precarious when we actually have it. It can leave a person open to other kinds of abuse or exploitation. Patterson explains that "the real antithesis to slavery in societies where the personalistic idiom of power was dominant was what may be called countervailing power." What we need are other powerful networks that we can escape into, ones that are able to absorb and protect us.

More than an abstract freedom, people need systems that can lift them up.

CHAPTER 7

Revolution

Tradition dictated that the oldest politician elected to the German Reichstag should preside over the parliament's new session. In 1932, that person was seventy-five-year-old Clara Zetkin.

On the day itself there was some doubt about whether she would be able to make it to the building at all. She had to be carried in on a stretcher, then lifted to her feet with the help of a cane, according to a journalist from *TIME* magazine. Grandmother Zetkin, as she had been dubbed, sweated with pain and fatigue. Two "big-hipped Amazonian" women supported her as she made her way up the stairs. She looked too weak even to pick up the Speaker's bell, let alone ring it, the report continued. Every part of her was unsteady. She wiped her forehead, drank some water.

And then she gave a speech that lasted more than forty minutes.

Zetkin was a member of Germany's Communist Party, a strong force in national politics for almost fifteen years. But the country had approached a turning point in its history. Adolf Hitler was in attendance that day at the Reichstag. Fascist thugs were congregating outside. The Nazis were a year away from coming into power. Once they did, the Communist Party would be banned. Thousands of its supporters would be killed or sent to concentration camps, adding to those already persecuted and murdered in the decades before.

But on the day of Zetkin's speech, there was still the faint hope that things might turn out differently, that citizens could be swayed toward another vision for Germany. The Russian revolutionary and Soviet leader Vladimir Lenin was once said to have remarked that the German communists had only one good man—and that was a woman: Clara Zetkin. She used her moment in the spotlight to rail against those who were seizing control of her country with empty promises of returning to some imagined glorious past. Her plea instead was for a fresh future, a radical alternative to what had gone before.

"The fight of the labouring masses against the disastrous suffering of the present is, at the same time, the fight for their full liberation," she declared, calling on ordinary workers to erase generations of historic oppression by rising up against exploitation by capitalists and imperialists. Echoing Karl Marx and Friedrich Engels, the philosophical founders of communism, she spoke about the millions of women who needed to be freed from the "the chains of sex slavery." For her, women's emancipation would be achieved through economic independence, not just from husbands and fathers but from every oppressor.

Like other communists of her era, Zetkin didn't consider herself a feminist. Far from it. She laughed at the idea that there was some universal sisterhood wrapping "a unifying ribbon around bourgeois ladies and female proletarians." Different women had different problems. It was impossible for the wealthy and privileged to understand the lives of ordinary working people, not least when women at the top of society directly benefited from the cheap labor of female servants and factory workers. So, she actively distanced herself from what she saw as the "bourgeois feminism" of the capitalist elites.

Zetkin's focus instead was on those at the very bottom of society's heap.

Years later, this would strike a chord with others, among them, the influential activist Angela Davis, who had been a member of both the US Communist Party and the Black Panthers. In her 1981 book *Women, Race & Class*, Davis explained that "working-class women and Black women alike were fundamentally linked to their men by the class exploitation and racist oppression which did not discriminate between the sexes." Women had long aligned themselves with powerful men to suppress the rights of other women. The racism of the American suffrage movement was one example. Liberation had to be for everyone, Davis argued, or it wasn't really liberation at all.

This was the promise of socialism.

It's a message that survives in feminist activism into the twenty-first century. In their 2019 manifesto *Feminism for the 99%*, the academics and organizers of the International Women's Strike in the United States, Cinzia Arruzza, Tithi Bhattacharya, and Nancy Fraser are clear that gender equality can't be achieved in a racist, imperialist society. "But we also understand," they write, "that the root of the problem is capitalism." What good is a feminism so diluted into the broader political landscape, they argue, that the best we can hope for is that a few women will smash glass ceilings and have as much power as the wealthiest men, while watching immigrant, working-class, and lower-caste women clear up the shattered glass on the floor underneath them?

The problem for Zetkin and other socialist women in the early twentieth century was that Communist Party leaders tended to be men, and they tended to speak with other men in mind. Even among revolutionaries, women came second. Until 1908, most parts of Germany legally barred women from joining political parties. The Communist Party, too, wasn't beyond nurturing a cult of masculinity wrapped around stereotypes of the macho, musclebound working man. As a prominent figure in the struggle, Zetkin tried to help her comrades remember their responsibility to women's liberation. At a major conference in Copenhagen in 1910 she helped propose an International Women's Day, still celebrated now. But male solidarity and misogyny in the upper ranks of communist leadership never completely disappeared.

For all these struggles, on that day in 1932 it was Clara Zetkin who had the world's attention. It's likely that most of the people in the Reichstag who heard her speech didn't share her political views. But she still commanded their respect. A journalist from the *New York Evening Post* wrote that when she finished speaking, "the galleries burst into wild applause that was not a political demonstration but a tribute to the purely physical courage of the old revolutionary."

She wouldn't survive to see the communist state she wanted in Germany. When the Nazis took power, Zetkin fled to Russia. She died there shortly afterward.

■　　■　　■

History doesn't stand still. More than a decade after Clara Zetkin's death, Germany would experience another political overhaul. And this one would finally bring her hope to reality.

In 1949, after its defeat in the Second World War, the country was divided into two parts. The larger, western portion of the country retained a capitalist economic system, under the authority of American, British, and French allies. This was now the Federal Republic of Germany. The smaller, eastern part became a satellite state of the Soviet Union. And this region was now known as the German Democratic Republic.

In the new socialist state that had been created, Zetkin arose from the history books as an icon. Her face was put on the ten-mark banknote and the twenty-mark coin. The German Democratic Republic would issue postage stamps with her image. East German cities would name streets after her. Angela Davis, too, was hailed as an anti-imperialist hero and featured on posters. Enormous crowds gathered to see her when she came to East Berlin in 1972.

The division between East and West Germany would last forty years until shortly after the fall of the Berlin Wall, in 1989, when the country was reunified. What happened in the meantime, in the Soviet Union from 1917 and then in other socialist states, was perhaps the biggest human experiment of modern times. In theory at least, the goal of the revolution was to fundamentally change how people thought about and behaved with each other, to rid them not just of the economic chains of oppression but of the mental chains as well.

In the process, every aspect of life would be challenged, from cultural traditions to ancient faiths. Soviet leaders encouraged atheism, in line with their conviction that religion was bourgeois and exploitative. In the German Democratic Republic, the number of people who identified as Protestant or Catholic fell from around 90 percent in 1950 to a little more than 30 percent in 1989. Literature, including children's books, reflected the anti-capitalist, anti-imperialist politics of the Soviet Union. So-called Red Westerns turned Hollywood movies on their heads by portraying Native Americans as the heroes and cowboys as the villains. The underdog was now the protagonist.

Everyone had work. Prices of goods were set by the state, not by markets, so life was affordable. But since Western imports were rare, this meant there weren't always enough of the things people wanted. Supply chains were unreliable. Occasionally, if there was overproduction, there would be a sudden glut of particular products. Writing about her experiences under communism, the Croatian journalist Slavenka Drakulić recalls "the shortages, the distinctive odors, the shabby clothing." A grown man, writes Drakulić, ate his first banana with the skin on because he didn't know he was supposed to peel it. That lack of bananas became a popular metaphor for everyday life in the Soviet Union, an existence in which otherwise ordinary goods had the potential to turn into luxuries.

But the worst of communism, as we know, weren't the shortages. Under the Russian leader Joseph Stalin, life in the Soviet Union was bloody and brutal, a seemingly endless string of purges, executions, rapes, and restrictions. Millions were sent to labor camps. To keep the system intact, there was widespread surveillance, next to no freedom of movement, no space for political dissent. Such was the horror that fascism and communism are today spoken about in the same breath. The political ideologies behind them couldn't have been more different, but as the journalist and historian Anne Applebaum has written, "If we don't feel at least as much revulsion for the crimes of communism as we do for the crimes of Nazism, we will be condemned to misunderstand both our own past and that of others."

The weight of those crimes sits heavily, as I see for myself when I travel to Germany. An old cobbled street in Berlin that was once dedicated to Clara Zetkin has since been given back its former name Dorotheenstrasse, after a Prussian princess. At the DDR Museum on the bank of the River Spree in Berlin, I'm offered a lesson on what a depressing police state the German Democratic Republic became—and how grateful we should all be that it has been left behind. An interrogation room and jail cell have been recreated for visitors to step inside. A rickety Trabant automobile is on display at the front of the museum, jokingly labeled "cardboard on wheels." From brutalist tower blocks to polyamide clothes, the portrait is of an authoritarian dystopia that struggled to stay afloat.

Yet, as long ago as state socialism feels now, there are still those who recall that era with a sense of wistfulness. Maybe we can't help but search for the light in the shade. It's the light our hearts want to remember. I hear one woman complain that her city declined after the fall of the Berlin Wall, leaving her adult children no choice but to leave to find work. At the DDR museum store, visitors eagerly snap up memorabilia—replica household objects and toys.

There are a few, too, who remember the radical hope that underpinned the socialist model. For a while, they had lived in a parallel universe, one in which a population temporarily followed entirely different rules from its neighbors. The Soviet Union was a place in which, for a brief moment, revolutionaries believed they could make real their egalitarian vision for the world. As badly as it turned out in the end, they did manage to achieve some of those goals. And the nostalgia for what wasn't so terrible about that time has led some to even revisit the socialist roots of many of today's struggles for equality. They can be seen in the ideals that Zetkin stood for more than a century ago: for women's right to vote, to be involved in politics, to go to university, to have legal equality in marriage, to be free of moral double standards around sexuality, and, above all, to not be exploited by anyone at all. In a sense, Zetkin was intersectional in her fight for change before the word existed.

When I visit Zetkin's former home to the north of Berlin, in Birkenwerder, Brandenburg—now preserved as a memorial—it's clear that I'm one of few people who make this pilgrimage. A bronze sculpture of her stands in the garden next to the empty street. Zetkin remains on the margins of women's history. She's rarely commemorated, even on International Women's Day. But for those who have made efforts to study state socialism in the twentieth century, as brutal as that era was, the archives reveal something remarkable. Gender relations in the Soviet Union did change. In among the rubble of old regimes, those original ideals resulted in some gains for women, even if they haven't always been well recognized.

A genuine attempt had been made in the twentieth century to smash the patriarchy.

■   ■   ■

In the autumn of 2018, my husband and I were sitting in a modern, sunny restaurant in the heart of Prague, the lunch guests of two Czech gender scholars. Parents to a young child we had left behind with grandparents in London to make this trip, we had just one thing on our minds: affordable childcare. We complained about how miserable it was to see our wages being drained by nursery fees just so we could have time to work. Other friends of ours, mostly women but a few men as well, had paused their careers to stay at home. I imagined it wasn't so different for families in the Czech Republic. Wasn't this the universal struggle, after all? Wasn't the inequity of childcare and housework the perennial thorn in the side of women's liberation?

From across the table, one of the women there smiled at us. "We remember when we had all the childcare we wanted," she said. "The issue we have now is that women want to stay at home and be traditional housewives!"

The history of feminism at this end of Europe wasn't the same as it was in Britain, where I had grown up. In former socialist states, the struggle had taken an entirely different trajectory. In North America and Western Europe, countries had long ago thrown their weight firmly behind democracy, individualism, and capitalism, accepting some degree of social inequality as the price to pay for these freedoms. Everyone couldn't have everything they wanted, but they would at least have a shot at working to get it. The state would occasionally step in to provide for people's basic needs, perhaps when it came to children's education or unemployment benefits. But by and large, women who wanted full equality with men were left to fight for piecemeal reform over decades.

Communists, on the other hand, wanted to see the state disappear altogether. All property would be commonly owned. There would be no hierarchies and no inequality. Everyone would work for the shared good in line with their talents. In the end, they hoped, the family would wither away as well. Instead of husband and wives, there would be equal, autonomous individuals, free to love as they chose with mutual respect for each other. Wider society would help raise children.

Until they achieved this radical utopia, communist revolutionaries settled for state socialism, a kind of halfway house in which those at the top of the Communist Party set policies and laws aimed at eliminating inequality as fast as possible. In reality, as we now know, these leaders ended up steering society with a crushing authoritarian hand, one that would turn out to be unimaginably ruthless. They would end up far from their ideals. But in the beginning at least, they did act quickly on some of their goals—particularly when it came to women's liberation.

"In all civilized countries, even the most advanced, women are actually no more than domestic slaves. Women do not enjoy full equality in any capitalist state, not even in the freest of republics," Vladimir Lenin had declared at the First All-Russia Congress of Working Women in 1918, having become head of the Soviet state after the revolution the year before. He would later write about how, for the married woman, "petty housework crushes, strangles, stultifies and degrades her, chains her to the kitchen and the nursery." Like Engels before him, he saw the struggle against oppression to be inside the home as well as outside it.

"One of the primary tasks of the Soviet Republic," Lenin announced, "is to abolish all restrictions on women's rights."

And that's precisely what it began to do. One of the first political changes that the communist leadership introduced when it took power in Russia was to put women on an equal legal footing with men, notes the British historian and political scientist Archie Brown. In 1917, all women were given the right to vote, a year before any women in Britain, and three years before any in the United States. Civil marriage replaced religious marriage. Divorce was made easier and cheaper. In 1920, Soviet Russia became the first country in the world to legalize abortion.

Gains in women's equality were precarious, however, as they were everywhere. The Soviet Union under Stalin would make abortion illegal in 1936 to raise falling birth rates, before legalizing it again in 1955 after Stalin had died. Russia and its neighbors had been deeply patriarchal for centuries. People wouldn't relinquish their old beliefs without a struggle. Stereotypes wouldn't just vanish. Gender inequalities and abuses inside the home would be largely neglected by Soviet policymakers. Tensions and contradictions like these would ultimately undermine the system. But for the time, the disruptions to gender norms in those early years broke new ground.

Ultimately, the class struggle still took center stage in Soviet Russia. Other forms of inequality were thought to be rooted in class divisions, so it was assumed they would all crumble together. Because of this foundational premise, freedom from oppression was believed to come through work. If women had their own incomes, they couldn't be trapped in marriages or families that didn't work for them, went the logic. Employment was their route to freedom. So, early in Soviet history, educational opportunities expanded for women as well as for men. Everyone, regardless of their gender, was given the right to paid employment. And they were expected to take it up. In 1936, the Soviet Politburo, the Communist Party's ultimate policy-making body, made it a criminal offence to deny a pregnant woman work or to lower her pay.

The Second World War saw women all over the world recruited into work traditionally done by men, but in the Soviet Union they also joined the military at rates not seen anywhere else. The historian Pamela Toler has written that the Soviet Union made the most dramatic use of women soldiers. Eight hundred thousand served as combatants in the Red Army, several thousand of them on the front as snipers, machine gunners, and tank crews, among other roles. More than a hundred thousand women were decorated for bravery during the war, she adds.

In Central and Eastern Europe, as state socialism expanded beyond Russia, women were encouraged to enroll in technical colleges. They became scientists and engineers. Families were provided with infant daycare and preschools as a matter of course. In the German Democratic Republic, the number of daycare places per thousand children soared from 13 in 1950 to 811 in 1986. Cheap public laundries and canteens took up at least some of the burden of housework and cooking.

Individual socialist states would adopt their own approaches depending on their circumstances. Slovakia, for example, was largely rural in the early 1950s. "The target there was to industrialize the country, and in order to do that they needed to shift women from family farms to factories and urban centers," I'm told by the gender scholar Blanka Nyklová at the Institute of

Sociology in Prague. To sell young women that proposition, the state linked urban life with "the idea of emancipation from the family and having the capacity to decide for yourself what your future's going to be. It does not have to be that you stay in the same village for your whole life with someone you don't necessarily want to marry."

Men became used to women working alongside them. Across almost all professions and industries, the idea of the working woman became normalized. And it remains that way to this day. "You are expected as a woman here to hold a job," says Nyklová.

But nowadays this part of socialist history has been largely shelved from public view, outside the memories of those who lived through it. Maybe there's a fear that talking about the positives of that time might betray a sympathy with former authoritarian regimes. But there's another barrier. If I knew relatively little about the lives of women in Central and Eastern Europe until I traveled to Germany, the Czech Republic, and Hungary and met them for myself, it was partly because of the ideological divide that went up between the East and the West after the Second World War. When the former British prime minister Winston Churchill described this in a speech in 1946 as an "iron curtain" descending over the region, the phrase stuck.

In the early years of the Cold War, there were few ways for those on the outside to know what was going on inside the Soviet Union. Communication was limited. It became a world behind a looking glass. To this day, archives from that era aren't easily accessible. Until the curtain fell, the only people who could offer much of a clue as to what was happening on the other side (aside from Soviet propagandists) were those who managed to leave.

■ ■ ■

Between 1950 and 1953, scholars at Harvard University, sponsored by the United States Air Force, interviewed hundreds of refugees and émigrés who had left the Soviet Union.

As the Americans put it, they hoped to understand "the social and psychological strengths and weaknesses of the Soviet system." Their goal was to figure out how state socialism managed to keep ticking, how much support it really had among its citizens, and whether it might be powerful enough to spread. Reams and reams of yellowing typewritten notes offer windows into how people felt about the seismic political shift they had lived through. These interviews, referred to by some academics simply as the "Harvard Project," have turned out to be one of the most revealing sources of information about the Soviet Union.

"Do you think that Soviet women in general want to work or not outside the home?" a Harvard interviewer probed.

"Women usually prefer the home situation, but in the Soviet Union conditions are such that women start to work at an early age," went the reply from one. "It does give them some independence. If they divorce, for example, then they have to work. It gives freedom to women. A woman feels free when she gets work." They went on to say that "to be only a housewife is something shameful. It is a trait of the petty bourgeoisie."

In another interview, a doctor was asked what the gender ratio was like when he was at medical school in Soviet Russia.

"There were more men than women when I studied but later there were more women than men and there were even special legal percentages on this score," he responded, implying that there had been quotas to encourage gender balance. "There were women who were big professors in the Soviet Union, even surgeons."

A fifty-six-year-old stenographer mentioned that women were treated absolutely equally under the educational system. "We had some excellent women chemists," she remarked. "In the Soviet Union there was no discrimination against women and they worked at the toughest jobs as well as men. They worked in the mines for example, underground."

Women began smoking in the streets after the revolution, according to one person. Other transcripts suggested that women felt free to initiate divorces, as men did, and weren't socially stigmatized for it.

Historians have to be careful with this sort of evidence. These interviews can't be viewed as entirely reliable because they were given by the people who most desperately wanted to leave the Soviet Union. But, then, perhaps this makes it all the more powerful that some of them so openly acknowledged how gender equality did exist for them in the Soviet Union—even when life was harsh in other ways. "Nothing is good except from the equality of men and women," said one middle-aged woman who was working as an economist, but felt frustrated at not being able to fully stretch herself intellectually.

The Harvard Project interviews leave little doubt that the socialist experiment in Russia had shaken up social norms. But what's just as revealing for scholars today is the prurient fascination of the American interviewers with the intimate details of Soviet women's everyday lives, the jobs they did, their relationships. Between the lines, it's impossible not to notice a concern that the communists might come for the United States next—and that the Soviet political system might actually prove attractive to women.

On the other side of the Iron Curtain, in American suburbia, life couldn't have been more different. In the 1950s, the same decade in which the Harvard Project interviews were being carried out, middle-class American women were being encouraged to give up work after they got married. Heterosexual marriage was seen as the only legitimate path through adulthood. Divorce was frowned upon. The historian Elaine Tyler May writes that, as paradoxical as it may sound, traditional gender roles were seen to underpin the *modern* post-war home in the United States. The country championed individualism, she notes, yet most people at that time chose to conform to social expectation. Of those who came of age during or after the Second World War, around 95 percent were married.

It hadn't always been this way. In 1909, thousands of textile workers in New York, many of them immigrants and Jewish women, led a strike to fight for better pay and working conditions. There was another garment workers' strike in Chicago in 1910. By 1920, according to the historian of gender and sexuality Lillian Faderman, women made up almost a third of the labor force in the United States. In the years leading up to the Second World War, the number of women in college education and in work outside the home went up. The image of a tough, muscly "Rosie the Riveter" was used to recruit women into the war effort.

But the end of the war saw a backlash against the working woman. The state needed families to have more children and for the men who had come back after fighting to have jobs to go to. The male breadwinner earning enough to keep a suburban housewife in comfort was now being promoted as the aspirational ideal, centuries after the Founding Fathers had first nurtured it as a cornerstone of American democracy. People were marrying at higher rates in the 1950s than in the years immediately before or after the war. A Gallup poll carried out in 1957, writes Faderman, found that 80 percent of Americans agreed that "a woman who chose not to marry was sick, neurotic, or immoral." Women's fashion designers, she adds, began emphasizing small waists and big hips and breasts. Magazines and books advised women on how to become better prospective wives and warned about the potential downsides for the children of working mothers.

The world of work in the United States had by then become so deeply skewed that it became difficult for some to even imagine women and men doing the same jobs. Male scientists and engineers had cultivated cultures that sought to associate ingenuity, rationality, and skill with masculinity, further marginalizing women who tried to break into their ranks. Gendered stereotypes were arguably as strong as they had ever been.

That's not to say that stereotypes didn't exist in the Soviet Union, too. They did, especially around women in management and leadership. Men were running the Communist Party even at the end of Soviet rule. Even so, women made up 64 percent of machine operators and 42 percent of locomotive and motor drivers in 1954. The proportion of doctors who were women rose from 10 percent in 1913 to 79 percent in 1959. By that year, too, almost every pharmacist in the Soviet Union was a woman.

■   ■   ■

"I remember going to the US in the 1990s and realizing that people actually cooked dinner," I'm told by Éva Fodor, an associate professor of gender studies at Central European University, based in Budapest and Vienna. "This was beyond my wildest imagination!"

Fodor was raised in Hungary under state socialism by urban, intellectual parents who both worked. "I had lunch in the school canteen, and I went home and I had a sandwich for dinner. So, my mother never cooked dinner," she says. "People took food home from canteens." Her parents would take their linens to the public laundry service, where they would be washed and returned to them for "almost no money." Most children she knew went to the kindergarten as soon as they were old enough. This was how middle-class families like hers tended to live. For families in smaller towns or more rural areas, these options were scarcer. But for the people in her social circle, the state provided at least some of the support for the work that needed to be done at home by shifting the load to subsidized communal services outside it.

The revolutionary idea of fully socializing domestic labor was taken up by the activist Angela Davis in her writing in 1981. Davis asked why work at home couldn't be drawn into the industrial economy in the same way that grocery production had gone from being arduous household labor on small family farms to something done at scale by big agricultural corporations and food manufacturers. "Teams of trained and well-paid workers, moving from dwelling to dwelling, engineering technologically advanced cleaning machinery, could swiftly and efficiently accomplish what the present-day housewife does so arduously and primitively." Streamlined this way, housework could be provided at a rate that everyone could afford.

Davis described it as one of the most closely guarded secrets of capitalist societies: "the possibility—the real possibility—of radically transforming the nature of housework."

This dream was of course nowhere near being realized anywhere in the world. But in socialist states in Europe there was at least an effort to come close, allowing women to work at the rates that they did. Éva Fodor has compared workplace gender inequality in Hungary, where she grew up, to its neighbor Austria, which wasn't a socialist state but had a similar cultural history to Hungary's before their political systems diverged after the Second World War. In 1949, roughly a fifth of university students in both countries were women. By the 1970s, Hungary had reached gender parity. Austria wouldn't get there until the end of the century. In 1982, only 5 percent of Hungarian women were classified as housewives. In Austria, it was 40 percent. Legislation into the 1970s required a married woman in Austria to seek permission from her husband before she could work.

The way Hungary achieved such rapid progress in gender equality, Fodor shows, was through a combination of legislation, propaganda, quotas, generous maternity leave, kindergartens and nurseries that were often located inside factories and workplaces, and social and health incentives tied to work, such as sick child leave and hot subsidized meals. Hungarian socialist state institutions played an important role in "reshaping, reducing, and redefining gender inequalities not only in the short but also in the long term," she writes. "Neither market forces, a higher degree of economic development, nor a more autonomous feminist movement achieved significant gender equality in Austria."

If the two countries were seen as cultural laboratories, it's clear which one delivered faster change: the socialist state that took the lead in introducing bold reforms.

Because of the widespread changes to patterns of labor in former socialist states, people still think differently about working women more than thirty years after the fall of the Iron Curtain. Germany's Institute for Employment Research found that, decades after reunification, the gender pay gap in eastern

Germany in 2016 was a little more than 6 percent, while in western Germany it was in excess of 23 percent. In the east German university city of Cottbus, in Brandenburg, the pay gap was slightly in favor of women.

"Socialist states have changed gender norms. The norm of women working for wages changed within the span of fifteen years," says Fodor. "It created a lasting change in attitude. The notion that women are working for wages is perfectly normal, women having a career or at least women finding meaning in work."

Fodor's colleague Jasmina Lukić, a professor of comparative literature and gender studies at Central European University, has written that, growing up under socialism in Belgrade, "it was unimaginable to think that my salary would be lower because I was a woman." Lukić recalls that when she moved to Canada in the 1970s as a student, the difference was such that she couldn't see herself reflected in the feminist struggles there. Her cultural experience until then had been worlds apart. "I was always offended that Daisy Duck persistently wanted to marry Donald Duck, who was such a dope, and that Minnie Mouse kept hitting the garage wall with her car." In her case, she writes, "my mother was the only one in my family who knew how to drive and my father was lacking in any form of technical knowledge and skills."

Today, while Western Europe and the United States continue to struggle with some of the lowest rates of women in science, engineering, and technology in the world, the same problem doesn't exist in parts of Central and Eastern Europe. The international scientific journal *Nature* reported in 2019 that, when judged by the proportion of published papers authored by women, Central and Eastern European universities were among the best in the world when it came to gender balance. Poland's Medical University of Lublin and University of Gdansk came first and fourth. The University of Belgrade came third. By contrast, Harvard University came 286th and the Federal Institute of Technology in Zurich was 807th.

The cultural legacy of normalizing women as scientists and engineers lingers across former socialist states. "If a girl says she wants to be an engineer, I don't think it's strange. I don't think people think that's odd," says Fodor, whose own mother had trained to be an engineer in the 1950s, when women in Hungary were being encouraged to study at technical colleges.

The computer scientist Hasmik Gharibyan at California Polytechnic State University has written that in the computer science department of Yerevan State University in the former Soviet republic of Armenia, the proportion of women never fell below 75 percent throughout the 1980s and 1990s. She and her co-author found it necessary to point out that "this is not a typo."

The Institute of Labor Economics in Bonn published a paper in 2018 showing that the gender gap in achievement in mathematics was smaller in eastern Germany than it was in western Germany. After 1991, former socialist states were sending more girls than other countries to compete at the International Mathematical Olympiad, an annual contest for high school students. The researchers explained that before reunification, girls had for generations been seeing different gender stereotypes depending on where they lived. In West Germany, boys and girls hadn't even followed the same curricula at school. In East Germany, between 1949 and 1989, one of the most popular magazines, the *Neue Berliner Illustrierte*, would show "professionally active and 'emancipated' women, working as journalists, professors, brigadiers or factory workers."

Similarly, studies looking at the many thousands of Jewish immigrants who moved to Israel from the former Soviet Union in the early 1990s have found that high school girls in this cohort were far more likely to choose to study science, technology, engineering, and mathematics than girls whose families hadn't moved from the former Soviet Union. Women from the former Soviet Union were also more likely to work full-time than both native-born Israelis and other immigrants, and to work in science and engineering. Researchers noticed that because they had been used to having plenty of childcare, these immigrants set up their own network of private daycare facilities with far longer operating hours than the ones otherwise available.

Women had essentially tried to recreate in Israel the childcare conditions they previously had under state socialism.

■　■　■

"What we want is to make easier the life of our housewives," Richard Nixon, then vice president of the United States, told Soviet leader Nikita Khrushchev in 1959 at the launch of an American cultural exhibition in Moscow. Nixon pointed with pride to the kitchen of a model home containing what was at that moment the height of domestic luxury: an integrated, front-loading automatic washing machine.

This encounter between Nixon and Khrushchev, both men holding court on what they thought women really wanted, came to be known as the "Kitchen Debate."

"Nixon insisted that American superiority in the cold war rested not on weapons, but on the secure, abundant family life of modern suburban homes," writes the historian Elaine Tyler May. More than a century after the last Founding Father had died, Nixon still believed that it was in the home that American women found happiness, freedom, and the good life.

Khrushchev told him in response that in the Soviet Union they didn't have this kind of "capitalist attitude toward women," treating people as transactional property to be kept at home in a kind of domestic bondage. Soviet women were free to work, to have independent lives, to leave their husbands. Societies had labored under myths of female inferiority and natural subordination for thousands of years. Now it was becoming clear just how vacuous those myths really were. The Soviet Union had shown that there were no natural constraints on what women could achieve given the opportunity. Outwardly at least, gender equality was brandished as a symbol of socialism's modernity compared to capitalism.

In reality, though, neither Nixon nor Khrushchev was telling the full story from the ground in their countries.

Plenty of women were employed in the United States, not least because they had no other option. As ever, the dream of female domesticity was available only to those who could afford it. But the dream itself was also beginning to show cracks. In her 1963 book *The Feminine Mystique*, Betty Friedan would capture the growing dissatisfaction of housewives, trapped in bubbles of romanticized domesticity, trying to live up to what was expected of them but not feeling fulfilled by it.

"The problem lay buried, unspoken, for many years in the minds of American women," wrote Friedan. "Each suburban wife struggled with it alone. As she made the beds, shopped for groceries, matched slipcover material, ate peanut butter sandwiches with her children, chauffeured Cub Scouts and Brownies, lay beside her husband at night—she was afraid to ask even of herself the silent question—'Is this all?'" Some of the women she interviewed had turned to alcohol or tranquilizers to numb their unhappiness. A disconnect had emerged between the image that the United States presented to the world and the mood of its own citizens.

More and more American women had sacrificed their professional dreams to stay at home. As Friedan noted, this could be measured in the dramatic plunge in the proportion of women in higher education. In 1920, 47 percent of American college students were women, she wrote. By 1958 that figure had fallen to 35 percent. Cataloguing the problems with America's ideal of the domesticated housewife, Friedan's book helped launch the women's liberation movement in the United States.

The irony was that much of what American feminists would be demanding, women in parts of the Soviet Union already had. And as early as 1896, almost seven decades before Friedan, Clara Zetkin had herself written about bourgeois housewives, "tired of living like dolls in doll houses."

American victory in the ideological gender battle of the Cold War counted on women being happy housewives, taking a back seat in public life, parking their careers for their families. "Political and economic elites really upheld the stay-at-home wife, breadwinner-homemaker model as a kind of unique symbol of Americans' success, as opposed to the Soviet model of women's emancipation and gender equality, which they saw as very, very threatening," I'm told by the University of Pennsylvania professor Kristen Ghodsee, who has researched women's roles under state socialism in Russia and Eastern Europe. "There was a real heavy pressure in the late forties and fifties to maintain the patriarchal nuclear family."

This left little room to maneuver for those who wanted anything else. At a time when it was dangerous for anyone to admit to having communist sympathies, it may have been expedient for Betty Friedan to play down her roots as a left-wing trade union journalist in the 1940s, suggests Ghodsee, and instead put the emphasis on her personal life as being the major influence on her work. In the United States, the idea of female emancipation had become so enmeshed with communist ideology that leaders were reluctant to concede anything to women's rights activists for fear of what this might mean politically. The thinking was that because the Soviets did it, it couldn't be done in the United States, explains Ghodsee.

Despite the long and vibrant tradition of women's rights activism in the United States, anti-discrimination legislation of the kind that existed in Soviet Russia since the Bolshevik Revolution wouldn't be introduced until the 1960s and 1970s. It took until 1973 for abortion to be decriminalized nationwide, and it has remained precarious even then.

According to Ghodsee, politics in the United States continues to be affected by the gender politics of the Cold War. She learned this the hard way in 2017 after writing an article for the *New York Times* with the controversial title "Why Women Had Better Sex Under Socialism." Ghodsee had argued that by making women less economically dependent on men, socialist states had given them a degree of agency and sexual freedom that they didn't have in capitalist countries. Women didn't feel compelled to marry for money or to stay in bad relationships, because they had paid work and state support. She expected some pushback from American critics. But not what actually came.

The article unleashed "a shitstorm of hatred and abuse and vitriol from the right wing of this country," she tells me. "It was awful, really awful. Death threats and rape threats."

Much of the criticism, says Ghodsee, came from conservatives and Christian evangelicals who believed that women were happier in the home, that women's rights had undermined families and damaged children. It wasn't just men who disagreed with her; it was women, too. "There's a whole kind of very conservative streak in the United States that thinks the fifties were the pinnacle of American superiority and that somehow it's rooted in the nuclear family." As far as they were concerned, a woman's place was and always had been in the home.

■   ■   ■

Soviet leader Nikita Khrushchev might have struck a raw nerve with Americans anxious about what state socialism could offer women. But in private, even the Soviets were uncertain about their own rhetoric. The men at the top of the Communist Party harbored doubts about the prospects for true gender equality.

In 1963, Russian engineer Valentina Tereshkova would become the first woman in space. On her return, Khrushchev wouldn't be able to resist a swipe at the West: "The bourgeoisie always claim that women are the weaker sex." Here was a female cosmonaut surviving possibly the most punishing physical journey a human could take. But as Tereshkova has disclosed in interviews since, the Soviet regime was actually so concerned about sending women into space that it would take them nineteen years to allow another woman to do it.

Just as there were cracks in the American ideal for women, so there were cracks in the Soviet one. Not everyone was happy in the jobs they had. As Slavenka Drakulić has written, women "had to work like men. . . . They worked on construction sites, on highways, in mines, in fields and in factories—the communist ideal was a robust woman who didn't look much different from a man." Party magazines, she observes, told women to be good workers and party members first. This didn't sit easily with those who had never signed up for it, or who yearned for a more traditional version of femininity.

In one dissident underground feminist magazine, a Russian writer declared: "WE WANT TO BE MOTHERS, WIVES, HOUSEWIVES—WOMEN AT LAST!"

The problem for both the East and the West was that women on each side were being forced to subscribe to a particular brand of womanhood, neither regime taking the time to find out what individual women wanted for themselves. While stereotypes of masculinity stayed intact (and largely the same) on both sides of the Iron Curtain, femininity became a battleground. Each side paraded their version as a sign of their own political superiority. In the Soviet Union, women were portrayed in official propaganda as round and rosy heroines riding tractors into the sunset, the historian Sheila Rowbotham has written. In popular culture in the West, meanwhile, Soviet women were caricatured as being devoid of womanliness, sometimes even sinister. They were "sitting behind desks in uniforms and judging men mercilessly."

Éva Fodor, like most scholars of the Soviet Union, is cautious of overstating communism's record on gender. Despite the stereotype of the strong, dominant Soviet woman, widespread misogyny persisted. Male leaders were suspicious of women banding together to demand rights separately from the socialist struggle. Women worked, but there was frequently a gendered division of labor that led to effective pay gaps. A large proportion of doctors were women, for instance, but surgeons were usually men—and surgeons were paid more.

There was still a firm sense of what made a woman a woman, and a man a man. Homosexuality wasn't decriminalized in East Germany until 1968, a year after it became legal in Britain. Even under a system ideologically committed to equality, there turned out to be limits to how far gender norms could be challenged. What was never accounted for was that humans don't start from scratch. We start with what we know, with legacies of tradition, honor, expectation, guilt, belief, and bias. There's only so much change we're able to accept in a short space of time.

Those failures could have been predicted. The old revolutionary Clara Zetkin herself didn't question that there should be a sexual division of labor within families. This wasn't only an ideological position she had chosen to take. It was a pragmatic one, too. A state needs citizens, and it needs people to give birth to and raise those citizens. This created a permanent tension between the rhetoric of women's emancipation and the state's demand to keep its population growing. The one belief that never disappeared throughout the history of communism in Russia and elsewhere was that women were mothers and carers first, even if they worked outside the home.

And this meant that women were hardly free of domestic drudgery. Work at home was often added to their work outside the home, creating an exhausting double burden that even supposedly enlightened socialist men were unwilling to share. Without so much as the respite of an integrated, front-loading automatic washing machine, Richard Nixon was right that life could be harder in some ways for Soviet women.

An article in the journal *New German Critique* in 1978 captured the problem. The number of unmarried women in East Germany at the time was rising. The birth rate was falling. Two-thirds of divorce applications were being filed by women. And one of the most common reasons for these breakups was apparent incompatibility of personality and outlook between husband and wife. The article speculated that "certainly a great deal of disagreement over the domestic division of labor must be part of that incompatibility."

Even so, the state neglected the division of labor inside people's homes for fear of alienating its social base—working men. "East German women came to rate employment as integral to their sense of self," writes Donna Harsch, a historian of twentieth-century Germany, in *The Revenge of the Domestic*, her book on women under state socialism. But nearly all Communist Party leaders were men, and "they benefited from the conventional, gendered division of domestic labor." Their commitment to making domestic work more equitable sometimes turned out to be little more than lip service. East Germany's *Family Law Book* of 1965 encouraged partners to take mutual responsibility for the household. But this rarely happened.

"The typical husband did not alter private habits to accommodate an employed wife," writes Harsch. There was an insistence that women and men be treated the same in their jobs outside the home. Inside the home, though, socialist leaders gently fell back on the belief that domestic gender roles were determined by biology. The socialist dream had been realized only part of the way.

The patriarchy could have been smashed. Instead, it was only dented. Trapped in a world in which they had paid employment and more rights, but few of the freedoms, goods, or labor-saving products available in the West, women in the Soviet Union understandably wondered whether the grass might be greener on the other side. In the end, their dissatisfaction became one of the many reasons people couldn't wait for the Iron Curtain to fall.

■   ■   ■

The decade after the collapse of state socialism in Central and Eastern Europe was instructive.

On the one hand, people were experiencing life without restrictions for the first time in decades. They could see friends and family in the West, they could travel, enjoy other cultures, buy goods from the rest of the world, read and publish what they wanted. They had bananas. In the rush to live life by new rules, there were some women who chose not to work now that they didn't have to. There was an uptick in those becoming full-time housewives and staying at home with their children. Research published by the Leibniz Institute for the Social Sciences shows that rates of women's labor participation fell by as much as 20 to 25 percent in thirteen Eastern European countries after 1989—a period when they were going up in Western Europe.

But as the reality of living in a newly capitalist society set in, the grass on the other side of the ideological divide turned out to be not quite as lush and green as people were expecting it to be.

"We had thought that after the revolution peaches would be different— bigger, sweeter, more golden," wrote the journalist Slavenka Drakulić in *How We Survived Communism and Even Laughed,* recalling the period after the Iron Curtain came down. People imagined they would be entering the glamorous world they had glimpsed furtively in Western movies and fashion magazines. Under capitalism, they thought they would be finally living life in full color rather than black and white.

"But as I stood in line at a stall in the street market I noticed that the peaches were just as green, small, and bullet-hard, somehow pre-revolutionary. The tomatoes were still far too expensive. The strawberries—still sour, the oranges—still dry and wrinkled."

After the end of European state socialism, as Éva Fodor and her colleagues have documented, most women quickly saw their living standards deteriorate. There was rising unemployment, poverty, and prostitution. For westerners, former Eastern European states became the go-to places for surrogates to carry babies, or for cheap nannies and housekeepers. In some areas, childcare facilities began to dwindle, making it harder for women to go to work—which could explain some of their falling employment rates. Within a couple of decades, the gains in gender equality that had been seen in socialist states in earlier years would be matched by Western Europe and the United States.

Most other European countries had by now adopted softer versions of some of the same socialist policies that had existed under the Soviet Union. Millions of people now benefited from paid parental leave, child benefit payments, universal healthcare, and subsidized higher education.

In 2017, the historian and gender scholar Susanne Kranz used archival records and personal interviews to build a portrait of the lives of ordinary women working in a huge office-equipment factory in the East German town of Sömmerda before and after the end of state socialism. Efforts to bring in equality between women and men had run so deep that even gender-specific grammatical forms that were (and still are) common in the German language weren't generally used, she explains. Working had become "part of an internalized self-perception," she writes. Almost all women were employed outside the home. More importantly, they couldn't imagine not being employed. By the mid-1990s, though, everyone in the factory was afraid of losing their jobs. One young mother was left fighting for her position in the company. "In the last months many ideals and dreams of a just society went down the drain," she said. "But the propriety and dignity of human beings—the respect for working women and mothers—cannot be derailed."

In the end, four out of five industrial jobs in Sömmerda were lost. Women were the hardest hit by these cuts.

Blanka Nyklová at the Institute of Sociology in Prague tells me that, in her country, older women she has interviewed who used to work in the chemical industry as researchers or lab technicians have seen their own children struggle to stay employed. "Their daughters are just screwed, smart women with degrees who are really at the end of their tethers because there's no nurseries."

This doesn't mean that people want to live under authoritarian communist regimes again. But if there is a longing for the old days of the Soviet Union, says Fodor, "the nostalgia is mainly for a caring state. People expect a state to take care of them." They expect pensions, welfare, and healthcare. But they also want some of the old services that brought people together, things like sports fields and canteens. The promise of state socialism was never comfort. It certainly wasn't luxury. But it did try to offer a community, a welfare net, and a guarantee of work that staved off some of the alienation that had made people vulnerable to abuse or exploitation—and this had been especially true for women.

"Socialism never completely defeated local patriarchies," writes Kristen Ghodsee. But it "did go a long way in *attempting* to create the conditions for women's full emancipation."

Like Fodor has in Hungary, Ghodsee has observed a degree of nostalgia among Bulgarians, too. In the early 2000s, some could be spotted buying Soviet-era memorabilia. "As kindergartens, hospitals, and schools have been systematically closed throughout the 1990s, Bulgarian women have been the ones responsible for providing care to children, the elderly, and the sick." For a few, she says, this has prompted fond memories of "the old system."

Nostalgia can work in strange ways. This "old system" was in fact a radically new one at the time. In Eastern and Central Europe, state socialism lasted less than two generations. That brief period of time was like hitting a reset button, beginning society again with new rules. Socialism proved that how the state was organized could have a profound impact on how people thought about themselves and each other, and it instituted that change perhaps more rapidly than any other regime has in history. Where it failed on gender equality was to forget that humans are cultural creatures, not automatons. We cling to our customs, our beliefs, even if we don't understand why we do. Instituting equality wasn't just a fight against capitalism. It was also a fight against the past.

And as old and comforting as socialism might feel now to some of those who lived through it, patriarchal traditions are older.

■   ■   ■

Local patriarchies weren't just undefeated under state socialism. Having survived in the background for decades, in the twenty-first century they began to reassert themselves more powerfully than before.

In the autumn of 2021, in a speech in front of his country's intellectual and wealthy elites, Russian president Vladimir Putin announced that the fight for equality around the world had "turned into aggressive dogmatism bordering on absurdity." This, he added, "is even worse than the agitprop department of the Central Committee of the Communist Party of the Soviet Union." Since taking power, Putin has become known as a defender of so-called "traditional" values, in favor of heterosexual families and against feminism and the rights of sexual and gender minorities.

Communism has been replaced by a new ideology, this time looking not to the possibility of a radical future but to reclaim the past.

Christianity is once again popular and visible in Russia. The same is true in former socialist states such as Poland and Hungary. Three decades of increasing restrictions on abortion in Poland after communism ended, resulting in what is now a near-total ban, have been presented as a return to "traditional" values—with the wholehearted support of the Catholic Church. In the same way that Putin has, other politicians also raise the specter of communism when they argue against gender equality. The Polish president, Andrzej Duda, has described the promotion of the rights of sexual minorities as an ideology even more destructive than communism.

Hungary has refused to ratify the Istanbul Convention, which aims to prevent and combat violence against women. I was in Budapest in 2018 not long after Prime Minister Viktor Orbán stopped public funding for higher education courses in gender studies, eight years after he also ended the requirement to erase gender stereotypes in the teaching of kindergarten children. There was a genuine fear among the academics I met there about who the government might come for next. State attacks on gay, lesbian, and transgender people had started to become particularly vicious. They became worse in subsequent years. "They relentlessly persecute them in the government-friendly media, every day, and I'm not exaggerating. *Every day* there is an article," Éva Fodor tells me. There is a general disdain nowadays, she adds, for feminism and independent civil organizations fighting for equal rights.

How did former socialist states become bastions of right-wing religious conservatism? It may be partly because nations need their populations to grow. They have always leaned on families to have as many children as possible, and enforcing strict gender norms and promoting heterosexual marriage have been useful in achieving that end. It's as true today as it was in ancient Athens, creating a constant tension for those in power.

"In the past few years, the Hungarian government has introduced a whole range of pro-natalist policies that give a lot of money to families with a lot of children. The more children you have, the more money you get," explains Fodor. Under one policy, a working mother of four or more children wouldn't have to pay income tax. Under another, state loans given to married couples are written off if they have three or more children.

But there's more to the rise of the conservative right than population concerns. After the fall of the Iron Curtain, people were also distrustful of anything that resembled communism. In an effort to forge new national identities distanced from the Soviet Union and its ideology, the struggle for gender equality suffered a reputational crisis. It was too closely linked to the former regime. Fodor tells me that for the first ten years after 1990, it was difficult to talk about women's rights. "Even the words we were using, like 'emancipation,' were words that had been usurped by the communist policy-makers, the socialist policymakers, and had been completely delegitimized."

It was in this environment that it became easier for populist strongmen to emerge, speaking a language of religion and nativism that appealed to those who had seen their cultures marginalized under the Soviet Union. Some wanted to reclaim what they thought they had lost. And patriarchy was tied up in those lost things. Communist Party policies in Central Asia, for instance, had sought to end old practices of polygamy and child marriage. In 1927, the Soviets had also banned Muslim women in these states from wearing the veil. There was an immediate backlash. Thousands of women in Uzbekistan were killed for unveiling or cooperating with the Communist Party, writes the historian of Central Asia Adrienne Edgar. In Turkmenistan, men rioted against their new divorce laws. "In response, the Soviet state adopted laws in the late 1920s making it a capital crime to murder or attempt to murder a woman because of her efforts to become emancipated."

When the Soviet Union collapsed, harking back to the past led inexorably to a return to several of the old patriarchal customs. In Kyrgyzstan, for instance, some have defended the practice of bride kidnapping as a local tradition, a symbol of Kyrgyz ways.

One paradox of this turn to tradition in post-socialist states is that, while being encouraged to maintain old-fashioned roles as wives and mothers at home, women generally haven't dropped out of work in as huge numbers as might be expected. In 1999, the economist Constantin Ogloblin, who has studied labor patterns in these countries for decades, found that, between 1994 and 1996, women in Russia were working at roughly the same rates as men were, and they were more likely to have been through higher education. Women made up more than three-quarters of economists in the country, and more than 90 percent of accountants and bookkeepers. By 2002, labor participation rates for women had fallen slightly, but this wasn't necessarily through choice. More than 90 percent of both men and women still wanted to work.

Similarly in Hungary, the state's support for families with children doesn't advise women to give up working outside the home. "So, this is not a back to the kitchen ideology; it's a policy that basically forces women to do more work," explains Fodor. Women are not being encouraged to become full-time housewives, not least because states are aware that both household finances and national economies would suffer if that were to happen. They are expected to work *and* to have plenty of children. Except this time under a capitalist system.

The tradition they've been sold by their new leaders isn't a return to the old days. Instead, it is a tradition that has been deliberately refitted to suit the needs of those in charge. They're not looking to bring back the past as it really was. What they're doing is using the past to strengthen their hand in the present. And this form of control—tinged with expedience and hypocrisy—is one of the enduring themes of patriarchal power.

CHAPTER 8

Transformation

Early on the eighth of May in 1980, the first woman to serve as a cabinet member in an Iranian government was killed by firing squad.

The year before, Iran had been in the midst of a revolution to overthrow the country's autocratic ruler, the shah, Mohammad Reza Pahlavi, and replace his monarchy with a republic. It was a movement that drew support from every section of society, from conservative Muslim clerics, who already had enormous influence over ordinary Iranians, to firebrand left-wing students and women's rights activists pushing for socioeconomic and gender equality. Tired of living under the shah's unyielding thumb, watching political opposition and debate repressed, millions were ready for change.

"For me at the time, this revolution would spell the end of tyranny. I was ready to give my life for it," I'm told by the Iranian sociologist Chahla Chafiq, who was active in the student movement. "I felt as if I were on the top of a very high mountain. The air I breathed seemed to be of a rare purity, the clear view before me promised the arrival of the most beautiful season I could have known. I could see our ranks of protesters growing day by day in the streets of Tehran.

"Freedom was just around the corner. And we were reaching it."

The revolution exposed how out of touch the shah had become with his own citizens. Sharply dressed in European suits, with a succession of glamorous lovers and wives, he had used oil revenues and close ties with the United States and Europe to industrialize Iran. People were encouraged to shed their traditions and embrace Western modernity. But it was too fast for some. Their fear was that Iran was losing itself while the shah squandered money on luxury cars and imported French food. Opposition began to coalesce around an exiled Muslim cleric, Ayatollah Ruhollah Khomeini, who promised a more religiously principled and culturally authentic future for the state, one without exploitation by foreign powers.

But like so many revolutions that century, only some ended up getting the change they wanted. "The transition from dream to nightmare was quite rapid," says Chafiq.

Khomeini returned from exile and established a theocracy. In the new Islamic Republic, laws that were seen to contravene Muslim teachings, or at least particular interpretations of them, were quickly revoked. Women's rights became an early casualty. Religious clerics pressed for a return to old-fashioned gender roles. Before long, women needed to have permission from male guardians to travel outside the country. Schools became segregated by gender. Abortion was banned. The legal age of marriage for girls was lowered from eighteen to nine, then later raised to thirteen, re-opening the door to child brides. Openly gay men faced severe punishment, even execution.

In 1936, the shah's father had taken the controversial decision to ban women from veiling in public. After the revolution, veiling became mandatory. Seeking a return to old ways, some Iranians welcomed this conservative turn. A memorial to the legendary Iranian activist Sediqeh Dowlatabadi—who had opened the first girls' school in the conversative city of Isfahan in 1918, and famously removed her veil in public when she returned from a women's rights conference in Paris in 1926—was vandalized. But for those who had wanted the revolution to give them more freedoms, not fewer, their pushback was swift. After compulsory veiling rules were announced, thousands of people gathered to march on the streets of the capital, Tehran.

"It was a huge demonstration with women—and men—from all professions there, students, doctors, lawyers. We were fighting for freedom: political and religious, but also individual," recalled the photographer Hengameh Golestan in an interview years later. Their protest wasn't about opposing the veil. For the Muslim women who wanted to wear it, the shah's earlier ban had caused shame and distress, sometimes secluding them further for fear of going out uncovered. This was about allowing women to decide for themselves what to wear. It was a question of personal autonomy.

"No man—not the Shah, not Khomeini, and not anyone else—will ever make me dress as he pleases," a lawyer, Farzaeh Nouri, told crowds, according to a reporter from the *New York Times*.

But the protests proved to be of no use. From that point on, women would be under surveillance by the morality police. It came as a shock to Chahla Chafiq. "I understood this reality the day a young boy in the street pointed his gun at me and asked me why I was not wearing the veil." Looking back on her photographs, Golestan realized that the protest was the last time women in Tehran walked the streets freely with their heads uncovered.

The British journalist James Buchan, who lived in Iran and has chronicled this period of history, writes that hundreds of thousands of Iranians ended up leaving the country for Turkey, Europe, and the United States over the next few years. Many of them were academics and professionals. For some, it was a matter of life or death.

Chafiq was among them. "I was very visible in the radical left-wing student movement. With the arrest of a number of my comrades, I was forced to go underground, living under a false name and changing my place of residence as soon as a possible intrusion of the Islamist political police appeared," she explains. "As the hunt for opponents continued to grow, I was forced, like many others, to go into exile." For three days she traveled by foot and by horse to Turkey before making her way to France, where she still lives.

Back in Iran, left-wing activists who were caught before they could flee found themselves imprisoned in coffin-like conditions, writes Buchan. "By the end of 1982, after over 5,000 young people had perished on the revolutionary gallows, the back of the revolt was broken."

It was clear by then that one oppressive state had been replaced by another.

There's relatively little publicly available information about Iran's first female cabinet minister, Farrokhroo Parsa, who was executed on May 8, 1980. What we do know is that she had been a trained medical doctor and biology teacher before entering politics, and always at the forefront of women's rights activism. Her mother is said to have been under house arrest when Parsa was born, for angering religious conservatives by publishing articles on gender equality. Parsa was among those who helped fight for Iranian women to have the vote. They were given that right in 1963, the same year that she was elected to Parliament, before being appointed minister of education.

After the revolution, Parsa became an immediate target for the Islamic Republic. During her trial in 1980, the charges against her included the bizarre accusation that she was "causing corruption and spreading prostitution." Within a few months of her arrest, she was found guilty and executed.

■　　■　　■

The question that hangs over us in the twenty-first century is how patriarchy manages to survive in the face of resistance. How can it be possible for women to fight so hard for change, to even be part of revolutionary struggles for equality, and still not achieve it? What is it about this form of oppression that gives it such force?

Today, many of Iran's most outspoken feminists have not felt safe enough to live in the country. Among them is Masih Alinejad, a journalist from a working-class family, the granddaughter of sharecroppers, who was briefly jailed and interrogated when she was a teenager for her part in producing political pamphlets. Later, as a reporter in Tehran, she became notorious for challenging Iran's political leaders, occasionally to their faces. Now she lives in New York, running an international campaign against mandatory veiling.

"I didn't have any plan, actually, to launch a movement against compulsory hijab from the beginning," Alinejad tells me.

It started when she posted a photograph of herself on social media in 2014, unveiled on a street in London. She was thrilled by the simple feeling of the wind in her hair. That moment opened a floodgate online, which would see more women across Iran do the same. In 2018, twenty-nine women were reportedly arrested after protesting the compulsory hijab. In 2019, the Iranian judiciary named Alinejad specifically when announcing that anyone found sharing online video footage of women removing their veils could face up to ten years in prison. In 2020, three activists—Mojgan Keshavarz, Yasaman Aryani, and her mother, Monireh Arabshahi—were imprisoned after handing out flowers to women metro passengers in Tehran while unveiled. Then, in September 2022, protests erupted across Iran when twenty-two-year-old Mahsa Amini died after being detained by Iran's morality police for wearing "unsuitable attire." Within weeks, hundreds were injured or killed, including a teenager, Nika Shahkarami. Schoolgirls and college students tore off their veils and staged sit-ins.

"Why do they do this?" Alinejad asks me. "I'm going to tell you why. Because without protesting, they have already been punished by the government." Whether they speak out or not, she says, women and girls suffer the daily indignity of being judged for wearing their veils inappropriately or not dressing "modestly" enough. In August 2021, a man was reported to have run over two women with his car because he felt they were not adequately covered, leaving them seriously injured.

"Women are being beaten up in the streets every day by morality police. You won't exist if you don't wear this small piece of cloth. So, that's why for women that was just enough. . . . They are fed up. They are really fed up with the religious dictatorship, with religion making the decision over their own bodies." Watching the screen adaptation of *The Handmaid's Tale*, Margaret Atwood's dystopian novel about a patriarchal religious state, Alinejad saw immediate parallels with Iran. "This is a fiction in the West, but this is my reality. This is our daily life."

Mandatory veiling has become less popular among everyday Iranians. But it's an issue that still divides people. As Alinejad explains in her memoir *The Wind in My Hair*, the 1979 revolution caused tensions within her own family. Her father enlisted in one of the volunteer arms of the Islamic Revolutionary Guards, setting up roadblocks to check that passing cars weren't carrying alcohol or music cassettes, which were seen by the regime as un-Islamic. Alinejad writes that one of his favorite insults was to say that her sinful ways would "make the devil blush." From childhood, she internalized the message that she would be punished if she took off her veil, if not on Earth, then by God. The decision to remove it was a profoundly difficult one.

"I didn't want to lose the link, the bond, between me and my community. I didn't want to break my mother's heart. I didn't want to break my father's heart. I didn't want to lose my family," she tells me, her voice unsteady.

As a result of Alinejad's activism, her family has come under pressure to denounce her. She herself has been the focus of smear campaigns, including accusations that she is a Western spy. In 2020, she was the target of an alleged kidnap attempt backed by the Iranian government. When her brother was arrested in Iran while she was in the United States, and later sentenced to eight years in prison, she felt so tortured by guilt that she wanted to commit suicide.

"Why should I feel guilty?" she asks. "Those who put these innocent people in jail for their civil disobedience, most peaceful civil disobedience, should feel guilty! Those who have beaten up women in the street for not wearing a proper hijab should feel guilty!"

Few could have guessed Iran would end up where it is. When the artist Andy Warhol visited Tehran in 1976 to do a portrait of the shah's wife, the empress, Farah Pahlavi, he saw a city in which women looked free to live as they chose. Among the urban elites at least, they wore makeup and miniskirts. Women and men could go to restaurants and movie theatres together. That decade, abortion was legalized. Women served in the army. Hundreds sat on local government councils.

Over the course of the twentieth century, efforts had been gradually ramping up to improve women's rights in Iran. By 1910, nearly fifty schools for girls had opened in Tehran, writes Janet Afary, a professor of religious studies at the University of California, Santa Barbara, and a historian of modern Iran.

Two decades later, radical newspapers and women's magazines were pushing back against polygamy, the veil, and easy divorces for men. Women clubbed together to raise money for girls' education. In 1933, more than fifty thousand pupils attended 870 girls' schools, she adds. By 1978, a third of university students were women. Around the same time, roughly half of Iran's teachers and medical students were women.

■   ■   ■

The question for scholars and feminists since the revolution in Iran has been how a country that had been making measurable progress on women's rights for decades could have managed to roll back on so many of those gains in just a few years.

It's a question that could extend just as easily to other parts of the world. From the conservative turn in Europe's former socialist states to the return of the Taliban in Afghanistan, societies that had once hoped to undermine patriarchal systems of government seem on the brink of accomplishing exactly the opposite. For every step toward women's liberation, there seems to be the risk of backlash.

In China between the 1950s and the 1970s, the Communist Party openly celebrated its commitment to gender equality. The country had the world's largest workforce of women. Today the party's survival is seen to hinge instead on a patriarchal authoritarianism, according to the journalist Leta Hong Fincher. "The Chinese government aggressively perpetuates traditional gender norms and reduces women to their roles as dutiful wives, mothers and baby breeders," she writes in her 2018 book about China's feminist awakening, *Betraying Big Brother*. Between 1990 and 2010, the average salary gap between urban men and women in China increased by ten percentage points. Universities have demanded higher entrance exam scores from women than from men in some courses, while at the same time "tightening ideological controls on gender and women's studies programs," adds Fincher. Feminist activists have been harassed, interrogated, even imprisoned.

In the United States, home to some of the most progressive social movements in the world, lawmakers in several states have for years sought to restrict access to abortion and undermine anything beyond a narrow definition of gender and the family. Even before the Supreme Court overturned the constitutional right to abortion in 2022, states including Texas and Oklahoma had passed some of the strictest abortion bills in the world. Republican politicians have leaned into "traditional" family values and railed against the teaching of sexual orientation and gender identity. At a rally in South Carolina in early 2022, as people waved "Save America" signs behind him, former president Donald Trump told crowds that his party would "proudly uphold the Judeo-Christian values and principles of our nation's founding."

The roots of this rhetoric lie in some of the earliest states and empires, built upon the need to grow populations, secure people's loyalties to the ruling elites, and breed warriors to expand or defend their territories. Laws and religions came to be built around the gendered principle that there were only two useful kinds of person: women who could bear and raise children and men who could fight. The diverse realities of human life had to be controlled, and the needs of the individual erased. Trump explained it himself in his speech in South Carolina: "The fate of any nation ultimately depends upon the willingness of its citizens to lay down, and they must do this, lay down their very lives to defend their country," he said. "We want our generals to think about winning wars, not to teach pronouns."

But that control over populations has always been unstable. There's no single moment when patriarchal values decisively "won." Instead, what we see all the way through history is resistance. As the Brooklyn-based author Gal Beckerman has written, "Change—the kind that topples social norms and uproots orthodoxies—happens slowly at first. People don't just cut off the king's head. For years and even decades they gossip about him, imagine him naked and ridiculous, demote him from deity to fallible to mortal."

It was simmering dissatisfaction like this that eventually led to the toppling of the shah in Iran in 1979. Many millions of everyday people fought with passion to see an end to his repressive regime—and they included women of all social and economic backgrounds. In the early days of the revolution at least, there was a brief moment when anything felt possible. The spirit of the time wasn't owned by conservative religious clerics alone.

"For many Iranian youth, it was an unforgettable moment," the researcher Masserat Amir-Ebrahimi has written. There "between the death of the old authority and the birth of the new one, public spaces became free spaces." Pop music was available alongside religious songs. Banned books were sold on the streets. Women left their family homes to join their comrades for months. There was a feeling that they were taking back their country from both the monarchy and from foreign forces. For young radical students like Chahla Chafiq the future was ripe with promise. In fact, Chafiq tells me, even Ayatollah Khomeini "was positively received by secular political groups, from the left to the liberals, because of his radical stance against the shah and his Western allies, especially America."

That moment was short-lived.

"Soon after the victory of the revolution, the political atmosphere changed," explains Amir-Ebrahimi. "Women and youth were the first targets of the Revolutionary Guards." The tragedy of Iran is that even though a bold social reset was attempted, patriarchal systems of control reasserted themselves anyway. For all the optimism of that moment, women's rights were on balance lost rather than gained. Many backed the Islamic Republic only to be betrayed by it.

"I hope you forgive us for the mistake we made," wrote the Nobel Peace Prize–winning human rights activist and lawyer Shirin Ebadi in an essay for the *Washington Post* four decades later. In 1970, Ebadi had been a judge. Under the Islamic Republic, she was demoted to clerk. But when the revolution was happening, her generation believed it was ushering in a new era of democracy and freedom. They hoped life would be better for everyone afterward, including for women. As Ebadi admits, it may have been a combination of idealism and naivete that allowed them to be misled by the promises of a leader who was as obviously conservative as Ayatollah Khomeini.

"The very day he started to implement the new laws on women I realized that even a religious leader can be deceitful," she writes. "The man who was supposed to be a savior became a dictator instead."

■   ■   ■

Among the many reasons that Ayatollah Khomeini slipped into power as seamlessly as he did, immediately fashioning the conservative religious state he wanted, was that other sources of political opposition had been almost entirely quashed before him, writes the historian Janet Afary. Under his drive to modernize the country, the shah had eventually given women the right to vote, allowed a few to serve as ministers and judges, and legalized abortion. But this wasn't purely out of a commitment to women's emancipation. His actions were designed to take the wind out of the political left and "present the possibility of social reform through a secular and authoritarian government."

He wouldn't tolerate any kind of grassroots activity, explains Afary, whether around labor rights or women's issues. Socialist groups had been banned long before the revolution began. Campaigners such as Farrokhroo Parsa, who was made a minister, were brought into government rather than being left to agitate outside it. By co-opting the women's rights agenda in Iran to some small degree, the Shah dampened more radical demands. He staved off opposition—but he could only manage it for a while. Come the revolution, this strategy in fact had devastating consequences for women's rights. By taking the steam out of Iran's vibrant twentieth-century grassroots feminist movements, the shah hadn't just fought off resistance to his own authority in the short-term; he had also made it harder for anyone in the future to challenge patriarchy in Iran.

Frances Hasso, a scholar of gender and sexuality in the Arab world at Duke University, describes the compromises that feminists make within patriarchal states as bargains with the devil. Reform from the inside may feel necessary and useful at the time, but the downside is that "fresh thinking on sexual and family life is foreclosed" in the process. It becomes harder to push for a bold reimagining of society when people have been pacified with smaller changes.

And as those who push for reform from within know, the smaller changes can come painfully slowly. Today, a woman's right to vote is a nonpartisan issue in most countries. It's uncontroversial. But it was only a little more than a century ago that expecting action on suffrage was considered radical, including in Europe and North America. The same is true of so many of the rights we now take for granted. In 1889, activists in the United States faced considerable resistance from local leaders when they tried to petition the state of Delaware to raise the age of consent for girls from seven years old to eighteen. The age of consent in the state had already been *lowered* in 1871 from ten. In Georgia, the age of consent remained ten until 1918. Some causes, including making marital rape a crime, continue to be controversial in other countries. Gradual shifts in the law and in public attitudes may feel like progress. They may even feel inevitable in hindsight. But if they're inevitable, why don't we reach them sooner?

This was the problem with Iranian reforms in the twentieth century. As everyone knew, under the ruling monarchy, women's rights would always be precarious because they were ultimately the gift of the shah, rather than the product of a society that was fairly and equally organized at its heart. The shah may have felt pressure from people around him to change the system, including from the women in his own family, but all power rested with him in the end. Women's emancipation would only ever come at his pace. Farrokhroo Parsa may have worked with the shah's regime to achieve practical change, but that change was always limited to what the shah would tolerate.

He was still the nation's patriarch.

In the meantime, writes Afary, the "lack of political democracy and independent trade unions in factories and workplaces pushed workers further into mosques and theological seminaries, the only places where grievances could still be aired." Religious clerics, already highly respected, became more important. Feminism was demonized multiple times over, in part by the clerics, but also because it was seen to be associated with out-of-touch urban elites and despised Western imperialists.

"In the second half of the twentieth century, radical intellectuals who had been committed to modernist ideologies, including greater social, economic and political rights for women, became disillusioned with Western democracy and feminism," Afary explains. By the end, for many, Ayatollah Khomeini represented the only feasible alternative to the shah. Instead of weaving women's rights and freedoms into the revolution, making the fight against patriarchy part of the mission, hostility toward feminism turned into "one of the main pillars of the new alliance."

■   ■   ■

"Revolutionary men with principles were not really different from the rest," reflects the protagonist in *Woman at Point Zero*, a 1983 translation of the novel by the Egyptian feminist and psychiatrist Nawal El Saadawi. "They used their cleverness to get, in return for principles, what other men buy with their money."

Occupied by foreign powers for decades, watching their country's sovereignty and wealth drained by their greed while at the same time being told they had inferior cultures and beliefs, Iranians (like so many in the Middle East, Asia, and Africa that century) were looking for a way to be "modern" without sacrificing their identities, without leaving behind what they saw as their histories and traditions. Before Ayatollah Khomeini came to power, people flocked to an influential and charismatic Paris-educated theologian who offered exactly that.

Ali Shariati was in some ways the intellectual force behind the revolution, writes Zohreh Sullivan, a professor of English who has researched colonialism and the Iranian diaspora. Shariati's call, she explains, was for a return "not to the self of a distant past, but a past that is present in the daily life of the people." He preached against capitalist Western culture—but also in favor of science and industry. He adopted the language of the European left, emphasizing the struggle against imperialism and the need to redistribute wealth more fairly—but within an Islamic framework. He supported women's equality with men to a degree—but denounced what he saw as female sexual exploitation in countries such as the United States.

This fresh, politicized brand of Islam held genuine appeal for those who saw Western capitalism as using "women's bodies to sell more commodities," writes Janet Afary. "Young women students began to wear the traditional Islamic headscarves and eagerly attended his sermons." Here was what looked to them like a culturally authentic, socially acceptable way to have agency and visibility within their faith. As many as 3,500 young people registered for a course of Shariati's lectures in 1971, according to the journalist James Buchan. "Shariati offered a vision of femininity—vigorous, loyal, chaste and companionable—that entranced many Iranian women."

His was, adds Sullivan, a revolutionary model of Islamic womanhood.

Shariati died of a heart attack before the Iranian revolution began. Ayatollah Khomeini's political convictions weren't quite the same, but Khomeini did choose to pepper his speeches with the kind of language that Shariati had used. He spoke about "colonialism," "exploitation," and "social revolution," explains Afary. Khomeini even mentioned the courage and independence of women. He told a reporter during the revolution that women would be "free in the Islamic Republic in the selection of their activities and their future and their clothing," adds Buchan.

This would turn out to be untrue. Khomeini may well have known it was untrue as he said it. He had long been wedded to a particular vision of the respectable, devout Muslim woman. And he had consistently opposed reforms under the shah that favored gender equality, including laws in the 1960s and 1970s to give women more divorce and child custody rights. But in its own way, the Islamic Republic did try to reconcile religion with radicalism, and tradition with modernity. For all the other restrictions women and girls would face, the regime supported girls' education and literacy. Segregating boys and girls in fact reassured conservative families who were worried about sending their daughters away to study. Eventually there would be no gender gap in university student numbers.

But there were tensions as well. "Our problems and miseries are caused by losing ourselves," Khomeini is quoted as once saying. The goal was to get Iran back to what it used to be. Inevitably, this meant a focus on tradition and religion. And for women, this translated into an emphasis on their roles as wives and mothers.

"Motherhood was politicized and valorized," writes Zohreh Sullivan. Birth rates shot up. Women's employment rates plummeted under the Islamic Republic, especially in government jobs. Men's employment rates rose. The effects of the state's legal changes to women's and children's rights have reverberated through the decades. In early 2021, the Statistical Center of Iran disclosed that there had been more than nine thousand child marriages registered in the country the previous summer, almost all of which involved girls between the ages of ten and fourteen.

Not unlike in ancient Athens, the state's integrity was invested in women's bodies, its moral health seen to be reflected in their behavior and dress. To be good Iranians, to truly reject foreign values, women needed to follow tradition. Even before Khomeini took power, this principle had become woven into how women behaved. At the height of the revolution, writes James Buchan, those who had never worn the black chador (a cloak that started to become customary in Iran from around the 1600s, loosely covering the whole body, exposing only the face, and held in place by hand) began to wear it to demonstrate their rejection of Western clothing and how much they identified with women in poorer and rural areas, who were more likely to veil.

The chador turned into a middle-class statement of solidarity with the working classes. This, in turn, was supported by the more religious and conservative elements in the revolutionary struggle against the shah, who had always wanted women to wear veils. Chahla Chafiq recalls that during protest marches, "little by little, I saw groups of women in black chadors growing up and walking at a distance from the men. Then, one day, our group was visited by men who were circulating among the demonstrators, advising them to build non-mixed ranks. They also told us that it would be good to wear the veil to show that the people were united against the shah."

Buchan writes that the shah's twin sister, Ashraf Pahlavi, who had played an active role in advancing women's rights in Iran, watched crowds of demonstrators on the streets below from a helicopter during the revolution. She slowly realized that a moving black mass below her was actually women wearing the dark chador, like the one her grandmother had worn.

"My God," she thought, "is this how it ends?"

The fact that women fighting for equality and freedom would choose to wear the all-encompassing chador, once rejected by Iranian women's rights activists, surprised onlookers not just outside Iran but also some within it. By that moment, though, this piece of clothing didn't mean what it had before.

There were other forces at play. Now the chador was associated not just with sexual modesty or religious devotion; it was also a visible mark of tradition. And at that moment, tradition was a symbol of political resistance.

■　■　■

When the revolution was over, every woman would have to learn to negotiate her own place in the new Islamic Republic.

In the coming decades, many would feel betrayed. Farrokhroo Parsa ended up being executed by the state, as we know. Thousands of women left the country. Others did the opposite, joining volunteer militias and becoming foot soldiers for the regime. Policewomen would patrol the streets to check that other women were following the state's modesty rules. They might stop those who showed too much hair or wore clothes that were too tight. A few would brandish batons against protestors. A small number of Iranian women secured places for themselves in the country's leadership. Among them were cheerleaders for the Islamic Republic, who fully subscribed to its patriarchal system of government. But there were also some who pushed strategically for reform, cutting their own bargains with the regime.

If there could have been a broader way to imagine the freedoms of Iranian women after the revolution, a way of having the religious coexist with the secular, for a political plurality that appreciated the diversity of women's lives and wishes, a way of retaining the rights women had already secured and expanding them, this had long before been stalled by the suppression of the secular left, feminism, and most other sources of opposition. This meant that in the new Islamic Republic, women's rights would again turn into the gifts of the men in charge.

Once it had been the ruling shah deciding what freedoms women would or wouldn't have; now it would be the male clerics. In this Iran, removing the veil would become the new symbol of political resistance.

■　■　■

The stranglehold of patriarchal power lies in how deeply woven it has become into so many of our cultures. More than anything, humans are cultural creatures. We feel the need to belong, to have a history, to feel that our existence has some meaning beyond ourselves. Without connections to the past, we would have no reference point on which to build our identities. But where do we turn when our cultures are both something we want to protect and the sources of our oppression?

The political scientist Partha Chatterjee notes that in movements against British rule in India more than a century ago, just as in Iran after the revolution, there was a fear that women might abandon their local traditions. "It is striking how much of the literature on women in the nineteenth century concerns the threatened Westernization of Bengali women," he writes. Men were given far more leeway to behave the way they chose. But the nationalist project for freedom was seen to be at risk if women in particular couldn't embody what the nation was supposed to represent. By living out their cultural traditions, as patriarchal as those traditions could be, they proved that the nation had resisted foreign control. For women, this "bound them to a new, and yet entirely legitimate, subordination."

As the Sri Lankan feminist scholar Kumari Jayawardena has written, women "still had to act as the guardians of national culture, indigenous religion and family traditions—in other words, to be both 'modern' and 'traditional.'"

It's the desire to hold onto something permanent, especially when life feels impermanent, that drives us to defend our cultures and religions. Over thousands of years, these have turned into our anchors in the world. But this is also why it's at moments of crisis, during revolution, upheaval, or war, that patriarchal power tends to double down. In modern-day Afghanistan, for instance, the influence of the Taliban may have been suppressed by foreign powers for a while, but as women's activists on the ground have urged the world to understand, conflict and disaster have only ended up making conservative voices stronger. Those were the voices that promised stability in the maelstrom, exploiting people's need to feel safe and secure when they were most vulnerable—while also expecting women to submit to a form of religious patriarchy even more repressive than Iran's.

"We saw the invasion and occupation as actually strengthening the hand of the ultraconservatives of Afghanistan, because they had this really powerful rallying cry of defending the country from foreign invaders," the women's rights activist Yifat Susskind told *The Nation* magazine in 2021. As she explained, "Decades and decades of war had created conditions that actually were inimical to the success of the Afghan women's movement."

As ethnic and religious nationalists have always known, there's nothing quite as powerful as having an enemy against which a people's sense of cultural identity can be asserted. In their 2020 book *The Future of Difference*, the sociologists Sabine Hark and Paula-Irene Villa describe how extremist nationalist parties across Europe have mobilized nativism in their appeals to local women in the face of increased immigration. They offer "vulnerable" white women the promise of protection from what have been described as "violent" foreign men coming from cultures incompatible with their own. They defend "the achievements of whichever 'we' is at stake—the nation, the people, the nuclear family, Christianity—against outsiders." Nationalism is this way spun into a toxic mix with xenophobia and patriarchy.

For some women, this brand of patriarchal nationalism has become a rallying cry. In the United States, researchers at George Washington University investigated those who took part in the far-right attack on the Capitol building in January 2021 (by March the following year, more than a hundred women had been arrested for crimes related to the siege). The researchers found that, in explaining their actions, the women often emphasized their roles as mothers, wives, and daughters in need of protection, or as protectors of their own children against external threats. By retreating into patriarchal concepts of American womanhood, they saw themselves as defending their culture.

The part we play in society is woven into our identities. That identity matters even more when we believe our societies might disintegrate if we fail to play the part. But when people are at once the keepers of culture and bound by it, the devastating consequence is that those who push back may be accused of not only betraying their society but also of betraying themselves.

In the process, the unthinkable can become thinkable. The practice of female genital mutilation, sometimes referred to as female circumcision, has been supported by older women who want to make sure their daughters are able to marry. But in 2007, when Arbore elders living in southern Ethiopia's Rift Valley decided to abolish female circumcision in their community under pressure from the government, charities, and missionaries, they met with resistance from the girls themselves. The social anthropologist Echi Gabbert, who happened to be present when this decision was made, documented one teenager's defense: "The culture of our father, our grandfathers. How we originated. We will not give it up," she told Gabbert. "This is our culture and we will not leave it.

"If our mothers should refuse to continue cutting us, we will cut ourselves."

■   ■   ■

In her 1994 memoir *Dreams of Trespass*, the late sociologist and feminist Fatima Mernissi chronicles a childhood in the middle of the twentieth century growing up in one of Morocco's last surviving harems in the ancient city of Fez. These harems were wealthy extended family homes, not unlike the matrilineal *taravads* of Kerala in India, except patriarchally organized. Brothers lived with their wives, sometimes polygamously; their sisters who were unmarried or divorced; and all their children. The women Mernissi describes, matter-of-factly without romanticizing them, are strong and smart. There are hardened warriors and former slaves among them. But here in the harem, they're all looking onto the same courtyard bounded by high walls, unable to leave without a man's permission.

Each woman sees her circumstances differently. Her mother rails at what she feels to be the absurdity of her existence. She's desperate to live independently and implores her daughter to imagine a new life for herself (which Mernissi does, leaving to study in the capital, Rabat, then Paris and the United States, later becoming a visiting professor at Berkeley and Harvard). Some of the older women, on the other hand, see the harem as a cultural institution that needs to be maintained. They tend to go along with what the men of the household want, Mernissi writes. Women outnumber the men in their household. But, as she observes, women's solidarity is a sensitive issue, "since the women rarely sided all together against the men."

Her mother accuses those who ally themselves with the men as being largely responsible for the women's suffering, like "wolves posing as sheep." If female solidarity really existed, she expresses bitterly, they wouldn't be in the harem at all.

Their ideological differences manifest subtly. Whatever each woman may feel about her circumstances, she finds ways to exercise agency. Kept in seclusion as much as possible, the women have separate spheres of work and leisure from the men. But Mernissi's mother defiantly cooks luxurious breakfasts for herself on occasion, instead of eating the communal food with everyone else. Another woman climbs acrobatically onto the high terrace, from where she can see the world around her. Others ride horseback and swim in the river. When they're together, though, something as simple as what to embroider on their clothes can become a bone of contention. A few of the women want to try out innovative new embroidery patterns, for instance. Others want to stick to old-fashioned ones out of respect for their ancestors, seeing themselves as keepers of these traditions.

Her aunt, Mernissi writes, "referred to the women as a group," but "deep down there was no cohesion at all. The split between the women was unbridgeable, with the conflict over the embroidery design emblematic of much deeper, antagonistic world views."

The problem, obvious to Mernissi even as a child, is that individuals want different things. In our personal pursuits of happiness, we make the compromises that work for us at the time, knowing that they may disappoint others with whom we might otherwise find solidarity. Women's politics don't exist purely along gender lines, any more than they do for men. This isn't always out of selfishness. It may just as often be about security or survival. But it can have the effect of aligning with the patriarchal systems around us, accepting tradition for the sake of tradition, selecting which rights we prioritize, negotiating loyalties around family, culture, nation, race, class, and caste. This conflict, perhaps, is what interrupts the prospect for solidarity.

In her book *Against White Feminism*, the lawyer and journalist Rafia Zakaria documents how empty she has found some claims of global sisterhood. The idea that women are always working in each other's interests, that they even know what each other's interests are, is one that rings particularly hollow in countries that have been subject to Western military invasions. If Western feminists really understood the needs of women, she argues, would they have defended military attacks by the United States on Afghanistan in the name of gender equality and female liberation, as some did? They imagined that Afghan women would want to be free of patriarchal control above all, when in that moment—like anyone in that moment—what they actually wanted was to be free of war.

"The small matter of devastating bombings that left thousands dead and more disabled, forever splintered families, and wrecked livelihoods was a necessary means to that shining feminist end," Zakaria writes. There was a failure to recognize that "Afghan women were inextricably connected to Afghan men," she explains. They weren't the enemy during war; they were husbands, brothers, and sons.

Part of the reason that Mernissi's family clung to its traditions was that Morocco had long been a target of foreign powers with an eye on colonizing the country. In her home, the burden fell on women to keep the old ways alive. Their own individual needs and desires didn't matter in that moment, not when there was a state to defend. Her father's excuse for not breaking away from the harem despite her mother's pleas was a familiar refrain: tradition.

"We live in difficult times, the country is occupied by foreign armies, our culture is threatened," he told her.

"All we have left is these traditions."

.   .   .

Moroccan harems became a thing of the past within Fatima Mernissi's own lifetime, but her upbringing had a profound impact on her career. Her work as a sociologist became dedicated to understanding the philosophies that undergird patriarchy, giving it such ideological force that some of the strongest women she knew not only felt resigned to it but defended it.

Following centuries of Muslim intellectuals before her, both men and women, Mernissi challenged the assumption that women's subordination was woven into her religion from the start, that it had some incontrovertible theological or historic basis. Culture and religion, the glue that held her childhood harem together, had never been static. What we think of as "tradition," she showed, has far shallower roots.

The evidence for this was abundant. Mernissi was told, for instance, that a woman couldn't rule a country under Muslim law. Yet her grandmother also informed her as a child that a Muslim woman who had been a slave had acceded to the Egyptian throne in 1250 after her husband died. When Mernissi's father hesitated in taking her to the mosque with him because she was a girl, her uncle reminded him that the Prophet Muhammad, whose life is used as a model for modern Muslims, had conducted prayers with a female child playing in front of him. In the seventh century, the prophet's own great-granddaughter Sukayna refused to wear a veil and was said to have married five or six times, never pledging obedience to any of her husbands.

"Women fled aristocratic tribal Mecca by the thousands to enter Medina, the Prophet's city in the seventh century, because Islam promised equality and dignity for all, for men and women, masters and servants," Mernissi wrote in *The Veil and the Male Elite*. "When I finished writing this book I had come to understand one thing: if women's rights are a problem for some modern Muslim men, it is neither because of the Koran nor the Prophet, nor the Islamic tradition, but simply because those rights conflict with the interests of a male elite." Patriarchy, far from being a return to the past, was in fact being constantly remade in the present, and sometimes with greater force than before.

Mernissi showed how, like in so many other parts of life, religion had over time become recruited into the service of power, laboring for the patriarchs. Like mythical claims about female and male natures, religiously sanctioned male domination had a strength of its own. Where philosophers and scientists had appealed to the authority of biology to paint women as inferior, religious men appealed to the authority of the divine.

"To fundamentalists, women symbolise ethnic and cultural purity," writes the sociologist Fatou Sow, who has researched how patriarchal ideas have spread in Senegal through interpretations of Islam that seek to push women out of spiritual leadership positions, promote female genital mutilation, and undermine matrilineal practices. "Fundamentalist groups manipulate religion for ideological and political means, and women's rights issues are a particular focus." The trick can be brazenly transparent: tradition is actively rewritten, and women are then supposed to follow it.

"Obedience to the patriarchal order is looked upon as a sign of commitment to God and religious faith," writes Sow.

As much as religion can feel like a set of beliefs that is fixed and eternal, religious meaning has always been manipulated to suit the politics of the day. The Catholic Church, for instance, has continually built and reinforced its case for "traditional" families, the role of women, and the gender binary. In 2004, before he became pope, Cardinal Joseph Ratzinger wrote a letter to Catholic bishops making his case against women priests. Ratzinger said that women seeking power for themselves led "to harmful confusion regarding the human person, which has its most immediate and lethal effects in the structure of the family."

He went on to make a direct reference to feminism: "Although a certain type of feminist rhetoric makes demands 'for ourselves,' women preserve the deep intuition of the goodness in their lives of those actions which elicit life, and contribute to the growth and protection of the other." Whether she accepted it or not, Ratzinger's reasoning went, every woman's true purpose was to support men and children.

Part of the privilege of having power is being able to pour your definition of what is moral, natural, or authentic into your own container. When the idealogues of the Islamic Republic constructed their new Iran, they were also interpreting religion in a way that suited their politics. This might explain the occasional inconsistencies in Ayatollah Khomeini's comments on women's rights. He had suggested before the revolution, in public at least, that women would have the freedom to wear what they wanted, to make their own personal choices—implying that this could be consistent with his faith. Whether or not this is what he actually intended, those rights never materialized. But when they didn't, that was also framed as a religiously motivated decision.

It's here that Mernissi's argument hits hardest. If it's ancient history, tradition, or an unchanging faith that justifies circumscribing women's lives, how is it possible for the patriarchs in the present to define what's acceptable and what isn't? How are they able to bend the past and tradition to their will, yet women who want greater rights and freedoms can't do the same?

■　■　■

Perhaps motivated by the hypocrisy she encountered, Fatima Mernissi became one of the founders of a school of thought known as Islamic feminism. As permanent as religion appeared to be, she argued that how we read it is shaped by our own time, and that it has always been that way. Mernissi studied the same texts as the conservative clerics but with different eyes, exposing their misinterpretations and ambiguities. As she interrogated history, she revealed that the Arab world was far more socially diverse in the past than people in the present acknowledged. She went so far as to suggest that, given the room for interpretation that has always existed, there was no reason why religious texts might not also be read in ways that were consistent with feminism.

There were once Islamic historians, Mernissi wrote, who "held that the Muslim family marked a break with earlier practices," including some "that were clearly anti-patriarchal." Ancient texts proved that women had enjoyed power and freedom. They included evidence, she argued, of a panorama of sexual rights women enjoyed in the past. There were unions in which children didn't belong to their biological fathers, and in which women could have more than one regular sexual partner. There were wives who were free to send away husbands they no longer wanted with simple ritual gestures. There were matrilineal marriages in which husbands stayed with their wives' tribes.

The anthropologist Andrey Korotayev, based at Moscow State University, confirmed in 1995 that there is evidence of matrilineal lineages in third-century southern Arabia. Texts exist in which the only listed family relatives of men are their brothers, and all the recorded descendants are of the women only. There's evidence, too, that women in these communities shared leadership with men.

Mernissi's approach is a radical one. But others have argued that there are limits to how far patriarchy in religion can really be challenged. Not all feminists are convinced that the world's major faiths can fully accommodate gender equality, especially when their teachings include passages that can only be interpreted as mandating male domination. The Quran, for instance, mentions a woman's "obedience" to her husband. The historian Kimberly Hamlin at Miami University, Ohio, details in *Free Thinker*, her biography of the American suffragist Helen Hamilton Gardener, how women's rights activists in the nineteenth century also had a tough time arguing against those in the United States who thought that women were naturally subordinate to men because the Bible said so.

"When nearly every biblical passage pertaining to women was so degrading, Gardener pondered, 'how anyone can be an absolutely orthodox Christian and a woman suffragist at the same time is always one of those conundrums that I have to give up,'" quotes Hamlin.

But activists like Gardener found they couldn't avoid religion if they wanted to pull the broad mass of people along with their demands in a country as religious as theirs. This was why the second half of the nineteenth century saw a string of high-profile feminist critiques and reinterpretations of Christianity, including publication of *The Woman's Bible*. Through efforts like these, they were able to find a route for feminism within their faith.

As Mernissi similarly recognized, once a society has been built on a theological basis, once it has positioned itself against other systems of thought, feminists have few places to turn for their rights except through religion. Muslim women needed to find a pragmatic way to assert their demands for equality. Her method turned out to be influential because it tackled the patriarchs on their own turf. It was a feminism that came from within the very culture it was trying to challenge. And it remains powerful to this day. The Egyptian-born journalist Mona Eltahawy has written about the joy of learning that the Middle East had a feminist heritage of its own, and that this heritage wasn't just imported from the West. "To a young woman struggling with forces she believed she could not stand up to, Mernissi's words were much-needed ammunition."

In their 2019 memoir *Unicorn*, the British Iraqi filmmaker and drag performer Amrou Al-Kadhi also thrills in finding an accepting place within Islam by independently studying religious texts. "As a queer boy in Islam class, the threat of going to hell because of who I was inside was a very real and perpetual anxiety," Al-Kadhi writes. "I've lived between the Middle East and London, and have felt too gay for Iraqis, and too Iraqi for gays." After attending an event hosted by queer Muslims, they began to learn about Islam's tradition of critical thinking and independent discussion. It was a revelation. "It's not Allah who forbade my queer identity, but the people who ignored the well of alternative potentials in the Quran."

That the stories we tell about ourselves can decide how we live is a thread that runs all the way through Mernissi's work. She asks how the world might look if we rewrote these stories, how an act of imagination can nudge the boundaries away from the restrictive, manipulated claims of society and the state. "Liberation starts with images dancing in your little head," she recalls her aunt Habiba telling her as a child. Those images can become words. "And words cost nothing!"

■   ■   ■

In the middle of the twentieth century, Lewis Alfred Coser, a left-wing sociologist who had fled Nazi Germany for the United States, made the argument that conflict within and between groups in societies, far from being a bad thing, is in fact what fosters social change. There's rarely a system that works for everyone in terms of status or wealth. Friction at the edges moves the dial, helping new ways of thinking emerge. He wrote that "societies do not die the way biological organisms do, for it is difficult to assign precise points of birth or death to societies as we do with biological organisms." What we're left with is constant struggle.

There are pushes for power, and there are those pushing against, at times giving rise to more restrictive and authoritarian societies, at other times less. What we call patriarchy can be thought of as a set of factors in that ongoing conflict. It's about people looking to assert dominance over others through claims to nature, history, and the divine. They are inventing and reinventing these claims all the time, sometimes succeeding, sometimes failing. But the fight for a fairer and more equal society is also constantly repositioning itself.

The Iran that existed before the revolution of 1979 wasn't extinguished with the Islamic Republic. In a generational analysis of what happened afterward, the sociologist Masserat Amir-Ebrahimi writes that the women of the revolution laid the ground for generations of women after them to become "the most transgressive agents of change." Though they had been pushed to the margins, they achieved change from those margins. These were the "rebellious mothers who struggled hard for their freedom and resisted the complete Islamization of public spaces. These women continued to attend the universities and go to work despite the limitations and frequent humiliations they faced.

"They maintained their individuality in the face of repression and punishment."

The shift can be seen within families themselves, adds the human rights lawyer Leila Alikarami. Born in Iran just before the revolution, she studied at the University of Tehran and is now based in London. Growing up, she recalls her grandmother treating her differently from her brother. She would prepare special cookies in the holidays, Alikarami tells me. "I loved these cookies." But her grandmother would always make a point of telling everyone that she had made them especially for her brother rather than for Leila and her sisters. "That was hurtful. I was always complaining to my dad, and I didn't want to visit her. But my dad explained to me that she's old, and she doesn't want to discriminate, she doesn't want to hurt you, but this is her nature. This is the environment that she grew in," she says. "She was in favor of boys."

By Alikarami's parents' generation, attitudes around gender had already changed. "My mum is totally different," she says. "When I'm talking to my mum, I can have a conversation with her. And also with other family members, they can have a conversation." Her family supported her education and her career. Iran's government remains socially conservative and there are still discriminatory laws in place that favor men. But how individuals choose to live, how they create space for themselves, is another matter. "People are educated now, and culturally they are ahead of the government."

Inheritance laws in Iran, for instance, state that sons are entitled to twice as much as daughters. But, Alikarami tells me, "I know in my own family that many men gave their equal shares to sons and daughters." In marriage contracts, too, some husbands are waiving the power they have over wives to stop them from working, traveling, or asking for divorce. If doing so means not having to pay a hefty dowry or perhaps enjoying a larger family income by having both partners work, men are more willing to negotiate.

This isn't always easy, she adds. On a practical level, notaries occasionally object to these kinds of contracts. Both men and their parents don't want to cede too much. "Sometimes they don't want to agree because they don't want to lose their power. Sometimes they say, okay, we waive our rights; we give you the right to divorce, we give you the right to work, the right to travel, but how can I justify this to my mum? Or to my family?" In one case she knows, a man agreed to waive his marriage rights only if his family weren't told what he was doing.

As the historian Janet Afary and the scholar of nationalism and identity Jesilyn Faust write in their 2021 book *Iranian Romance in the Digital Age*, despite how heavily the Iranian government has promoted families and traditional motherhood, there has been a decline in marriage, particularly arranged marriages. In Tehran in 2018, there was one divorce for every three marriages. In 2016, more than 60 percent of all single households in the city belonged to women. Forty years since the Islamic Republic was founded, there are some women who are financially supporting their families.

The revolution may not have delivered the change for which women once fought, but nor could it stop it.

This mirrors some of the trends seen across the Middle East, North Africa, and South Asia, add Afary and Faust. Marriage and birth rates are falling. Fewer people are choosing conventional arranged marriages. Women are on average better educated and more employed than they were four decades ago. When they have the opportunity to claim their freedoms, women seize them. In February 2022, a rail company advertising for female drivers in Saudi Arabia reported that it received twenty-eight thousand applications for thirty jobs.

As birth rates fall, daughters have become more cared for by families, and more investment has gone into their education. Nowhere is this clearer than in China. After its coercive one-child policy was introduced in 1979, marriageable women became scarcer. As a result, in some regions of the country, women began to realize they could negotiate the terms on which they got married. Instead of having to move in with their husbands' families, as is customary in most of China, a few persuaded their husbands to move in with them—in effect, forcing matrilocality. As Biye Gao, a gender scholar at SOAS University of London, has documented, based on her fieldwork in Hunan province, a practice known in the local dialect as *zhaolang* sees children born into these families named after their mothers rather than their fathers.

The Chinese women who Biye Gao interviewed tended to be far more economically independent, especially because they had their own relatives around to help take care of their children. She describes one woman's situation as being similar to that of a "surrogate son" within her own family. She had upended the usual gender role. And with it, she found "the transformative power to challenge the oppressive state" when it tried to penalize her for having a second child—incidentally, a daughter.

Globally, birth rates have been declining for more than fifty years, from a peak of more than five births per woman in the 1960s to fewer than two and a half today, according to data from the World Bank. Even in China, despite the anguish caused by the government's former one-child policy, when given the choice to have more babies, women are opting to have fewer anyway. Instead of rising after a two-child policy was rolled out, the birth rate has fallen since 2016. The freedom to have as few children as people want has become one of the most bitterly contested between states and their citizens.

Gender boundaries, so forcefully policed by patriarchal societies and states for centuries, are also being challenged on every front. As of the summer of 2022, same-sex marriages were legal in thirty-one countries. In 2014, the Indian Supreme Court recognized the official existence of a third gender, following a path already paved by Nepal and Bangladesh. "Today, for the first time I feel very proud to be an Indian," the transgender activist Laxmi Narayan Tripathi told reporters.

■   ■   ■

Patriarchal customs aren't the only ones we have.

In the matrilineal societies of the Khasi Hills in Meghalaya, India, despite proposals to change inheritance laws to benefit sons and daughters equally, there's a determination not to kill off the old traditions that prioritize daughters. People there feel that matriliny is so tightly woven into the ethnic fabric of Khasi life that losing it might mean sacrificing their identity. The sociologist Tiplut Nongbri told me that even the senior Khasi men she's spoken with don't want to see an end to their matrilineal ways of life.

"They feel that it would be disastrous for society," she said, because it would disrupt the bedrock on which families are built. As an Indigenous tribal community already under threat, it's their cultural survival that has come to matter above all. Both men and women in the Khasi Hills have become invested in defending women's rights against an encroaching patriarchy.

The south Indian state of Kerala—where matriliny was officially abolished in 1976—meanwhile has come full circle. The region has positioned itself in the twenty-first century as a beacon for women's empowerment. In 2013, a twenty-four-acre "Gender Park" was established in the city of Kozhikode, formerly Calicut, with a museum and feminist library exploring women's history, including the stories of transgender women. Eight years later, a government primary school in one Kerala district introduced a gender-neutral uniform for its children, comprising three-quarter-length trousers and shirts. Broadly welcomed by politicians and celebrities, Kerala's matrilineal traditions were mentioned as one reason for the school's decision. Other schools have followed suit.

Tradition, I come to realize, is as we choose to make it.

Decades ago, a similar realization animated the work of anticolonial theorist and psychiatrist Frantz Fanon. "I am not a prisoner of history. I should not seek there for the meaning of my destiny," he wrote in his book *Black Skin, White Masks*. "I am my own foundation." We already possess the tools for creating the world we want.

Yet, whether it's ancient Greece and Rome or ancient India and North America, we look to the past as though it contains a magic formula for how we should live. But the past was neither better nor worse than what we have now; it was just more varied. As far back as we can see, humans have landed on rainbows of different ways of organizing themselves, always negotiating the rules around gender and its meaning. Nothing was static. Over millennia, though, we've been pushed gradually into believing that there are just a few ways in which humans can live—to the point where we now feel that the social patterns we follow must be natural rather than man-made.

At the end of this journey—one that has taken me from deep time all the way to our turbulent present—I'm left wondering if the radical societies we create now could someday form the basis of tomorrow's habits and customs. How can we rediscover our capacity to be socially nimble? We've developed an inertia when it comes to bold social and political change. We resign ourselves to the systems and institutions we have, even when we know they're not working. Standing at the precipice, we look back and feel terrified at what we might lose.

Imagine everything we could gain.

AFTERWORD

At least as long ago as antiquity, military leaders learned that one of the most effective ways to secure power over people was to use a strategy of "divide and rule." Separating out smaller groups created distrust and made it harder for them to form alliances. Their loyalties shifted from each other to those in charge. It was a tactic so devastatingly successful that it's seen all the way through history, thought to have been used by Julius Caesar in Rome and also by the British Empire.

Division is part of what gives patriarchy its power. The damage wrought by gendered oppression isn't just economic or physical; it's emotional and psychological. The effect of alienating daughters from parents, emotionally distancing wives from husbands, and demonizing those who don't conform to narrow gender norms has been to foster fear and hatred of the very people in whom we might otherwise find comfort. We know that it's possible to love and trust other human beings—our survival as a social species has depended on it—but one effect of this form of divide and rule has been to make us believe that we can't.

It subverts our closest relationships.

Patriarchal power is, in one sense, no different from any other system of control. What sets it apart is that it operates even at the level of the family. Its Machiavellian force lies in the fact that it can turn the people nearest to us into the enemy. The evolution of this strategy can be traced through the practices of patriliny and patrilocality, which separated women from their childhood kin, and in the dehumanizing brutality of captive taking. We can draw threads between that history of detachment and control all the way to some of our more recent laws and beliefs. But we can't assume that this has been the same all over the world. None of it was automatic. In some regions, patriarchal systems are thousands of years old. In others, they've become established only in the last few centuries.

Patriarchy as a single phenomenon doesn't really exist, then. There are instead, more accurately, many *patriarchies* formed by threads subtly woven through different cultures in their own way, working with local power structures and existing systems of inequality. States institutionalized human categorization and gendered laws; slavery influenced patrilocal marriage; empires exported gendered oppression to nearly every corner of the globe; capitalism exacerbated gender disparities; and religions and traditions are still being manipulated to give psychological force to the notion of male domination. Fresh threads are being woven into our social fabrics even now. If we are ever going to build a truly fair world, everything will need to be unpicked.

Faced with a task this monumental, the fight for our equality can feel like a war of attrition. I myself have spoken at law firms and banks to women who want to know how they can move up the corporate ladder in sexist work environments, all the while oblivious to those cleaning up their offices after them for subsistence wages.

We're yet to invent political systems that nurture the needs of the individual over the demands of the state, that cushion every one of us from the blows of this world. Even when all our laws are as fair as we can make them, when we've moved beyond our gender stereotypes to accept all people as they are, after our languages and cultures reflect values of equality, this doesn't mean there won't still be those out there trying to assert power over others in some new way.

As interminable as this struggle might seem, though, there's a beauty to be found in it nonetheless. When we fight for equality, we don't just fight for ourselves. We fight for others. And much of the time, that fight does get us somewhere. Without it, our lives could be so much worse. As a science writer who spends most of her time thinking about human nature, I find this to be the most extraordinary part of us. While researching this book, I've met and read the work of people who have laid down their lives and careers for the idea of human dignity and freedom. As much as we can't bear to be treated unfairly, most of us can't bear for others to be treated unfairly either—including strangers we've never met. We share in their pain. We want to help.

If we're ever to repair the damage caused by patriarchal power, we can do it only by nurturing this shared humanity—the part of us that manages to love even when there are those seeking to divide and rule. Some still claim that oppression is somehow woven into who we are, that humans are inherently selfish and violent, that entire categories of people are naturally dominant or subordinate. I have to ask: Would we care about each other so much if that were true?

ACKNOWLEDGMENTS

I n 2017, I wrote a book on the science of sex and gender, *Inferior: How Science Got Women Wrong*, which included a chapter on male domination. The question I was asked most often by readers afterward was: If we haven't always been male dominated, how do we explain the widespread stranglehold of patriarchy? That response is what set this book in motion. What I didn't anticipate was that I'd be writing most of it during a pandemic, traveling in the brief windows of time when it was safe and interviewing people by phone or online.

I would like to thank the following people for giving me their valuable time for firsthand interviews, and in some cases also fielding follow-up questions and other queries: Amy Parish, Frans de Waal, Steven Goldberg, Robin Jeffrey, Manu Pillai, Tiplut Nongbri, Nicole Creanza, Adam Kuper, Brian Steele, Awhenjiosta Myers, Jennifer Nez Denetdale, Ruth Tringham, Reşit Ergener, Miriam Robbins Dexter, Cynthia Eller, Colin Renfrew, Karina Croucher, Ian Hodder, Fidan Ataselim, Melek Önder, Kristian Kristiansen, Pontus Skoglund, Sarah Pomeroy, Stephanie Budin, James Scott, Rebecca Futo Kennedy, Alwin Kloekhorst, Faiza Haikal, Andrew Bayliss, Walter Penrose, Fairuz Choudhury, Benaifer Bhandari, Catherine Cameron, Blanka Nyklová, Éva Fodor, Kristen Ghodsee, Chahla Chafiq, Masih Alinejad, and Leila Alikarami.

I'm deeply grateful to those who provided support and wisdom in other ways. Sabahattin Alkans was my experienced guide through Anatolia, and the Alexander von Humboldt Foundation allowed me to spend time in Berlin. The Logan Nonfiction Program fellowship in New York gave me much-needed time away from the pressures of home life, as well as a community of other nonfiction creators. And the Society of Authors generously supported my research with a K. Blundell Trust grant.

I am also indebted to the New York Public Library; my wonderful friend Jess Wade, who has been my champion for years; the endless kindness of Alex O'Brien; and the generous help and advice of Paige Bethmann, Tim Power, Susan Perkins, Fiona Jordan, Tim Requarth, Paramita Nath, Donna Harsch, Janet Afary, Shomsia Ali, Rafil Kroll-Zaidi, Ruta Nimkar, Neda Sepehrnoush, and Pippa Goldschmidt.

My career has rested for a while now in the hands of Louise Haines at 4th Estate, Amy Caldwell at Beacon Press, and Peter Tallack and Tisse Takagi at the Science Factory, and they've never shown me anything but wholehearted faith and encouragement. I hope I never let them down.

Mariyam Haider was my first fact-checker, skillfully catching errors that were sometimes even in academic source material. She has been a sounding board and a friend along the journey. This book, and my previous two, would have been far weaker without the sharp eye and countless hours of Pete Wrobel, who has a unique talent for collecting information and never forgetting it. I'll never be able to thank him enough for his generosity and wisdom. Thank you, too, to my brilliant copyeditors, Susan Lumenello at Beacon Press and Kate Johnson at 4th Estate.

Finally, love and gratitude to my patient and beautiful family: my parents and parents-in-law; my son, Aneurin; my husband, Mukul; and my sisters, Rima and Monica. Every book I write brings me a little closer to understanding the world as it is, and it's a world I want to be better for each of them.

REFERENCES

INTRODUCTION

Pinney, Christopher. *'Photos of the Gods': The Printed Image and Political Struggle in India*. London: Reaktion Books, 2004.

Ramayya, Nisha. *States of the Body Produced by Love*. Newcastle upon Tyne: Ignota Books, 2019.

Ramos, Imma. *Tantra: Enlightenment to Revolution*. London: Thames & Hudson and the British Museum, 2020.

Dalmiya, Vrinda. "Loving Paradoxes: A Feminist Reclamation of the Goddess Kali." *Hypatia*, vol. 15, no. 1, Winter 2000, pp. 125–50.

Merelli, Annalisa. "Kali Is the 3,000-Year-Old Feminist Icon We Need Today." *Quartz*, 8 January 2020, https://qz.com/1768545/hinduisms-kali-is-the -feminist-icon-the-world-desperately-needs/ (last accessed 7 June 2022).

Appiah, Kwame Anthony. "Digging for Utopia." *New York Review of Books*, 16 December 2021.

Learned Sir Robert Filmer Baronet. *Patriarcha; of the Natural Power of Kings*. London: Richard Chiswell, 1680.

Millett, Kate. *Sexual Politics* (1970). Urbana: University of Illinois Press, 2000.

Walby, Sylvia. *Theorizing Patriarchy*. Oxford: Basil Blackwell, 1990.

Beechey, Veronica. "On Patriarchy." *Feminist Review*, no. 3, 1979, pp. 66–82.

Punit, Itika Sharma. "Social Distancing from House Helps Is Exposing the Indian Family's Unspoken Sexism." *Quartz India*, 26 March 2020, https://qz.com /india/1823823/with-coronavirus-lockdown-working-indian-women-face -family-sexism (last accessed 23 April 2021).

Nagaraj, Anuradha. "Wages for Housewives: Party's Manifesto Pledge Stirs Debate in India." Reuters, 7 January 2021. https://www.reuters.com/article/us-india -women-politics-idUSKBN29C1TQ (last accessed 15 May 2021).

Mohanty, Chandra Talpade. "Under Western Eyes: Feminist Scholarship and Colonial Discourses." *Feminist Review*, no. 30, Autumn 1988, pp. 61–88.

Ortner, Sherry B. "Gender Hegemonies." *Cultural Critique*, no. 14, Winter 1989–1990, pp. 35–80.

Jones-Rogers, Stephanie E. *They Were Her Property: White Women as Slave Owners in the American South*. New Haven, CT: Yale University Press, 2019.

Lerner, Gerda. "Placing Women in History: Definitions and Challenges." *Feminist Studies*, vol. 3, nos. 1–2, Autumn 1975, pp. 5–14.

MacKinnon, Catharine A. *Toward a Feminist Theory of the State* (1989). Cambridge, MA: Harvard University Press, 1991.

Delphy, Christine. *Close to Home: A Materialist Analysis of Women's Oppression* (1984). New York: Verso Books, 2016.

Rosaldo, Michelle Zimbalist. "The Use and Abuse of Anthropology: Reflections on Feminism and Cross-Cultural Understanding." *Signs*, vol. 5, no. 3, Spring 1980, pp. 389–417.

CHAPTER 1: Domination

Le Guin, Ursula K. "A War Without End." In *Utopia*, by Thomas More. London: Verso, 2016.

Saini, Angela. *Inferior: How Science Got Women Wrong and the New Research That's Rewriting the Story*. London: 4th Estate, 2017.

Parish, Amy Randall. "Female Relationships in Bonobos (*Pan paniscus*)." *Human Nature*, no. 7, March 1996, pp. 61–96.

Parish, Amy R., Frans B. M. de Waal, and David Haig. "The Other 'Closest Living Relative': How Bonobos (*Pan paniscus*) Challenge Traditional Assumptions about Females, Dominance, Intra- and Intersexual Interactions, and Hominid Evolution." *Annals of the New York Academy of Sciences*, vol. 907, no. 1, April 2000, pp. 97–113.

de Waal, Frans. *Different: Gender Through the Eyes of a Primatologist*. London: Granta, 2022.

Smith, Jennifer E., et al. "Obstacles and Opportunities for Female Leadership in Mammalian Societies: A Comparative Perspective." *Leadership Quarterly*, no. 31, 2020.

Goldberg, Steven. *The Inevitability of Patriarchy*. New York: William Morrow, 1973.

Darwin, Charles. *The Descent of Man and Selection in Relation to Sex* (1874). Project Gutenberg edition, 1999, updated 2021.

Wilson, Edward O. "Human Decency Is Animal." *New York Times*, 12 October 1975, p. 272.

Smuts, Barbara. "The Evolutionary Origins of Patriarchy." *Human Nature*, vol. 6, no. 1, March 1995, pp. 1–32.

Delphy, Christine. *Close to Home: A Materialist Analysis of Women's Oppression* (1984). New York: Verso Books, 2016.

Leacock, Eleanor. "Review of *The Inevitability of Patriarchy*, by Steven Goldberg." *American Anthropologist*, vol. 76, no. 2, June 1974, pp. 363–65.

Maccoby, Eleanor E. "Sex in the Social Order: Review of *The Inevitability of Patriarchy*, by Steven Goldberg." *Science*, vol. 182, no. 4111, November 1973, pp. 469–71.

"Number of Countries Where the De Facto Highest Position of Executive Power Was Held by a Woman from 1960 to 2021." *Statista*, November 2021. https://www.statista.com/statistics/1058345/countries-with-women-highest-position-executive-power-since-1960 (last accessed 14 January 2022).

"Women in Politics: 2020." UN Women, 1 January 2020. https://www.unwomen.org
/sites/default/files/Headquarters/Attachments/Sections/Library/Publications
/2020/Women-in-politics-map-2020-en.pdf (last accessed 3 March 2022).

Parish, Amy R. "Two Sides of the Same Coin: Females Compete and Cooperate."
Archives of Sexual Behavior, published online 22 November 2021.

Morris-Drake, Amy, Julie M. Kern, and Andrew N. Radford. "Experimental
Evidence for Delayed Post-Conflict Management Behaviour in Wild Dwarf
Mongooses." *Elife*, no. 10, 2 November 2021, p. e69196.

van Leeuwen, Edwin J. C., et al. "A Group-Specific Arbitrary Tradition in Chimpanzees (*Pan troglodytes*)." *Animal Cognition*, Issue 17, June 2014, pp. 1421–25.

Vince, Gaia. "Smashing the Patriarchy: Why There's Nothing Natural About Male
Supremacy." *The Guardian*, 2 November 2019.

Thompson, Melissa Emery. "How Can Non-Human Primates Inform Evolutionary Perspectives on Female-Biased Kinship in Humans?" *Philosophical Transactions of the Royal Society B*, vol. 374, no. 1780, 2 September 2019.

Sommer V. and A. R. Parish. "Living Differences." In *Homo Novus—A Human
Without Illusions* (Frontiers Collection), edited by Ulrich J. Frey, Charlotte
Störmer, and Kai P. Willführ. Berlin: Springer, 2010.

Jeffrey, Robin. "Matriliny, Women, Development—and a Typographical Error."
Pacific Affairs, vol. 63, no. 3, Autumn 1990, pp. 373–77.

Jeffrey, Robin. "Governments and Culture: How Women Made Kerala Literate."
Pacific Affairs, vol. 60, no. 3, Autumn 1987, pp. 447–72.

Roser, Max, and Esteban Ortiz-Ospina. "Literacy." Our World in Data, last revised
20 September 2018. https://ourworldindata.org/literacy (last accessed 4 November 2021).

"At 96.2%, Kerala Tops Literacy Rate Chart; Andhra Pradesh Worst Performer at
66.4%." *Economic Times*, 8 September 2020. https://economictimes.indiatimes
.com/news/politics-and-nation/at-96-2-kerala-tops-literacy-rate-chart-andhra
-pradesh-worst-performer-at-66-4/articleshow/77978682.cms?utm_source
=contentofinterest&utm_medium=text&utm_campaign=cppst (last accessed 24
October 2021).

Schneider, David M., and Kathleen Gough. *Matrilineal Kinship*. Berkeley: University of California Press, 1961.

Lowes, Sara. "Kinship Structure & Women: Evidence from Economics." *Daedalus*,
vol. 149, no. 1, Winter 2020, pp. 119–33.

Khalil, Umair, and Sulagna Mookerjee. "Patrilocal Residence and Women's Social
Status: Evidence from South Asia." *Economic Development and Cultural Change*,
vol. 67, no. 2, January 2019, pp. 401–38.

Dube, Leela. "Matriliny and Women's Status." *Economic and Political Weekly*, vol. 36,
no. 33, August 2001, pp. 3144–47.

Jordan, Fiona M., et al. "Matrilocal Residence Is Ancestral in Austronesian Societies." *Proceedings of the Royal Society B*, vol. 276, no. 1664, 7 June 2009, pp.
1957–64.

Kutty, Madhavan. *The Village Before Time* (1991), translated from Malayalam by
Gita Krishnankutty. New Delhi: IndiaInk, 2000.

Verjus, Anne. "The Empire of the Nairs: A Society Without Marriage nor Paternity." Talk delivered at Consortium on Revolutionary Era, Charleston, SC,
23–25 February 2017.

Pillai, Manu S. *The Ivory Throne: Chronicles of the House of Travancore*. India: Harper-Collins, 2016.

Arunima, G. "Matriliny and Its Discontents." *India International Centre Quarterly*, vol. 22, nos. 2/3, Summer–Monsoon 1995, pp. 157–67.

Starkweather, Kathrine, and Monica Keith. "One Piece of the Matrilineal Puzzle: The Socioecology of Maternal Uncle Investment." *Philosophical Transactions of the Royal Society B*, vol. 374, no. 1780, 2 September 2019.

Ly, Goki, et al. "From Matrimonial Practices to Genetic Diversity in Southeast Asian Populations: The Signature of the Matrilineal Puzzle." *Philosophical Transactions of the Royal Society B*, vol. 374, no. 1780, 2 September 2019.

Chakravarti, Uma. "Whatever Happened to the Vedic *Dasi*? Orientalism, Nationalism, and a Script for the Past." In *Recasting Women: Essays in Colonial History*, edited by Kumkum Sangari and Sudesh Vaid. New Delhi: Kali for Women, 1989.

Moore, Lewis. *Malabar Law and Custom*. Madras: Higginbotham & Co., 1905.

Moore, Melinda A. "A New Look at the Nayar Taravad." *Man*, vol. 20, no. 3, September 1985, pp. 523–41.

Fuller, C. J. "The Internal Structure of the Nayar Caste." *Journal of Anthropological Research*, vol. 31, no. 4, Winter 1975, pp. 283–312.

Nongbri, Tiplut. "Kinship Terminology and Marriage Rules: The Khasi of North-East India." *Sociological Bulletin*, vol. 62, no. 3, September–December 2013, pp. 413–30.

Nongbri, Tiplut. "Family, Gender and Identity: A Comparative Analysis of Trans-Himalayan Matrilineal Structures." *Contributions to Indian Sociology*, vol. 44, nos. 1–2, 2012, pp. 155–78.

Pakyntein, Valentina. "Gender Preference in Khasi Society: An Evaluation of Tradition, Change and Continuity." *Indian Anthropologist*, vol. 30, nos. 1–2, June and December 2000, pp. 27–35.

Marak, Queenbala, and Jangkhomang. "Matriliny and the Megalithic Practices of the Jaintias of Meghalaya." *Indian Anthropologist*, vol. 42, no. 2, July–December 2012, pp. 67–82.

Banerjee, Roopleena. "'Matriarchy' and Contemporary Khasi Society." *Proceedings of the Indian History Congress*, vol. 76, 2015, pp. 918–30.

Karmakar, Rahul. "Matrilineal Meghalaya to Give Land Rights to Men." *The Hindu*, 26 October 2021. https://www.thehindu.com/news/national/other-states/matrilineal-meghalaya-to-give-land-rights-to-men/article37175110.ece (last accessed 14 November 2021).

Das, Mohua. "Meet the Men's Libbers of Meghalaya." *Times of India*, 27 August 2017. http://timesofindia.indiatimes.com/articleshow/60237760.cms?utm_source=contentofinterest&utm_medium=text&utm_campaign=cppst (last accessed 14 November 2021).

Krishna, Geetanjali. "The Second Sex." *The Caravan*, 31 May 2012. https://caravanmagazine.in/lede/second-sex (last accessed 14 November 2021).

Allen, Timothy. "Meghalaya, India: Where Women Rule, and Men Are Suffragettes." BBC News, 19 January 2012. https://www.bbc.com/news/magazine-16592633 (last accessed 14 November 2021).

Gokhale, Nitin A. "Motherdom's Prodigals." *Outlook*, 5 February 2022. https://www.outlookindia.com/magazine/story/motherdoms-prodigals/215463 (last accessed 5 March 2022).

Gopalakrishnan, Manasi. "Men in India's Matrilineal Khasi Society Demand More Rights." DW.com, 23 November 2020. https://www.dw.com/en/india-khasi -men-rights/a-55704605 (last accessed 14 November 2021).

Roy, David. "Principles of Khasi Culture." *Folklore*, vol. 47, no. 4, December 1936, pp. 375–93.

"David Roy's Contributions Finally Get Due Acknowledgement." *The Shillong Times*, 23 December 2012. https://theshillongtimes.com/2012/12/23/david -roys-contributions-finally-get-due-acknowledgement/ (last accessed 5 November 2021).

Krier, Jennifer. "The Marital Project: Beyond the Exchange of Men in Minangkabau Marriage." *American Ethnologist*, vol. 27, no. 4, November 2000, pp. 877–97.

Blackwood, Evelyn. "Representing Women: The Politics of Minangkabau Adat Writings." *Journal of Asian Studies*, vol. 60, no. 1, February 2001, pp. 125–49.

Chadwick, R. J. "Matrilineal Inheritance and Migration in a Minangkabau Community." *Indonesia*, no. 51, April 1991, pp. 47–81.

Abdullah, Taufik. "Adat and Islam: An Examination of Conflict in Minangkabau." *Indonesia*, no. 2, October 1966, pp. 1–24.

Sanday, Peggy Reeves. *Women at the Center: Life in a Modern Matriarchy*. Ithaca, NY: Cornell University Press, 2002.

Arunima, G. *There Comes Papa: Colonialism and the Transformation of Matriliny in Kerala, Malabar, c. 1850–1940*. New Delhi: Orient Longman Private Limited, 2003.

Abraham, Janaki. "'Matriliny Did Not Become Patriliny!': The Transformation of Thiyya 'Taravad' Houses in 20th-Century Kerala." *Contributions to Indian Sociology*, vol. 51, no. 3, September 2017, pp. 287–312.

Stone, Linda. *Kinship and Gender: An Introduction*. Boulder, CO: Westview Press, 1997.

Surowiec, Alexandra, Kate T. Snyder, and Nicole Creanza. "A Worldwide View of Matriliny: Using Cross-Cultural Analyses to Shed Light on Human Kinship Systems." *Philosophical Transactions of the Royal Society B*, vol. 374, no. 1780, 2 September 2019.

Graeber, David, and David Wengrow. *The Dawn of Everything: A New History of Humanity*. London: Allen Lane, 2021.

Graeber, David, and David Wengrow. "Are We City Dwellers or Hunter-Gatherers?" *New Humanist*, 14 January 2019. https://newhumanist.org.uk /articles/5409/are-we-city-dwellers-or-hunter-gatherers (last accessed 20 November 2020).

Stoeltje, Beverly J. "Asante Queen Mothers: A Study in Female Authority." *Annals of the New York Academy of Sciences*, vol. 810, no. 1, June 1997, pp. 41–71.

Waihong, Choo. *The Kingdom of Women: Life, Love and Death in China's Hidden Mountains*. London: I. B. Tauris, 2017.

Suzman, James. *Affluence Without Abundance: The Disappearing World of the Bushmen*. New York: Bloomsbury, 2017.

Boehm, Christopher. "Egalitarian Behavior and Reverse Dominance Hierarchy." *Current Anthropology*, vol. 34, no. 3, June 1993, pp. 227–54.

Phillips, Anne. *Unconditional Equals*. Princeton, NJ: Princeton University Press, 2021.

CHAPTER 2: Exception

"Today in History: The Seneca Falls Convention." Library of Congress. https://www.loc.gov/item/today-in-history/july-19 (last accessed 2 April 2020).

"Report of the Woman's Rights Convention, Held at Seneca Falls, New York, July 19th and 20th, 1848. Proceedings and Declaration of Sentiments." Library of Congress. https://www.loc.gov/resource/rbcmil.scrp4006702/?sp=16 (last accessed 2 April 2020).

Haraway, Donna. "Situated Knowledges: The Science Question in Feminism and the Privilege of Partial Perspective." *Feminist Studies*, vol. 14, no. 3, Autumn 1988, pp. 575–99.

"Old New York Diorama." American Museum of Natural History. https://www.amnh.org/exhibitions/permanent/theodore-roosevelt-memorial/hall/old-new-york-diorama#fullscreen (last accessed 3 May 2020).

McGuire, Randall H. "Archeology and the First Americans." *American Anthropologist*, New Series, vol. 94, no. 4, December 1992, pp. 816–36.

Kuper, Adam. *The Invention of Primitive Society: Transformation of an Illusion*. New York: Routledge, 1988.

Steele, Brian. "Thomas Jefferson's Gender Frontier." *Journal of American History*, vol. 95, no. 1, June 2008, pp. 17–42.

Kerber, Linda K. "Separate Spheres, Female Worlds, Woman's Place: The Rhetoric of Women's History." *Journal of American History*, vol. 75, no. 1, June 1988, pp. 9–39.

de Tocqueville, Alexis. *Democracy in America, Volume II* (1840). Translation here: https://xroads.virginia.edu/~Hyper/DETOC/CH3_12.htm (last accessed 1 February 2021).

Hogan, Margaret A., and C. James Taylor, editors. *My Dearest Friend: Letters of Abigail and John Adams*. Cambridge, MA: Belknap Press of Harvard University Press, 2007.

Mill, Harriet Hardy Taylor. *Enfranchisement of Women*. Reprinted from the *Westminster Review*, July 1851. London: Trubner and Co., 1868.

Kerber, Linda K. "The Paradox of Women's Citizenship in the Early Republic: The Case of Martin vs. Massachusetts, 1805." *American Historical Review*, vol. 97, no. 2, April 1992, pp. 349–78.

Global Campaign for Equal Nationality Rights. https://equalnationalityrights.org/the-issue/the-problem (last accessed 9 May 2022).

Reed, Patricia. "The Role of Women in Iroquoian Society." *NEXUS*, vol. 10, no. 1, 1992, pp. 61–87.

Delsahut, Fabrice, and Thierry Terret. "First Nations Women, Games, and Sport in Pre- and Post-Colonial North America." *Women's History Review*, vol. 23, no. 6, August 2014, pp. 976–95.

Alonso, Harriet Hyman. "Peace and Women's Issues in U.S. History." *OAH Magazine of History*, vol. 8, no. 3, Spring 1994, pp. 20–25.

Details about the Haudenosaunee Confederacy from the website https://www.haudenosauneeconfederacy.com (last accessed 2 April 2020).

Mann, Barbara A. "The Lynx in Time: Haudenosaunee Women's Traditions and History." *American Indian Quarterly*, vol. 21, no. 3, Summer 1997, pp. 423–49.

Beauchamp, William Martin. "Iroquois Women." *Journal of American Folklore*, vol. 13, no. 49, 1900, pp. 81–91.

Denetdale, Jennifer Nez. "Chairmen, Presidents, and Princesses: The Navajo Nation, Gender, and the Politics of Tradition." *Wicazo Sa Review*, vol. 21, no. 1, January 2006, pp. 9–28.

Denetdale, Jennifer Nez. "Return to 'The Uprising at Beautiful Mountain in 1913': Marriage and Sexuality in the Making of the Modern Navajo Nation." In *Critically Sovereign: Indigenous Gender, Sexuality, and Feminist Studies*, edited by Joanne Barker. Durham, NC: Duke University Press, 2017.

Yellowhorse, Sandra. "My Tongue Is a Mountain: Land, Belonging and the Politics of Voice." *Genealogy*, vol. 4, no. 112, November 2020.

Ligaya, Mishan. "Before There Was Man; Before There Was Woman." *New York Times Style Magazine*, 20 February 2022.

Blackwood, Evelyn. "Sexuality and Gender in Certain Native American Tribes: The Case of Cross-Gender Females." *Signs*, vol. 10, no. 1, 1984, pp. 27–42.

Niro, Shelley, Keller George, and Alan Brant. "An Aboriginal Presence: Our Origins." Canadian Museum of History. https://www.historymuseum.ca/cmc/exhibitions/aborig/fp/fpz2f22e.html (last accessed 19 April 2020).

Lopez, Barry, and Oren Lyons. "The Leadership Imperative: An Interview with Oren Lyons." *Mānoa*, vol. 19, no. 2, Maps of Reconciliation: Literature and the Ethical Imagination, Winter 2007, pp. 4–12.

Wagner, Sally Roesch. *Sisters in Spirit: Haudenosaunee (Iroquois) Influence on Early American Feminists*. Summertown, TN: Native Voices Book Publishing, 2001.

"Report of the Woman's Rights Convention, Held at Seneca Falls, New York, July 19th and 20th, 1848. Proceedings and Declaration of Sentiments." Library of Congress. https://www.loc.gov/resource/rbcmil.scrp4006702/?sp=16 (last accessed 2 April 2020).

Jacobs, Renée. "The Iroquois Great Law of Peace and the United States Constitution: How the Founding Fathers Ignored the Clan Mothers." *American Indian Law Review*, vol. 16, no. 2, 1991, pp. 497–531.

Corey, Mary E. "Writing and 'Righting' the History of Woman Suffrage." In *The Best of New York Archives: Selections from the Magazine, 2001–2011*. New York State Archives Partnership Trust, 2001, pp. 101–5.

Gage, Matilda Joslyn. "The Remnant of the Five Nations." *Evening Post*, 24 September 1875. https://nyshistoricnewspapers.org/lccn/sn83030390/1875-09-24/ed-1/seq-1 (last accessed 18 May 2020).

Tooker, Elisabeth. "Lewis H. Morgan and His Contemporaries." *American Anthropologist*, vol. 94, no. 2, June 1992, pp. 357–75.

Morgan, Lewis Henry. *Ancient Society; or Researches in the Lines of Human Progress from Savagery through Barbarism to Civilization*. New York: Henry Holt & Company, 1877.

Service, Elman R. "The Mind of Lewis H. Morgan." *Current Anthropology*, vol. 22, no. 1, February 1981, pp. 25–43.

Engels, Friedrich. *The Origin of the Family, Private Property and the State*. Chicago: Charles H. Kerr & Company, 1902.

"Remarks Concerning the Savages of North America, [Before 7 January 1784]." Founders Online, National Archives. https://founders.archives.gov/documents/Franklin/01-41-02-0280 (last accessed 12 March 2022) [Original source: *The Papers of Benjamin Franklin*, vol. 41, *16 September 1783 to 29 February 1784* (New Haven, CT: Yale University Press, 2014), pp. 412–23].

Landsman, Gail H. "The 'Other' as Political Symbol: Images of Indians in the Woman Suffrage Movement." *Ethnohistory*, vol. 39, no. 3, Summer 1992, pp. 247–84.

Pettigrew, William A., and David Veevers. *The Corporation as a Protagonist in Global History, c. 1550–1750.* Global Economic History Series, vol. 16. Leiden: Brill, 2019.

Stansell, Christine. "Women, Children, and the Uses of the Streets: Class and Gender Conflict in New York City, 1850–1860." *Feminist Studies*, vol. 8, no. 2, Summer 1982, pp. 309–35.

Bret, David. *Doris Day: Reluctant Star.* London: J. R. Books, 2008.

Zagarri, Rosemarie. "Morals, Manners, and the Republican Mother." *American Quarterly*, vol. 44, no. 2, June 1992, pp. 192–215.

Zagarri, Rosemarie. "The Significance of the 'Global Turn' for the Early American Republic: Globalization in the Age of Nation-Building." *Journal of the Early Republic*, vol. 31, no. 1, Spring 2011, pp. 1–37.

Jaffe, Alexandra. "Trump Honors 'Great Patriot,' Conservative Icon Phyllis Schlafly." NBC News, September 10, 2016. https://www.nbcnews.com/politics/2016 -election/donald-trump-honor-conservative-icon-phyllis-schlafly-funeral-n646101.

Fletcher, Alice. "The Legal Condition of Indian Women." Speech at the First Convention of the International Council of Women, Albaugh's Opera House, Washington, DC, 29 March 1888.

Ryan, Melissa. "Others and Origins: Nineteenth-Century Suffragists and the 'Indian Problem.'" In *Susan B. Anthony and the Struggle for Equal Rights*, edited by Christine L. Ridarsky and Mary M. Huth. Rochester, NY: Boydell & Brewer, 2012, pp. 117–44.

Griffith, Elisabeth. *In Her Own Right: The Life of Elizabeth Cady Stanton.* New York: Oxford University Press, 1985.

Hamad, Ruby. *White Tears/Brown Scars: How White Feminism Betrays Women of Colour.* London: Trapeze, 2020.

"Voting Rights for Native Americans." Classroom Materials at the Library of Congress, Library of Congress. https://www.loc.gov/classroom-materials/elections /right-to-vote/voting-rights-for-native-americans/. (last accessed 12 August 2022).

Shoemaker, Nancy. "The Rise or Fall of Iroquois Women." *Journal of Women's History*, vol. 2, no. 3, Winter 1991, pp. 39–57.

Leacock, Eleanor. "Interpreting the Origins of Gender Inequality: Conceptual and Historical Problems." *Dialectical Anthropology*, vol. 7, no. 4, February 1983, pp. 263–84.

Fiske, Jo-Anne. "Colonization and the Decline of Women's Status: The Tsimshian Case." *Feminist Studies*, vol. 17, no. 3, Autumn 1991, pp. 509–35.

Ghosh, Durba. "Gender and Colonialism: Expansion or Marginalization?" *Historical Journal*, vol. 47, no. 3, September 2004, pp. 737–55.

Pember, Mary Annette. "Death by Civilization." *The Atlantic*, 8 March 2019. https:// www.theatlantic.com/education/archive/2019/03/traumatic-legacy-indian -boarding-schools/584293 (last accessed 12 March 2022).

Sacks, Karen Brodkin. "Toward a Unified Theory of Class, Race, and Gender." *American Ethnologist*, vol. 16, no. 3, August 1989, pp. 534–50.

CHAPTER 3: Genesis

Weil, Simone. *The Need for Roots: Prelude to a Declaration of Duties Towards Mankind* (1952). London: Routledge, 2005.

Balter, Michael. *The Goddess and the Bull; Çatalhöyük: An Archaeological Journey to the Dawn of Civilization*. New York: Free Press, 2005.

Belmonte, Cristina. "This Stone Age Settlement Took Humanity's First Steps Toward City Life." *History Magazine, National Geographic*, 26 March 2019. https://www.nationalgeographic.com/history/magazine/2019/03–04/early-agricultural -settlement-catalhoyuk-turkey (last accessed 21 June 2020).

"Neolithic Site of Çatalhöyük." United Nations Educational, Scientific and Cultural Organization's World Heritage Convention website. https://whc.unesco .org/en/list/1405 (last accessed 21 June 2020).

Nakamura, Carolyn, and Lynn Meskell. "Articulate Bodies: Forms and Figures at Çatalhöyük." *Journal of Archaeological Method and Theory*, vol. 16, no. 3, 2009, pp. 205–30.

Meskell, Lynn, and Carolyn Nakamura. *Çatalhöyük 2005 Archive Report*, pp. 161–88. https://web.stanford.edu/group/figurines/cgi-bin/omeka/files/original/f9bcd 1d615efc93fcd1fe897640ebbc1.pdf (last accessed 9 August 2020).

Hodder, Ian. "James Mellaart 1925–2012." In *Biographical Memoirs of Fellows of the British Academy*, XIV. London: The British Academy, 2015, pp. 411–20.

Mellaart, James. "A Neolithic City in Turkey." *Scientific American*, vol. 210, no. 4, April 1964, pp. 94–105.

Barstow, Anne. "The Uses of Archaeology for Women's History: James Mellaart's Work on the Neolithic Goddess at Çatal Hüyük." *Feminist Studies*, vol. 4, no. 3, October 1978, pp. 7–18.

Stone, Merlin. *When God Was a Woman* (originally published as *The Paradise Papers*). London: Harcourt Brace Jovanovich, 1978.

Eisler, Riane. *The Chalice and the Blade: Our History, Our Future*. New York: HarperCollins, 1988.

Steinem, Gloria. "Wonder Woman." In *The Superhero Reader*, edited by Charles Hatfield, Jeet Heer, and Kent Worcester. Jackson: University Press of Mississippi, 2013, pp. 203–10.

Gimbutas, Marija. *The Living Goddesses*, edited and supplemented by Miriam Robbins Dexter. Berkeley: University of California Press, 2001.

Steinfels, Peter. "Idyllic Theory of Goddesses Creates Storm." *New York Times*, 13 February 1990, Science Section, p. 1.

Dexter, Miriam Robbins. "The Roots of Indo-European Patriarchy: Indo-European Female Figures and the Principles of Energy." In *The Rule of Mars: Readings on the Origins, History and Impact of Patriarchy*, edited by Cristina Biaggi. Manchester, CT: Knowledge, Ideas & Trends, 2006, pp. 143–54.

Christ, Carol Patrice. "'A Different World': The Challenge of the Work of Marija Gimbutas to the Dominant World-View of Western Cultures." *Journal of Feminist Studies in Religion*, vol. 12, no. 2, Fall 1996, pp. 53–66.

Tringham, Ruth. "Review of Archeology: *The Civilization of the Goddess: The World of Old Europe*. Marija Gimbutas (Joan Marler, ed.)." *American Anthropologist*, vol. 95, no. 1, March 1993, pp. 196–97.

"Episode 1: Joseph Campbell and the Power of Myth." BillMoyers.com, 21 June 1988. https://billmoyers.com/content/ep-1-joseph-campbell-and-the-power -of-myth-the-hero's-adventure-audio (last accessed 18 March 2022).

Eller, Cynthia. *The Myth of Matriarchal Prehistory: Why an Invented Past Won't Give Women a Future*. Boston: Beacon Press, 2000.

Butler, Judith. *Gender Trouble: Feminism and the Subversion of Identity*. New York: Routledge, 1999.

Meskell, Lynn. "Goddesses, Gimbutas and 'New Age' Archaeology." *Antiquity*, vol. 69, no. 262, March 1995, pp. 74–86.

Thornton, Bruce. "The False Goddess and Her Lost Paradise." *Arion: A Journal of Humanities and the Classics*, vol. 7, no. 1, Spring–Summer 1999, pp. 72–97.

Keller, Mara Lynn. "Gimbutas's Theory of Early European Origins and the Contemporary Transformation of Western Civilization." *Journal of Feminist Studies in Religion*, vol. 12, no. 2, Fall 1996, pp. 73–90.

Gero, Joan M., and Margaret W. Conkey. *Engendering Archaeology: Women and Prehistory*. Oxford: Blackwell, 1991.

Conkey, Margaret W., and Ruth E. Tringham. "Archaeology and the Goddess: Exploring the Contours of Feminist Archaeology." In *Feminisms in the Academy: Rethinking the Disciplines*, edited by Abigail Stewart and Domna Stanton. Ann Arbor: University of Michigan Press, 1995.

Belcher, Ellen H. "Identifying Female in the Halaf: Prehistoric Agency and Modern Interpretations." *Journal of Archaeological Method and Theory*, vol. 23, no. 3, September 2016, pp. 921–48.

Hays-Gilpin, Kelley. "Feminist Scholarship in Archaeology." *Annals of the American Academy of Political and Social Science*, vol. 571, September 2000, pp. 89–106.

Hodder, Ian. "Women and Men at Çatalhöyük." *Scientific American*, vol. 290, no. 1, January 2004, pp. 76–83.

Hodder, Ian. "Çatalhöyük: The Leopard Changes Its Spots; A Summary of Recent Work." *Anatolian Studies*, vol. 64, 2014, pp. 1–22.

Bolger, Diane. "The Dynamics of Gender in Early Agricultural Societies of the Near East." *Signs*, vol. 35, no. 2, Winter 2010, pp. 503–31.

Molleson, Theya. "The Eloquent Bones of Abu Hureyra." *Scientific American*, vol. 271, no. 2, 1994, pp. 70–75.

Pilloud, Marin A., and Clark Spencer Larsen. "'Official' and 'Practical' Kin: Inferring Social and Community Structure from Dental Phenotype at Neolithic Çatalhöyük, Turkey." *American Journal of Physical Anthropology*, vol. 145, no. 4, August 2011, pp. 519–30.

Larsen, Clark Spencer, et al. "Bioarchaeology of Neolithic Çatalhöyük Reveals Fundamental Transitions in Health, Mobility, and Lifestyle in Early Farmers." *Proceedings of the National Academy of Sciences*, vol. 116, no. 26, 25 June 2019, pp. 12615–23.

Schmidt, Klaus. "Göbekli Tepe—The Stone Age Sanctuaries; New Results of Ongoing Excavations with a Special Focus on Sculptures and High Reliefs." *Documenta Praehistorica*, vol. 37, 31 December 2011, pp. 239–56.

Rountree, Kathryn. "Archaeologists and Goddess Feminists at Çatalhöyük: An Experiment in Multivocality." *Journal of Feminist Studies in Religion*, vol. 23, no. 2, Fall 2007, pp. 7–26.

CHAPTER 4: Destruction

"Emine Bulut: Anger in Turkey over Mother's Murder." BBC News, 23 August 2019. https://www.bbc.co.uk/news/world-europe-49446389 (last accessed 25 August 2020).

Bruton, F. Brinley. "Turkey's President Erdogan Calls Women Who Work 'Half Persons.'" NBC News, 8 June 2016. https://www.nbcnews.com/news/world /turkey-s-president-erdogan-calls-women-who-work-half-persons-n586421 (last accessed 19 March 2022).

"Turkey President Erdogan: Women Are Not Equal to Men." BBC News, 24 November 2014. https://www.bbc.com/news/world-europe-30183711 (last accessed 19 March 2022).

Belge, Burçin. "Women Policies Erased from Political Agenda." Bianet.org. http:// bianet.org/english/women/130607-women-policies-erased-from-political -agenda (last accessed 9 September 2020).

Butler, Daren, Orhan Coskun, and Birsen Altayli. "Turkey Considering Quitting Treaty on Violence Against Women: Ruling Party." Reuters, 5 August 2020. https://www.reuters.com/article/us-turkey-women/turkey-considering -quitting-treaty-on-violence-against-women-ruling-party-idUSKCN2511QX (last accessed 9 September 2020).

Yalcinalp, Esra. "Turkey Erdogan: Women Rise Up over Withdrawal from Istanbul Convention." BBC News, 26 March 2021. https://www.bbc.co.uk/news/world -europe-56516462 (last accessed 3 May 2021).

Kandiyoti, Deniz. "End of Empire: Islam, Nationalism and Women in Turkey." In *Women, Islam & the State*, edited by Deniz Kandiyoti. London: Palgrave Macmillan, 1991.

Göknar, Erdağ. "Turkish-Islamic Feminism Confronts National Patriarchy: Halide Edib's Divided Self." *Journal of Middle East Women's Studies*, vol. 9, no. 2, Spring 2013, pp. 32–57.

Lowenthal, David. *The Past Is a Foreign Country—Revisited.* Cambridge: Cambridge University Press, 2015.

Peterson, Jane. "Domesticating Gender: Neolithic Patterns from the Southern Levant." *Journal of Anthropological Archaeology*, vol. 29, 2010, pp. 249–64.

Hagelberg, Erika, et al. "Introduction. Ancient DNA: The First Three Decades." *Philosophical Transactions of the Royal Society of London. Series B, Biological Sciences,* vol. 370, 2015.

Haak, Wolfgang, et al. "Ancient DNA from the First European Farmers in 7500-Year-Old Neolithic Sites." *Science*, vol. 310, 11 November 2005, pp. 1016–18.

Kristiansen, Kristian. *Archaeology and the Genetic Revolution in European Prehistory.* Cambridge: Cambridge University Press, 2022.

Haak, Wolfgang, et al. "Massive Migration from the Steppe Was a Source for Indo-European Languages in Europe." *Nature*, vol. 522, 11 June 2015, pp. 207–11.

Reich, David. "Ancient DNA Suggests Steppe Migrations Spread Indo-European Languages." *Proceedings of the American Philosophical Society*, vol. 162, no. 1, March 2018, pp. 39–55.

Tassi, Francesca, et al. "Genome Diversity in the Neolithic Globular Amphorae Culture and the Spread of Indo-European Languages." *Proceedings of the Royal Society B*, vol. 284, 29 November 2017.

Allentoft, Morton E., et al. "Population Genomics of Bronze Age Eurasia." *Nature*, vol. 522, 1 June 2015, pp. 167–72.

Reich, David. *Who We Are and How We Got Here: Ancient DNA and the New Science of the Human Past.* Oxford: Oxford University Press, 2018.

Heyd, Volker. "Kossinna's Smile." *Antiquity*, vol. 91, no. 356, 2017, pp. 348–59.

Mallory, Fintan. "The Case Against Linguistic Palaeontology." *Topoi: An International Review of Philosophy*, 12 February 2020.

Hakenbeck, Susanne E. "Genetics, Archaeology and the Far Right: An Unholy Trinity." *World Archaeology*, vol. 51, no. 4, 2019, pp. 517–27.

Furholt, Martin. "Massive Migrations? The Impact of Recent aDNA Studies on Our View of Third Millennium Europe." *European Journal of Archaeology*, vol. 21, no. 2, May 2018, pp. 159–91.

Furholt, Martin. "Mobility and Social Change: Understanding the European Neolithic Period After the Archaeogenetic Revolution." *Journal of Archaeological Research*, vol. 29, January 2021, pp. 481–535.

Toler, Pamela D. *Women Warriors: An Unexpected History*. Boston: Beacon Press, 2019.

Haas, Randall, et al. "Female Hunters of the Early Americas." *Science Advances*, vol. 6, no. 45, 4 November 2020.

Wei-Haas, Maya. "Prehistoric Female Hunter Discovery Upends Gender Role Assumptions." *National Geographic* online, 4 November 2020. https://www .nationalgeographic.com/science/2020/11/prehistoric-female-hunter-discovery -upends-gender-role-assumptions (last accessed 17 November 2020).

Hedenstierna-Jonson, Charlotte, et al. "A Female Viking Warrior Confirmed by Genomics." *American Journal of Physical Anthropology*, vol. 164, no. 4, December 2017, pp. 853–60.

"An Officer and a Gentlewoman from the Viking Army in Birka." EurekAlert! press release, 8 September 2017. https://www.eurekalert.org/pub_releases/2017–09 /su-a0a090817.php (last accessed 18 November 2020).

Bolger, Diane, editor. *Gender Through Time in the Ancient Near East*. Lanham, MD: AltaMira Press, 2008.

Bolger, Diane, and Rita P. Wright. "Gender in Southwest Asian Prehistory." In *A Companion to Gender Prehistory*, edited by Diane Bolger. Oxford: Wiley-Blackwell, 2012.

Goldberg, Amy, et al. "Ancient X Chromosomes Reveal Contrasting Sex Bias." *Proceedings of the National Academy of Sciences*, vol. 114, no. 10, 7 March 2017, pp. 2657–62.

Kristiansen, Kristian, et al. "Re-Theorising Mobility and the Formation of Culture and Language Among the Corded Ware Culture in Europe." *Antiquity*, vol. 91, no. 356, 2017, pp. 334–47.

"Steppe Migrant Thugs Pacified by Stone Age Farming Women." *Science Daily*, 4 April 2017. https://www.sciencedaily.com/releases/2017/04/170404084429.htm (last accessed 2 May 2021).

Anthony, David W. *The Horse, the Wheel, and Language: How Bronze-Age Riders from the Eurasian Steppes Shaped the Modern World*. Princeton, NJ: Princeton University Press, 2007.

Barras, Colin. "History of Violence." *New Scientist*, 30 March 2019, pp. 29–33.

Scorrano, Gabriele, et al. "The Genetic and Cultural Impact of the Steppe Migration into Europe." *Annals of Human Biology*, vol. 48, no. 3, May 2021, pp. 223–33.

Ammerman, Albert J. "Comment on 'Ancient DNA from the First European Farmers in 7500-Year-Old Neolithic Sites.'" *Science*, vol. 312, 30 June 2006, p. 1875.

de Barros Damgaard, Peter, et al. "The First Horse Herders and the Impact of Early Bronze Age Steppe Expansions into Asia." *Science*, vol. 360, no. 6396, 29 June 2018.

Mathieson, Iain, et al. "The Genomic History of Southeastern Europe." *Nature*, vol. 555, 8 March 2018, pp. 197–203.

Wilkin, Shevan, et al. "Dairying Enabled Early Bronze Age Yamnaya Steppe Expansions." *Nature*, vol. 598, September 2021, pp. 629–33.

Carpenter, Jennifer. "Archaeologists Uncover a Neolithic Massacre in Early Europe." *Science*, 17 August 2015. https://www.science.org/content/article /archaeologists-uncover-neolithic-massacre-early-europe (last accessed 21 March 2022).

Meyer, Christian, et al. "The Massacre Mass Grave of Schöneck-Kilianstädten Reveals New Insights into Collective Violence in Early Neolithic Central Europe." *Proceedings of the National Academy of Sciences*, vol. 112, no. 36, August 2015, pp. 11217–22.

Silva, Marina, et al. "A Genetic Chronology for the Indian Subcontinent Points to Heavily Sex-Biased Dispersals." *BMC Evolutionary Biology*, vol. 17, no. 88, 23 March 2017.

Balaresque, Patricia, et al. "Y-Chromosome Descent Clusters and Male Differential Reproductive Success: Young Lineage Expansions Dominate Asian Pastoral Nomadic Populations." *European Journal of Human Genetics*, vol. 23, 14 January 2015, pp. 1413–22.

Krause, Johannes, and Thomas Trappe. *A Short History of Humanity: A New History of Old Europe*, translated by Caroline Waight. New York: Random House, 2021.

Karmin, Monika, et al. "A Recent Bottleneck of Y Chromosome Diversity Coincides with a Global Change in Culture." *Genome Research*, vol. 25, no. 4, 2015, pp. 459–66.

Zeng, Tian Chen, et al. "Cultural Hitchhiking and Competition Between Patrilineal Kin Groups Explain the Post-Neolithic Y-Chromosome Bottleneck." *Nature Communications*, vol. 9, 25 May 2018.

Knipper, Corina, et al. "Female Exogamy and Gene Pool Diversification." *Proceedings of the National Academy of Sciences*, vol. 114, no. 38, 19 September 2017, pp. 10083–88.

Reich, David. "Social Inequality Leaves a Genetic Mark." *Nautilus*, 29 March 2018. http://nautil.us/issue/58/self/social-inequality-leaves-a-genetic-mark (last accessed 21 November 2020).

Underhill, Peter A., et al. "The Phylogenetic and Geographic Structure of Y-Chromosome Haplogroup R1a." *European Journal of Human Genetics*, vol. 23, 2015, pp. 124–31.

Onon, Urgunge. *The Secret History of the Mongols: The Life and Times of Chinggis Khan* (ca 13th c.). London: RoutledgeCurzon, 2001.

McLynn, Frank. *Genghis Khan: His Conquests, His Empire, His Legacy*. Boston: Da Capo Press, 2015.

Zerjal, Tatiana, et al. "The Genetic Legacy of the Mongols." *American Journal of Human Genetics*, vol. 72, no. 3, 1 March 2003, pp. 717–21.

Moore, Laoise T., et al. "A Y-Chromosome Signature of Hegemony in Gaelic Ireland." *American Journal of Human Genetics*, vol. 78, no. 2, February 2006, pp. 334–38.

Sjögren, Karl-Göran, et al. "Kinship and Social Organization in Copper Age Europe. A Cross-Disciplinary Analysis of Archaeology, DNA, Isotopes, and Anthropology from Two Bell Beaker Cemeteries." *BioRxiv* 863944, 11 December

2019 (pre-print). Now published in *PLOS ONE*; doi: 10.1371/journal.pone .0241278.

Schroeder, Hannes. "Unraveling Ancestry, Kinship, and Violence in a Late Neolithic Mass Grave." *Proceedings of the National Academy of Sciences*, vol. 116, no. 22, May 2019, pp. 10705–10.

De Nicola, Bruno. *Women in Mongol Iran: The Khatuns, 1206–1335*. Edinburgh: Edinburgh University Press, 2017.

Lazaridis, Iosif, et al. "Genetic Origins of the Minoans and Mycenaeans." *Nature*, vol. 548, 2 August 2017, pp. 214–18.

CHAPTER 5: Restriction

Pompeii graffiti: Location IX.8.3, House of the Centennial; in the latrine near the front door, Reference 5243: "Secundus defecated here." Location II.7, Gladiator Barracks, Reference 8792b: "Antiochus hung out here with his girlfriend Cithera."

Rabinowitz, Nancy Sorkin, and Lisa Auanger, editors. "Introduction." In *Among Women: From the Homosocial to the Homoerotic in the Ancient World*. Austin: University of Texas Press, 2002.

Katz, Marilyn. "Ideology and 'The Status of Women' in Ancient Greece." *History and Theory*, vol. 31, no. 4, December 1992, pp. 70–97.

Katz, Marilyn A. "Sappho and Her Sisters: Women in Ancient Greece." *Signs*, vol. 25, no. 2, Winter 2000, pp. 505–31.

Blundell, Sue. *Women in Ancient Greece*. Cambridge, MA: Harvard University Press, 1995.

Roy, J. "'Polis' and 'Oikos' in Classical Athens." *Greece & Rome*, vol. 46, no. 1, April 1999, pp. 1–18.

Aristotle. *Politics*, 2nd ed., translated by Carnes Lord. Chicago: University of Chicago Press, 2013.

Hesiod. *The Homeric Hymns and Homerica*, with an English translation by Hugh G. Evelyn-White. In *Works and Days*. Cambridge, MA: Harvard University Press, 1914.

Morris, Ian. "Archaeology and Gender Ideologies in Early Archaic Greece." *Transactions of the American Philological Association (1974–2014)*, vol. 129, 1999, pp. 305–17.

Pomeroy, Sarah B. *Goddesses, Whores, Wives, and Slaves: Women in Classical Antiquity*. London: Pimlico, 1975.

Osborne, Robin. "Law, the Democratic Citizen and the Representation of Women in Classical Athens." *Past & Present*, no. 155, May 1997, pp. 3–33.

Ramsey, Gillian. "Hellenistic Women and the Law: Agency, Identity, and Community." In *Women in Antiquity: Real Women Across the Ancient World*, edited by Stephanie Lynn Budin and Jean Macintosh Turfa. London: Routledge, 2016.

Lardinois, André, and Laura McClure, editors. *Making Silence Speak: Women's Voices in Greek Literature and Society*. Princeton, NJ: Princeton University Press, 2001.

Dossey, Leslie. "Wife Beating and Manliness in Late Antiquity." *Past & Present*, no. 199, May 2008, pp. 3–40.

Rousseau, Jean-Jacques. *Emile, or On Education* (1762), translated by Barbara Foxley. London: J. M. Dent and Sons, 1921.

Scheidel, Walter. "The Most Silent Women of Greece and Rome: Rural Labour and Women's Life in the Ancient World (II)." *Greece & Rome*, vol. 43, no. 1, October 1995, pp. 1–10.

Food and Agriculture Organization of the United Nations. *FAO Policy on Gender Equality 2020–2030*. FAO: Rome, 2020.

Davis, Angela Y. *Women, Race & Class*. New York: Random House, 1981.

Alesina, Alberto, et al. "On the Origins of Gender Roles: Women and the Plough." *Quarterly Journal of Economics*, vol. 128, no. 2, May 2013, pp. 469–530.

Tauger, Mark B. "Not by Grain Alone." *Agricultural History*, vol. 92, no. 3, Summer 2018, pp. 429–35.

Bolger, Diane. "The Dynamics of Gender in Early Agricultural Societies of the Near East." *Signs*, vol. 35, no. 2, Winter 2010, pp. 503–31.

Burton, Michael L., and Douglas R. White. "Sexual Division of Labor in Agriculture." *American Anthropologist*, vol. 86, no. 3, September 1984, pp. 568–83.

Scott, James C. *Against the Grain: A Deep History of the Earliest States*. New Haven, CT: Yale University Press, 2017.

"Gender and Sexuality: Ancient Near East." In *The Oxford Encyclopedia of the Bible and Gender Studies*, edited by Ilona Zsolnay. Oxford Biblical Studies Online, http://www.oxfordbiblicalstudies.com/article/opr/t453/e48 (last accessed 12 April 2022).

Lerner, Gerda. *The Creation of Patriarchy*. New York: Oxford University Press, 1986.

Hunter, Virginia. "Review: *The Origins of Patriarchy: Gender and Class in the Ancient World*." *Labour/Le Travail*, vol. 22, Fall 1988, pp. 239–46.

Meyers, Carol L. "Was Ancient Israel a Patriarchal Society?" *Journal of Biblical Literature*, vol. 133, no. 1, Spring 2014, pp. 8–27.

Rohrlich, Ruby. "State Formation in Sumer and the Subjugation of Women." *Feminist Studies*, vol. 6, no. 1, Spring 1980, pp. 76–102.

Crawford, Harriet E. W. *The Sumerian World*. London: Routledge, 2013.

Beavis, Mary Ann. "Christian Origins, Egalitarianism, and Utopia." *Journal of Feminist Studies in Religion*, vol. 23, no. 2, Fall 2007, pp. 27–49.

Michals, Debra, editor. "Deborah Sampson (1760–1827)." National Women's History Museum, 2015. https://www.womenshistory.org/education-resources /biographies/deborah-sampson (last accessed 27 April 2022).

Assante, Julia. "The Kar.Kid/Harimtu, Prostitute or Single Woman? A Reconsideration of the Evidence." *Ugarit-Forschungen*, no. 30, 1998, pp. 5–96.

Budin, Stephanie Lynn. *The Myth of Sacred Prostitution in Antiquity*. Cambridge: Cambridge University Press, 2008.

Lerner, Gerda. "The Origin of Prostitution in Ancient Mesopotamia." *Signs*, vol. 11, no. 2, Winter 1986, pp. 236–54.

Kennedy, Rebecca Futo. *Immigrant Women in Athens: Gender, Ethnicity, and Citizenship in the Classical City*. New York: Routledge, 2014.

Kennedy, Rebecca Futo. "Strategies of Disenfranchisement: 'Citizen' Women, Minor Heirs and the Precarity of Status in Attic Oratory." In *Voiceless, Invisible, and Countless: Subordinate Experience in Ancient Greece, 800–300 BCE*, edited by S. Gartland and D. Tandy (under review at Oxford University Press).

McCaffrey, Kathleen. "The Female Kings of Ur." In *Gender Through Time in the Ancient Near East*, edited by Diane Bolger. Lanham, MD: AltaMira Press, 2008, pp. 173–215.

Gilligan, Carol, and Naomi Snider. *Why Does Patriarchy Persist?* Cambridge: Polity Press, 2018.

Scott, James C. *Domination and the Arts of Resistance: Hidden Transcripts*. New Haven, CT: Yale University Press, 1990.

Zeitlin, Froma I. "The Dynamics of Misogyny: Myth and Mythmaking in the *Oresteia.*" *Arethusa*, vol. 11, nos. 1–2, 1978, pp. 149–84.

Nathan, Dev, Govind Kelkar, and Yu Xiaogang. "Women as Witches and Keepers of Demons: Cross-Cultural Analysis of Struggles to Change Gender Relations." *Economic and Political Weekly*, vol. 33, no. 44, October–November 1998, pp. WS58–69.

Vlassopoulos, Kostas. "Free Spaces: Identity, Experience and Democracy in Classical Athens." *Classical Quarterly*, vol. 57, no. 1, May 2007, pp. 33–52.

Rantala, Jussi, editor. *Gender, Memory, and Identity in the Roman World*. Amsterdam: Amsterdam University Press, 2019.

McLynn, Frank. *Genghis Khan: His Conquests, His Empire, His Legacy*. Boston: Da Capo Press, 2015.

Song Min, Choi. "Mandatory Military Service Extends to Women." *Daily NK*, 28 January 2015. https://www.dailynk.com/english/mandatory-military-service -extends (last accessed 6 April 2022).

Bayliss, Andrew. *The Spartans*. Oxford: Oxford University Press, 2020.

Pomeroy, Sarah B. "Spartan Women Among the Romans: Adapting Models, Forging Identities." *Memoirs of the American Academy in Rome. Supplementary Volumes*, vol. 7, 2008, pp. 221–34.

Penrose, Walter Duvall, Jr. *Postcolonial Amazons: Female Masculinity and Courage in Ancient Greek and Sanskrit Literature*. Oxford: Oxford University Press, 2016.

Holmes, Brooke. *Gender: Antiquity and Its Legacy*. London: I. B. Tauris, 2012.

Lepowsky, Maria. "Women, Men, and Aggression in an Egalitarian Society." *Sex Roles*, vol. 30, February 1994, pp. 199–211.

Ghisleni, Lara, et al. "Introduction to 'Binary Binds': Deconstructing Sex and Gender Dichotomies in Archaeological Practice." *Journal of Archaeological Method and Theory*, vol. 23, no. 3, September 2016, pp. 765–87.

Matić, Uroš. "(De)Queering Hatshepsut: Binary Bind in Archaeology of Egypt and Kingship Beyond the Corporeal." *Journal of Archaeological Method and Theory*, vol. 23, no. 3, September 2016, pp. 810–31.

Golden, Mark, and Peter Toohey. *Sex and Difference in Ancient Greece and Rome*. Edinburgh: Edinburgh University Press, 2003.

Laqueur, Thomas. *Making Sex: Body and Gender from the Greeks to Freud*. Cambridge, MA: Harvard University Press, 1992.

Olson, Kelly. "Masculinity, Appearance, and Sexuality: Dandies in Roman Antiquity." *Journal of the History of Sexuality*, vol. 23, no. 2, May 2014, pp. 182–205.

Bucar, Elizabeth M. "Bodies at the Margins: The Case of Transsexuality in Catholic and Shia Ethics." *Journal of Religious Ethics*, vol. 38, no. 4, December 2010, pp. 601–15.

Oyewumi, Oyeronke. *The Invention of Women: Making an African Sense of Western Gender Discourses*. Minneapolis: University of Minnesota Press, 1997.

Plato. *The Republic*, translated by Benjamin Jowett. New York: Modern Library, 1982.

Harvard Law Review Association. "Patriarchy Is Such a Drag: The Strategic Possibilities of a Postmodern Account of Gender." *Harvard Law Review*, vol. 108, no. 8, June 1995, pp. 1973–2008.

Surtees, Allison, and Jennifer Dyer, editors. *Exploring Gender Diversity in the Ancient World*. Edinburgh: Edinburgh University Press, 2020.

Von Stackelberg, Katharine T. "Garden Hybrids: Hermaphrodite Images in the Roman House." *Classical Antiquity*, vol. 33, no. 2, October 2014, pp. 395–426.

Fletcher, Judith. "The Virgin Choruses of Aeschylus." In *Virginity Revisited: Configurations of the Unpossessed Body*, edited by Bonnie MacLachlan and Judith Fletcher. Toronto: University of Toronto Press, 2007.

CHAPTER 6: Alienation

Euripides. *Hecuba*, translated by William Arrowsmith. In *Euripides III*. Chicago: University of Chicago Press, 1955.

Home Office and the Rt. Hon. Karen Bradley MP. "Coercive or Controlling Behaviour Now a Crime." Gov.UK, 29 December 2015. https://www.gov.uk /government/news/coercive-or-controlling-behaviour-now-a-crime (last accessed 27 February 2021).

Bhatt, Archana Pathak. "The Sita Syndrome: Examining the Communicative Aspects of Domestic Violence from a South Asian Perspective." *Journal of International Women's Studies*, vol. 9, no. 3, May 2008, pp. 155–73.

Adiga, Aravind. *The White Tiger*. London: Atlantic Books, 2008.

Anukriti S., et al. "Curse of the Mummy-ji: The Influence of Mothers-in-Law on Women in India." *American Journal of Agricultural Economics*, vol. 102, no. 5, October 2020, pp. 1328–51.

Karmaliani, Rozina, et al. *Report: Understanding Intimate Partner Violence in Pakistan Through a Male Lens*. London: Overseas Development Institute, March 2017.

Coffey, Diane. "When Women Eat Last." *The Hindu*, 3 January 2017. https://www .thehindu.com/opinion/op-ed/When-women-eat-last/article16978948.ece (last accessed 27 April 2021).

de Beauvoir, Simone. *The Second Sex* (1949). London: Vintage Classics, 1997.

Jayawardena, Kumari. *Feminism and Nationalism in the Third World* (1986). London: Verso, 2016.

Lerner, Gerda. *The Creation of Patriarchy*. New York: Oxford University Press, 1986, p. 87.

International Labour Organization. *Global Estimates of Modern Slavery: Forced Labour and Forced Marriage*. Geneva: ILO/Walk Free Foundation, September 2017. https://www.ilo.org/global/publications/books/WCMS_575479/lang —en/index.htm (last accessed 9 March 2021).

"Child Marriage Around the World: Infographic." UNICEF, 11 March 2020. https://www.unicef.org/stories/child-marriage-around-world (last accessed 9 March 2021).

"Improvements Introduced to Marriage Registration System." UK.gov, 4 May 2021. https://www.gov.uk/government/news/improvements-introduced-to -marriage-registration-system (last accessed 12 May 2021).

Stretton, Tim, and Krista J. Kesselring, editors. *Married Women and the Law: Coverture in England and the Common Law World*. Montreal: McGill-Queen's University Press, 2013.

Levin, Bess. "Samuel Alito's Antiabortion Inspiration: A 17th-Century Jurist Who Supported Marital Rape and Had Women Executed." *Vanity Fair* online, 3 May

2022. https://www.vanityfair.com/news/2022/05/samuel-alito-roe-v-wade -abortion-draft (last accessed 19 May 2022).

Deuteronomy 21:10–25:19. Bible, New International Version.

Gelb, I. J. "Prisoners of War in Early Mesopotamia." *Journal of Near Eastern Studies*, vol. 32, nos. 1–2, January–April 1973, pp. 70–98.

Colley, Linda. "Going Native, Telling Tales: Captivity, Collaborations and Empire." *Past & Present*, no. 168, August 2000, pp. 170–93.

Cameron, Catherine M. *Captives: How Stolen People Changed the World*. Lincoln: University of Nebraska Press, 2016.

"World of Domesday: The Social Order." National Archives. https://www.nation alarchives.gov.uk/domesday/world-of-domesday/order.htm (last accessed 17 April 2022).

Rossiter, W. S. *A Century of Population Growth: From the First Census to the Twelfth Census of the United States; 1790-1900*. United States Census Bureau. https:// www2.census.gov/library/publications/decennial/1900/century-of-growth /1790-1900-century-of-growth-part-1.pdf (last accessed 22 September 2022).

Hochschild, Adam. *Bury the Chains: Prophets and Rebels in the Fight to Free an Empire's Slaves*. Boston: Houghton Mifflin, 2005.

Helgason, Agnar, et al. "Estimating Scandinavian and Gaelic Ancestry in the Male Settlers of Iceland." *American Journal of Human Genetics*, vol. 67, no. 3, September 2000, pp. 697–717.

Cocks, Tim, and Issac Abrak. "Nigeria's Boko Haram Threatens to Sell Kidnapped Schoolgirls." Reuters, 5 May 2014. https://www.reuters.com/article/uk-nigeria -girls-protester/nigerias-boko-haram-threatens-to-sell-kidnapped-schoolgirls -idUKKBN0DL0LH20140505 (last accessed 15 May 2021).

Mbah, Fidelis. "Nigeria's Chibok Schoolgirls: Five Years On, 112 Still Missing." AlJazeera.com, 14 April 2019. https://www.aljazeera.com/news/2019/4/14 /nigerias-chibok-schoolgirls-five-years-on-112-still-missing (last accessed 25 September 2021).

Taylor, Lin. "Nearly 10,000 Yazidis Killed, Kidnapped by Islamic State in 2014, Study Finds." Reuters, 9 May 2017. https://www.reuters.com/article/us-mideast -crisis-iraq-yazidis-idUSKBN18527I (last accessed 15 March 2021).

"Kyrgyzstan: Fury over Death of 'Bride Kidnapping' Victim." BBC News, 8 April 2021. https://www.bbc.co.uk/news/world-asia-56675201 (last accessed 23 April 2021).

Taylor, Lin. "One in Five Girls and Women Kidnapped for Marriage in Kyrgyzstan: Study." Reuters, 2 August 2017. https://www.reuters.com/article/us -kyrgyzstan-women-bride-kidnapping-idUSKBN1AH5GI (last accessed 15 March 2021).

Becker, Charles M., Bakhrom Mirkasimov, and Susan Steiner. "Working Paper No. 35: Forced Marriage and Birth Outcomes." University of Central Asia, Institute of Public Policy and Administration, 2016. https://www.ucentralasia.org /Content/Downloads/Forced%20Marriage%20and%20Birth%20outcomes %20updated.pdf (last accessed 12 May 2021).

Steiner, Susan, and Charles M. Becker. "How Marriages Based on Bride Capture Differ: Evidence from Kyrgyzstan." *Demographic Research*, vol. 41, no. 20, 22 August 2019, pp. 579–92.

Arabsheibani, Reza, Alma Kudebayeva, and Altay Mussurov. "Bride Kidnapping and Labour Supply Behaviour of Married Kyrgyz Women." IZA Institute of Labor Economics, Discussion Paper No. 14133, 3 March 2021. https://papers .ssrn.com/sol3/Delivery.cfm/dp14133.pdf?abstractid=3794079&mirid=1 (last accessed 31 March 2021).

Rowbotham, Sheila. *Women, Resistance and Revolution: A History of Women and Revolution in the Modern World* (1972). New York: Verso Books, 2013.

Patterson, Orlando. *Slavery and Social Death: A Comparative Study* (1982). Cambridge, MA: Harvard University Press, 2018.

Patterson, Orlando. "Trafficking, Gender & Slavery: Past and Present." Speech delivered at The Legal Parameters of Slavery: Historical to the Contemporary conference. Published by the Charles Hamilton Houston Institute, Harvard Law School, Cambridge, MA, 2011.

Delphy, Christine. *Close to Home: A Materialist Analysis of Women's Oppression* (1984). New York: Verso Books, 2016.

Abramowicz, Sarah. "English Child Custody Law, 1660–1839: The Origins of Judicial Intervention in Paternal Custody." *Columbia Law Review*, vol. 99, no. 5, June 1999, pp. 1344–92.

Folbre, Nancy. *Rise and Decline of Patriarchal Systems: An Intersectional Political Economy*. New York: Verso Books, 2021.

Garcia, Manon. *We Are Not Born Submissive: How Patriarchy Shapes Women's Lives*. Princeton, NJ: Princeton University Press, 2021.

Ephesians 5:24. Bible, New International Version.

Human Rights Watch. *"Everything I Have to Do Is Tied to a Man": Women and Qatar's Male Guardianship Rules*. New York: HRW, 29 March 2021. https://www.hrw .org/report/2021/03/29/everything-i-have-do-tied-man/women-and-qatars -male-guardianship-rules (last accessed 31 March 2021).

Mernissi, Fatima. *Beyond the Veil: Male-Female Dynamics in Modern Muslim Society, Revised Edition*. Bloomington: Indiana University Press, 1987.

Holzman, Donald. "The Place of Filial Piety in Ancient China." *Journal of the American Oriental Society*, vol. 118, no. 2, April–June 1998, pp. 185–99.

Corno, Lucia, Eliana La Ferrara, and Alessandra Voena. "Discussion Paper: Female Genital Cutting and the Slave Trade." Centre for Economic Policy Research, London, December 2020.

World Health Organization. "Female Genital Mutilation." 3 February 2020. https://www.who.int/news-room/fact-sheets/detail/female-genital-mutilation (last accessed 15 May 2021).

Kandiyoti, Deniz. "Bargaining with Patriarchy." *Gender and Society*, vol. 2, no. 3, September 1988, pp. 274–90.

Afzal, Nazir. *The Prosecutor: One Man's Pursuit of Justice for the Voiceless*. London: Ebury Press, 2020.

Nwaubani, Adaobi Tricia. "Letter from Africa: Freed Boko Haram 'Wives' Return to Captors." BBC News, 26 July 2017. https://www.bbc.co.uk/news/world -africa-40704569 (last accessed 15 March 2021).

Patterson, Orlando. *Freedom in the Making of Western Culture, Volume I: Freedom*. New York: Basic Books, 1991.

Martin, Debra L., Ryan P. Harrod, and Misty Fields. "Beaten Down and Worked to the Bone: Bioarchaeological Investigations of Women and Violence in the Ancient Southwest." *Landscapes of Violence*, vol. 1, no. 1, art. 3, 2010.

Leonetti, Donna L., et al. "In-Law Conflict: Women's Reproductive Lives and the Roles of Their Mothers and Husbands Among the Matrilineal Khasi." *Current Anthropology*, vol. 48, no. 6, December 2007, pp. 861–90.

Rohrlich, Ruby. "State Formation in Sumer and the Subjugation of Women." *Feminist Studies*, vol. 6, no. 1, Spring 1980, pp. 76–102.

Gilligan, Carol, and Naomi Snider. *Why Does Patriarchy Persist?* Cambridge: Polity Press, 2018.

CHAPTER 7: Revolution

Luxemburg, Rosa. "The Socialisation of Society," December 1918, translated from German by Dave Hollis. Marxists.org. https://www.marxists.org/archive/luxemburg/1918/12/20.htm (last accessed 25 April 2022).

"Germany: New Reichstag." *TIME*, 12 September 1932. http://content.time.com/time/subscriber/article/0,33009,744331,00.html (last accessed 30 May 2021).

Zetkin, Clara. "Fascism Must Be Defeated." SocialistWorker.org, 10 January 2014. http://socialistworker.org/2014/01/10/fascism-must-be-defeated (last accessed 30 May 2021).

Zetkin, Clara. *Clara Zetkin: Selected Writings* (1984). Chicago: Haymarket Books, 2015.

Dollard, Catherine L. "Socialism and Singleness: Clara Zetkin." In *The Surplus Woman: Unmarried in Imperial Germany, 1871–1918*. New York: Berghahn Books, 2009, pp. 164–75.

Boxer, Marilyn J. "Rethinking the Socialist Construction and International Career of the Concept 'Bourgeois Feminism.'" *American Historical Review*, vol. 112, no. 1, February 2007, pp. 131–58.

Harsch, Donna. "Approach/Avoidance: Communists and Women in East Germany, 1945–9." *Social History*, vol. 25, no. 2, May 2000, pp. 156–82.

Davis, Angela Y. *Women, Race & Class*. New York: Random House, 1981.

Arruzza, Cinzia, Tithi Bhattacharya, and Nancy Fraser. *Feminism for the 99%: A Manifesto*. London: Verso, 2019.

Kaplan, Temma. "On the Socialist Origins of International Women's Day." *Feminist Studies*, vol. 11, no. 1, Spring 1985, pp. 163–71.

Evans, Richard J. "Theory and Practice in German Social Democracy 1880–1914: Clara Zetkin and the Socialist Theory of Women's Emancipation." *History of Political Thought*, vol. 3, no. 2, 1982, pp. 285–304.

Breuer, Rayna. "How Angela Davis Became an Icon in East Germany." DW.com, 12 October 2020. https://www.dw.com/en/how-angela-davis-became-an-icon-in-east-germany/a-55237813 (last accessed 14 July 2021).

Drakulić, Slavenka. *How We Survived Communism and Even Laughed*. London: Random House, 1993.

Hoffmann, David L. "The Great Socialist Experiment? The Soviet State in Its International Context." *Slavic Review*, vol. 76, no. 3, Fall 2017, pp. 619–28.

Applebaum, Anne, and Anatol Lieven. "Was Communism as Bad as Nazism?" *Prospect*, 20 October 2020.

Addelmann, Quirin Graf, and Gordon Freiherr von Godin, editors. *DDR Museum Guide: A Companion to the Permanent Exhibition*. Berlin: DDR Museum Verlag GmbH, 2017.

Funk, Nanette. "Feminism and Post-Communism." *Hypatia*, vol. 8, no. 4, Autumn 1993, pp. 85–88.

Goldman, Wendy Z. *Women, the State, and Revolution: Soviet Family Policy and Social Life, 1917–1936*. Cambridge: Cambridge University Press, 1993.

Smith, Hedrick. "In Soviet Union, Day Care Is the Norm." *New York Times*, 17 December 1974. https://www.nytimes.com/1974/12/17/archives/in-soviet-union -day-care-is-the-norm.html (last accessed 6 February 2022).

Lenin, V. I. Speech at the First All-Russia Congress of Working Women, 19 November 1918. Marxists.org, https://www.marxists.org/archive/lenin/works /1918/nov/19.htm (last accessed 18 April 2022).

Brown, Archie. *The Rise and Fall of Communism*. London: Bodley Head, 2009.

Ruthchild, Rochelle Goldberg. "Women and Gender in 1917." *Slavic Review*, vol. 76, no. 3, Fall 2017, pp. 694–702.

Bauer, Raymond A., Alex Inkeles, and Clyde Kluckhohn. *How the Soviet System Works: Cultural, Psychological and Social Themes*. Cambridge, MA: Harvard University Press, 1956.

Harvard Project on the Soviet Social System Online. Harvard Library. https:// library.harvard.edu/sites/default/files/static/collections/hpsss/index.html (last accessed 30 May 2021).

Transcripts referred to Schedule A, vol. 2, Case 11 (interviewer J.R., type A3); Schedule A, vol. 32, Case 91/(NY)1124 (interviewer M.S., type A4); Schedule B, vol. 22, Case 607 (interviewer M.F.); and Schedule B, vol. 23, Case 67 (interviewer K.G.).

May, Elaine Tyler. *Homeward Bound: American Families in the Cold War Era*. New York: Basic Books, 1988.

Faderman, Lillian. *Woman: The American History of an Idea*. New Haven, CT: Yale University Press, 2022.

"Postwar Gender Roles and Women in American Politics." Essay from the *Women in Congress, 1917–2006* exhibition. History, Art & Archives, United States House of Representatives, 2007. https://history.house.gov/Exhibitions-and -Publications/WIC/Historical-Essays/Changing-Guard/Identity/ (last accessed 2 June 2021).

Bix, Amy Sue. *Girls Coming to Tech! A History of American Engineering Education for Women*. Cambridge, MA: MIT Press, 2013.

Ruthchild, Rochelle. "Sisterhood and Socialism: The Soviet Feminist Movement." *Frontiers: A Journal of Women Studies*, vol. 7, no. 2, 1983, pp. 4–12.

Fodor, Éva. "The State Socialist Emancipation Project: Gender Inequality in Workplace Authority in Hungary and Austria." *Signs*, vol. 29, no. 3, Spring 2004, pp. 783–813.

Fuchs, Michaela, et al. "IAB Discussion Paper 201911: Why Do Women Earn More Than Men in Some Regions? Explaining Regional Differences in the Gender Pay Gap in Germany." Institute for Employment Research, Nuremberg, Germany, 2019.

Lukić, Jasmina. "One Socialist Story, or How I Became a Feminist." *Aspasia*, vol. 10, no. 1, Ten Years After: Communism and Feminism Revisited, edited by Francisca de Haan, March 2016, pp. 135–45.

Guglielmi, Giorgia. "Eastern European Universities Score Highly in University Gender Ranking." *Nature*, 29 May 2019.

Eveleth, Rose. "Soviet Russia Had a Better Record of Training Women in STEM Than America Does Today." *Smithsonian Magazine*, 12 December 2013.

https://www.smithsonianmag.com/smart-news/soviet-russia-had-a-better -record-of-training-women-in-stem-than-america-does-today-180948141 (last accessed 8 June 2021).

Ghazibyan, Hasmik, and Stephan Gunsaulus. "Gender Gap in Computer Science Does Not Exist in One Former Soviet Republic: Results of a Study." *Association for Computing Machinery Special Interest Group on Computer Science Education Bulletin*, vol. 38, no. 3, June 2006, pp. 222–26.

Lippmann, Quentin, and Claudia Senik. "Math, Girls and Socialism." *Journal of Comparative Economics*, vol. 46, no. 3, May 2018, pp. 874–88.

Friedman-Sokuler, Naomi, and Claudia Senik. "From Pink-Collar to Lab Coat: Cultural Persistence and Diffusion of Socialist Gender Norms." IZA Discussion Papers 13385, Institute of Labor Economics, Bonn, Germany, June 2020.

Friedan, Betty. *The Feminine Mystique*. New York: W. W. Norton, 1963.

Gosse, Van. "Betty Friedan." In *The Movements of the New Left, 1950–1975: A Brief History with Documents*. The Bedford Series in History and Culture. New York: Palgrave Macmillan, 2005.

Horowitz, Daniel. "Rethinking Betty Friedan and the *Feminine Mystique*: Labor Union Radicalism and Feminism in Cold War America." *American Quarterly*, vol. 48, no. 1, March 1996, pp. 1–42.

Ghodsee, Kristen Rogheh. *Why Women Have Better Sex Under Socialism: And Other Arguments for Economic Independence*. New York: Nation Books, 2018.

Ghodsee, Kristen. "Opinion: Why Women Had Better Sex Under Socialism." *New York Times*, 12 August 2017.

Ghosh, Pallab. "Valentina Tereshkova: USSR Was 'Worried' About Women in Space." BBC News, 17 September 2015. https://www.bbc.co.uk/news/science -environment-34270395 (last accessed 30 May 2021).

Schuster, Alice. "Women's Role in the Soviet Union: Ideology and Reality." *Russian Review*, vol. 30, no. 3, July 1971, pp. 260–67.

Schulte, Elizabeth. "Clara Zetkin, Socialism and Women's Liberation." Socialist-Worker.org, 7 March 2014. https://socialistworker.org/2014/03/07/clara -zetkin-and-socialism (last accessed 23 April 2022).

Rowbotham, Sheila. *Women, Resistance and Revolution: A History of Women and Revolution in the Modern World* (1972). New York: Verso Books, 2013.

Honeycutt, Karen. "Clara Zetkin: A Socialist Approach to the Problem of Woman's Oppression." *Feminist Studies*, vol. 3, nos. 3/4, Spring–Summer 1976, pp. 131–44.

Sudau, Christel, and Biddy Martin. "Women in the GDR." *New German Critique*, no. 13, Winter 1978, pp. 69–81.

Harsch, Donna. *The Revenge of the Domestic: Women, the Family, and Communism in the German Democratic Republic*. Princeton, NJ: Princeton University Press, 2006.

UN Development Fund for Women. *The Story Behind the Numbers: Women and Employment in Central and Eastern Europe and the Western Commonwealth of Independent States*. UNIFEM, March 2006. https://www.refworld.org/ docid/46cadad40.html (last accessed 18 June 2021).

Fodor, Éva, and Anikó Balogh. "Back to the Kitchen? Gender Role Attitudes in 13 East European Countries." *Zeitschrift für Familienforschung (Journal of Family Research)*, vol. 22, no. 3, 2010, pp. 289–307.

Kranz, Susanne. "'Der Sozialismus Siegt': Women's Ordinary Lives in an East German Factory." *Journal of International Women's Studies*, vol. 18, no. 4, 2017, pp. 50–68.

Ghodsee, Kristen. "Red Nostalgia? Communism, Women's Emancipation, and Economic Transformation in Bulgaria." *L'Homme*, vol. 15, no. 1, January 2004, pp. 23–36.

"Vladimir Putin Meets with Members of the Valdai Discussion Club. Transcript of the Plenary Session of the 18th Annual Meeting." Valdai Club, 22 October 2021. https://valdaiclub.com/events/posts/articles/vladimir-putin-meets-with-members-of-the-valdai-discussion-club-transcript-of-the-18th-plenary-session (last accessed 23 April 2022).

Kirchick, James. "Why Putin's Defense of 'Traditional Values' Is Really a War on Freedom." *Foreign Policy*, 3 January 2014. https://foreignpolicy.com/2014/01/03/why-putins-defense-of-traditional-values-is-really-a-war-on-freedom (last accessed 23 April 2022).

Neumeyer, Joy. "Poland's Abortion Ban Protests Changed the Country Forever." *Foreign Policy*, 8 November 2021. https://foreignpolicy.com/2021/11/08/poland-abortion-ban-women-strike-catholic-religion-progressive-politics (last accessed 10 February 2022).

"Polish Election: Andrzej Duda Says LGBT 'Ideology' Worse Than Communism." BBC News, 14 June 2020. https://www.bbc.co.uk/news/world-europe-53039864 (last accessed 2 July 2021).

"Hungary to Stop Financing Gender Studies Courses: PM Aide." Reuters, 14 August 2018. https://www.reuters.com/article/us-hungary-government-education/hungary-to-stop-financing-gender-studies-courses-pm-aide-idUSKBN1KZ1Mo (last accessed 18 June 2021).

Fodor, Éva. *The Gender Regime of Anti-Liberal Hungary*. Cham, Switzerland: Palgrave Macmillan, 2022.

Edgar, Adrienne. "Bolshevism, Patriarchy, and the Nation: The Soviet 'Emancipation' of Muslim Women in Pan-Islamic Perspective." *Slavic Review*, vol. 65, no. 2, Summer 2006, pp. 252–72.

Borbieva, Noor O'Neill. "Kidnapping Women: Discourses of Emotion and Social Change in the Kyrgyz Republic." *Anthropological Quarterly*, vol. 85, no. 1, Winter 2012, pp. 141–69.

Ogloblin, Constantin G. "The Gender Earnings Differential in the Russian Transition Economy." *Industrial and Labor Relations Review*, vol. 52, no. 4, July 1999, pp. 602–27.

Ogloblin, Constantin. "The Sectoral Distribution of Employment and Job Segregation by Gender in Russia." *Regional and Sectoral Economic Studies*, vol. 5, no. 2, 2005, pp. 5–18.

CHAPTER 8: Transformation

Bahrami, Ardavan. "A Woman for All Seasons: In Memory of Farrokhrou Parsa." Iranian.com, 9 May 2005. http://www.iranian.com/ArdavanBahrami/2005/May/Parsa/index.html (last accessed 12 January 2022).

Abdorrahman Boroumand Center for Human Rights in Iran. "Farrokhru Parsa." https://www.iranrights.org/memorial/story/34914/farrokhru-parsa (last accessed 12 January 2022).

Childress, Diana. *Equal Rights Is Our Minimum Demand: The Women's Rights Movement in Iran, 2005*. Minneapolis: Twenty-First Century Books, 2011.

Esfandiari, Golnaz. "Hijabs & Harassment: How Iran Soured Its 'Sisters' on the Revolution." Radio Free Europe, 23 February 2019. https://www.rferl.org/a/hijabs-harassment-how-iran-soured-its-sisters-on-the-revolution/29786447.html (last accessed 12 January 2022).

Cain, Sian. "Hengameh Golestan's Best Photograph: Iranian Women Rebel Against the 1979 Hijab Law." *The Guardian*, 3 September 2015. https://www.theguardian.com/artanddesign/2015/sep/03/hengameh-golestans-best-photograph-iranian-women-rebel-against-the-1979-hijab-law (last accessed 14 January 2022).

"100,000 Iranian Women March Against the Hijab Law in 1979 Tehran." *Flashbak*, 14 October 2017. https://flashbak.com/100000-iranian-women-march-hijab-law-1979-tehran-388136 (last accessed 13 January 2022).

Ibrahim, Youssef M. "'Death to Despotism Under Any Cover,' Was the Cry Last Week." *New York Times*, 11 March 1979. https://www.nytimes.com/1979/03/11/archives/irans-new-women-rebel-at-returning-to-the-veil.html (last accessed 26 January 2022).

Buchan, James. *Days of God: The Revolution in Iran and Its Consequences*. New York: Simon & Schuster, 2012.

Jecks, Nikki. "'I Was Iran's Last Woman Minister.'" BBC News, 19 August 2009. http://news.bbc.co.uk/2/hi/middle_east/8207371.stm (last accessed 16 January 2022).

Alinejad, Masih. *The Wind in My Hair: My Fight for Freedom in Modern Iran*. New York: Little, Brown, 2018.

Dehghan, Saeed Kamali. "Tehran Hijab Protest: Iranian Police Arrest 29 Women." *The Guardian*, 2 February 2018. https://www.theguardian.com/world/2018/feb/02/tehran-hijab-protest-iranian-police-arrest-29-women (last accessed 21 January 2022).

Ceasefire Centre for Civilian Rights. *Beyond the Veil: Discrimination Against Women in Iran*. London: Ceasefire Centre for Civilian Rights, Centre for Supporters of Human Rights, and Minority Rights Group International, September 2019. https://www.ceasefire.org/wp-content/uploads/2019/09/Beyond-the-Veil_CEASEFIRE_MRG_Iran_EN_Sept19.pdf (last accessed 13 February 2022).

"Flower Protest in Paris for Iranian No-Headscarf Activist." Associated Press, 8 March 2021. https://apnews.com/article/paris-iran-middle-east-womens-rights-2cc61bf90a93907a9bbf2b47a3d9d91d (last accessed 16 January 2022).

"Iran Man 'Drives Car into Two Women' for 'Not Wearing Hijab.'" *New Arab*, 11 August 2021. https://english.alaraby.co.uk/news/iran-man-drives-car-two-women-not-wearing-hijab (last accessed 21 January 2022).

"Iran Protests Spread, Death Toll Rises as Internet Curbed." Reuters, 21 September 2022. https://www.reuters.com/world/middle-east/four-iranian-police-officers-injured-one-assistant-killed-after-protests-irna-2022-09-21/ (last accessed 22 September 2022).

Rasmussen, Sune Engel. "Iran Protests Erupt After Teenage Demonstrator's Death." *Wall Street Journal*, 5 October 2022. https://www.wsj.com/articles/iran-protests-erupt-anew-after-a-teenage-protesters-death-11664993771.

Gritten, David. "Iran Protests: Schoolgirls Heckle Paramilitary Speaker." BBC News, 6 October 2022. https://www.bbc.com/news/world-middle-east -63143504.

Wright, Robin. "Iran's Kidnapping Plot Exposes Its Paranoia." *New Yorker*, 19 July 2021. https://www.newyorker.com/news/daily-comment/irans-kidnapping -plot-exposes-its-paranoia (last accessed 13 February 2022).

Fazeli, Yaghoub. "Iranian Journalist Masih Alinejad's Brother Sentenced to 8 Years in Prison: Lawyer." *Al Arabiya English*, 16 July 2020. https://english.alarabiya .net/News/middle-east/2020/07/16/Iranian-journalist-Masih-Alinejad-s -brother-sentenced-to-8-years-in-prison-Lawyer (last accessed 21 January 2022).

Washburn, Dan. "Interview: What It Was Like to Travel to Iran with Andy Warhol in 1976." *Asia Blog*, Asia Society, 22 October 2013. https://asiasociety.org/blog /asia/interview-what-it-was-travel-iran-andy-warhol-1976 (last accessed 20 May 2022).

Afary, Janet. "Steering Between Scylla and Charybdis: Shifting Gender Roles in Twentieth Century Iran." *NWSA Journal*, vol. 8, no. 1, Spring 1996, pp. 28–49.

Fincher, Leta Hong. *Betraying Big Brother: The Feminist Awakening in China*. London: Verso, 2018.

Kasakove, Sophie. "What's Happening with Abortion Legislation in States Across the Country." *New York Times*, 14 April 2022. https://www.nytimes.com/article /abortion-laws-us.html (last accessed 2 May 2022).

"Oklahoma Passes Bill Banning Most Abortions After Conception." BBC News, 20 May 2022. https://www.bbc.com/news/world-us-canada-61517135 (last accessed 21 May 2022).

Trump, Donald. "Former President Trump in Florence, South Carolina." C-SPAN .org, 12 March 2022. https://www.c-span.org/video/?518447-1/president -trump-florence-south-carolina (last accessed 2 May 2022).

Gessen, Masha. "Family Values." *Harper's Magazine*, March 2017.

Beckerman, Gal. *The Quiet Before: On the Unexpected Origins of Radical Ideas*. New York: Crown, 2022.

Amir-Ebrahimi, Masserat. "The Emergence of Independent Women in Iran: A Generational Perspective." In *Iranian Romance in the Digital Age: From Arranged Marriage to White Marriage*, edited by Janet Afary and Jesilyn Faust. London: I. B. Tauris, 2021.

Ebadi, Shirin. "I Thought the Iranian Revolution Would Bring Freedom. I Was Wrong." *Washington Post*, 25 February 2020. https://www.washingtonpost.com /opinions/2020/02/25/i-thought-iranian-revolution-would-bring-freedom-i -was-wrong (last accessed 14 January 2022).

Hasso, Frances Susan. "Bargaining with the Devil: States and Intimate Life." *Journal of Middle East Women's Studies*, vol. 10, no. 2, Spring 2014, pp. 107–34.

"The Age of Consent and Rape Reform in Delaware." *Widener Law Blog*, Delaware Library, 7 July 2014. https://blogs.lawlib.widener.edu/delaware/2014/07/07 /the-age-of-consent-and-rape-reform-in-delaware (last accessed 9 February 2022).

Freedman, Estelle B. *Redefining Rape: Sexual Violence in the Era of Suffrage and Segregation*. Cambridge, MA: Harvard University Press, 2013.

El Saadawi, Nawal. *Woman at Point Zero*. London: Zed Books, 1983.

Sullivan, Zohreh T. "Eluding the Feminist, Overthrowing the Modern? Transformations in Twentieth-Century Iran." In *Remaking Women: Feminism and Modernity in the Middle East,* edited by Lila Abu-Lughod. Princeton, NJ: Princeton University Press, 1998, pp. 215–42.

Kar, Mehrangiz, and Azadeh Pourzand. "Iranian Women in the Year 1400: The Struggle for Equal Rights Continues." Atlantic Council, Issue Brief, 2021.

Osanloo, Arzoo. "Lessons from the Suffrage Movement in Iran." *Yale Law Journal* (Forum), vol. 129, 20 January 2020.

Borjian, Maryam. "The Rise and Fall of a Partnership: The British Council and the Islamic Republic of Iran (2001–09)." *Iranian Studies,* vol. 44, no. 4, July 2011, pp. 541–62.

"Statistics Center of Iran: More Than 9,000 Child Marriages Were Registered in the Summer of 1999." RFI, 2 January 2021. https://bit.ly/321K7zD (last accessed 3 February 2022).

Sadeghi, Fatemeh. "Foot Soldiers of the Islamic Republic's 'Culture of Modesty.'" *Middle East Research and Information Project,* no. 250, Spring 2009.

Chatterjee, Partha. *The Nation and Its Fragments: Colonial and Postcolonial Histories.* Princeton, NJ: Princeton University Press, 1993.

Chatterjee, Partha. "The Nationalist Resolution of the Women's Question." In *Recasting Women: Essays in Colonial History,* edited by Kumkum Sangari and Sudesh Vaid. New Delhi: Kali for Women, 1989.

Chattopadhyay, Shreya. "As the US Leaves Afghanistan, Anti-War Feminists Push a New Approach to Foreign Policy." *The Nation,* 9 August 2021. https://www.thenation.com/article/world/afghanistan-feminist-foreign-policy (last accessed 19 February 2022).

Hark, Sabine, and Paula-Irene Villa. *The Future of Difference: Beyond the Toxic Entanglement of Racism, Sexism and Feminism.* London: Verso, 2020.

Matfess, Hilary, and Devorah Margolin. *The Women of January 6th: A Gendered Analysis of the 21st Century American Far-Right.* Washington, DC: Program on Extremism, George Washington University, April 2022.

Razavi, Shahra, and Anne Jenichen. "The Unhappy Marriage of Religion and Politics: Problems and Pitfalls for Gender Equality." *Third World Quarterly,* vol. 31, no. 6, 2010, pp. 833–50.

Gabbert, Echi Christina. "Powerful Mothers, Radical Daughters: Tales About and Cases of Women's Agency Among the Arbore of Southern Ethiopia." *Paideuma,* no. 60, 2014, pp. 187–204.

Mernissi, Fatima. *Dreams of Trespass: Tales of a Harem Girlhood.* New York: Basic Books, 1994.

Zakaria, Rafia. *Against White Feminism: Notes on Disruption.* New York: W. W. Norton, 2021.

Mernissi, Fatima. *Beyond the Veil: Male-Female Dynamics in Modern Muslim Society,* Revised Edition. Bloomington: Indiana University Press, 1987.

Mernissi, Fatima. *The Veil and the Male Elite: A Feminist Reinterpretation of Women's Rights in Islam.* New York: Addison-Wesley, 1991.

Sow, Fatou. "Fundamentalisms, Globalisation and Women's Human Rights in Senegal." *Gender and Development,* vol. 11, no. 1, May 2003, pp. 69–76.

Ratzinger, Joseph Cardinal. "Letter to the Bishops of the Catholic Church on the Collaboration of Men and Women in the Church and in the World." Vatican,

31 May 2004. https://www.vatican.va/roman_curia/congregations/cfaith/documents/rc_con_cfaith_doc_20040731_collaboration_en.html (last accessed 17 February 2022).

Seedat, Fatima. "Islam, Feminism, and Islamic Feminism: Between Inadequacy and Inevitability." *Journal of Feminist Studies in Religion*, vol. 29, no. 2, Fall 2013, pp. 25–45.

Golley, Nawar Al-Hassan. "Is Feminism Relevant to Arab Women?" *Third World Quarterly*, vol. 25, no. 3, 2004, pp. 521–36.

Korotayev, Andrey. "Were There Any Truly Matrilineal Lineages in the Arabian Peninsula?" *Proceedings of the Seminar for Arabian Studies*, vol. 25, 1995, pp. 83–98.

Bakhshizadeh, Marziyeh. "Three Streams of Thought in the Near East and Iran and Their Views on Women's Rights." In *Changing Gender Norms in Islam Between Reason and Revelation*. Opladen, Germany: Verlag Barbara Budrich, 2018, pp. 101–12.

Hamlin, Kimberly A. *Free Thinker: Sex, Suffrage, and the Extraordinary Life of Helen Hamilton Gardener*. New York: W. W. Norton, 2020.

Eltahawy, Mona. *Headscarves and Hymens: Why the Middle East Needs a Sexual Revolution*. New York: Farrar, Straus and Giroux, 2015.

Al-Kadhi, Amrou. *Unicorn: The Memoir of a Muslim Drag Queen*. London: 4th Estate, 2019.

Coser, Lewis A. "Social Conflict and the Theory of Social Change." *British Journal of Sociology*, vol. 8, no. 3, September 1957, pp. 197–207.

Alikarami, Leila. *Women and Equality in Iran: Law, Society and Activism*. London: I. B. Tauris, 2019.

"Inheritance Law." Iran Data Portal. https://irandataportal.syr.edu/inheritance-law (last accessed 13 February 2022).

Afary, Janet, and Jesilyn Faust, editors. *Iranian Romance in the Digital Age: From Arranged Marriage to White Marriage*. London: I. B. Tauris, 2021.

Barlow, Rebecca, and Shahram Akbarzadeh. "Women's Rights in the Muslim World: Reform or Reconstruction?" *Third World Quarterly*, vol. 27, no. 8, 2006, pp. 1481–94.

Kandiyoti, Deniz. *Gendering the Middle East: Emerging Perspectives*. Syracuse, NY: Syracuse University Press, 1996.

Mir-Hosseini, Ziba. "The Conservative: Reformist Conflict over Women's Rights in Iran." *International Journal of Politics, Culture, and Society*, vol. 16, no. 1, Fall 2002, pp. 37–53.

Ortiz-Ospina, Esteban, and Max Roser. "Marriages and Divorces." OurWorld InData.org. https://ourworldindata.org/marriages-and-divorces (last accessed 19 February 2022).

"Saudi Arabia: 28,000 Women Apply for 30 Train Driver Jobs." BBC News, 17 February 2022. https://www.bbc.com/news/world-middle-east-60414143 (last accessed 17 February 2022).

Gao, Biye. "State, Family and Women's Reproductive Agency in China." *feminists @law*, vol. 6, no. 2, 2017.

Yip, Waiyee. "China: The Men Who Are Single and the Women Who Don't Want Kids." BBC News, 25 May 2021. https://www.bbc.co.uk/news/world-asia-china-57154574 (last accessed 2 May 2022).

World Bank. "Fertility Rate, Total (Births per Woman)." https://data.worldbank
.org/indicator/SP.DYN.TFRT.IN (last accessed 19 February 2022).

Human Rights Campaign Foundation. "Marriage Equality Around the World."
https://www.hrc.org/resources/marriage-equality-around-the-world (last accessed 2 May 2022).

"India Court Recognises Transgender People as Third Gender." BBC News, 15
April 2014. https://www.bbc.com/news/world-asia-india-27031180 (last accessed 19 February 2022).

Karmakar, Rahul. "Matrilineal Meghalaya to Give Land Rights to Men." *The
Hindu*, 26 October 2021. https://www.thehindu.com/news/national/other
-states/matrilineal-meghalaya-to-give-land-rights-to-men/article37175110.ece
(last accessed 14 November 2021).

Jacob, Jeemon. "How a Kerala School Has Set the Trend with Gender-Neutral
Uniform." *India Today*, 16 November 2021. https://www.indiatoday.in/india
-today-insight/story/how-a-kerala-school-has-set-the-trend-with-gender
-neutral-uniform-1877283-2021-11-16 (last accessed 19 November 2021).

"Now, Gender Neutral Uniforms for Plus One Students of Balussery School." *The
Hindu*, 18 December 2021. https://www.thehindu.com/news/cities/kozhikode
/now-gender-neutral-uniforms-for-plus-one-students-of-balussery-school
/article37954516.ece (last accessed 5 March 2022).

Fanon, Frantz. *Black Skin, White Masks* (1952), translated by Charles Lam Mark-
man. London: Pluto Press, 1986.

INDEX

Adams, Abigail, 35
Adams, John, 35
Adiga, Aravind, 133
Afary, Janet, 181–82, 184–85, 187, 199–200
Afghanistan, impacts of conflict on conservative voices, 190, 193
Africa: Asantewaa, Nana Yaa, 25–26; Boko Haram, 138, 147–48; forced marriage in Niger, 135; matrilineal belt, 17
Afzal, Nazir, 147
Against White Feminism (Zakaria), 193
Agamemnon, 121
agriculture: and gender inequality, 83, 110–12; slow establishment of, 89
Alikarami, Leila, 198–99
Alinejad, Masih, 180–81
Alito, Samuel, 135–36
Al-Kadhi, Amrou, 197
Amazons, 121
American Museum of Natural History, "Old New York" diorama, 30–31, 34
Amina, queen of Zazzau, 115
Amini, Mahsa, 180
Amir-Ebrahimi, Masserat, 183–84, 198
Amma, Karthiyayani, 18
Anatolia, Land of Mother Goddess (Ergener), 58
Ancient Society (Morgan), 43
"Anglo-American Womanhood," 48
animal behavior studies, 11–12
Anthony, David, 91–94, 98
anthropology, Western: early explorations and questions, 36; male domination, 5; matriliny as paradox, 19, 24–25. *See also* archaeology; Çatalhöyük, Turkey; Gimbutas, Marija; Indigenous peoples
Appiah, Kwame Anthony, 2
Applebaum, Anne, 155
Arabshahi, Monireh, 180
archaeology: feminist, 73–75; gender biases, 77, 90; Halaf figurines, 74–75;

underlying assumptions, 72, 75. *See also* anthropology, Western; Çatalhöyük, Turkey; evolutionary biology; Gimbutas, Marija
Aristophanes, 121, 123
Aristotle, 105–6, 123, 127–28
Arruzza, Cinzia, 152–53
Arunima, G., 18
Aryani, Yasaman, 180
"Aryan" race, 43, 87
Asante people, Ghana, xi, 25–26
Asantewaa, Nana Yaa, xi, 25–26
Assante, Julia, 115–17
Ataselim, Fidan, 82–83
Athena, 66, 128
Athens, ancient, 104–5, 119–27, 129
Athwal, Surjit, 147
Atwood, Margaret, 181
Augustus, 119–20

Bachofen, Johann Jakob, 43–46
Bandaranaike, Sirimavo, xi, 14
"Barbara," as a name, 139
Barstow, Anne Llewellyn, 60–61
Bayliss, Andrew, 123–24
Beauchamp, William Martin, 39
Beckerman, Gal, 183
Beechey, Veronica, 3
Belcher, Ellen, 74
Betraying Big Brother (Fincher), 182
Bhattacharya, Tithi, 152–53
the Bible, 196–97
biological difference, 4–5, 27–28, 40
"biology is destiny" idea. *See* evolutionary biology
Birka, Sweden, grave of female warrior, x, 90
birth rates, policies addressing, 157–58, 170, 180, 187–88, 200–201
Black Skin, White Masks (Fanon), 202
Blackstone, William, 135